The Collyhurst Kid

A Brat's Tales

Brendan M. Ramsbottom

The Collyhurst Kid.

Or

A Brat's Tales.

By

Brendan M. Ramsbottom.

For

May and Paddy

(Mum & Dad)

All rights reserved. No part of this book may be reproduced or transmitted in any form or by any means without permission in writing from the author.

Introduction.

I don't know what possesses an ordinary person to start writing about their life – but I have to confess to being possessed.

For me it began around 1987. At that time I was a teacher at the Sutherland High School in Heywood. I taught English, some General Studies and managed groups of disaffected youngsters but I received my allowances for serving the school as a Head of Year. I loved my job and cared greatly for the school. It has since been erased from the face of the earth – progress?

Around this time the teachers' unions were in dispute with the then Tory Government, about the number of hours we were working and what they could expect us to do as part of the job. Suddenly teachers, like me, who had never stinted on their time during or after school hours, found themselves leaving school at the end of the day and during the lunch hour. For me and many others it was an inconvenience but we all agreed that the government were insensitive. That because they perceived that there were a handful of teachers who did the bare minimum they tarred us all with the same brush and expected us to prove we put in the time we were already putting in! Good will evaporated and I believe that in subjects like sport we're still paying the price for that government's bloody mindedness!

Anyway to cut a long story short I began occupying myself during the lunch hour by walking out from school onto the Pilsworth

Industrial Estate, in Heywood. During the average lunch time I'd cover maybe two or three miles.

It was during these walks that I began reminiscing and then formulating some of those memories into the stories contained in this very personal collection.

The tales deal with the very simple pleasures and experiences of a very average boy born into the Manchester of the 1950's to Irish parents. If you're not born for the greatness that becomes a Churchill or a Kennedy it seems to me that the greatness in your life is provided by those you rub shoulders with during your passage through this life. I have been blessed to have been associated with some of the finest people to ever walk this earth. They may not have been nation makers or shakers but they made this world of ours a better place and it is they I recall in these tales of my days.

Because the stories are so personal they may not appeal to everyone, so if you're the kind of person who asks, "What happens next?" they're probably not for you – because nothing much happens "next" in any of them!

For those of you with patience, determination and the willingness to continue although nothing much happens, I hope you achieve some measure of pleasure from them and, you never know, perhaps they might even trigger you to jot down some of your own reminiscences.

Good luck and God Bless.

Brendan M Ramsbottom 2011

p.s. Five years' after writing the above and publishing my book of memories I once again put pen to paper. I think the trigger was one of those who read my original text, wrote a review of it on Amazon and complained that he'd got it because he thought it was about Collyhurst and felt that it was more about Ireland. This new edition attempts to address this matter. I have added sections that accord more with an autobiographical account of my life which means more about all of the places I lived: Collyhurst, Middleton, Heywood, Rochdale and Todmorden; and worked: St. Wilfrid's Whitworth, the Sutherland High School Heywood, the Queen Elizabeth School Middleton and Hopwood Hall College Rochdale.

I hope that if you read the last edition and enjoyed it that you will also find the new stuff of interest. If you are completely new to the text I sincerely hope that you enjoy it all and that the seams attaching the earlier anecdotal memories to these new insertions aren't too bumpy a ride for you.

My aim continues to be to illustrate the enjoyment to be had in a normal life and perhaps to encourage you, dear reader to have a go yourself.

Brendan M Ramsbottom 2016

Contents

1. Golden Days.
2. Feed thy Neighbour.
3. You Never Forget.
4. Early Memories.
5. The Collyhurst Years: the 1950's – 1965.
6. Presidential Exchange.
7. Ballykilleen, Cloonfad.
8. The Kiernan's at Number 98.
9. Crossing the Bridge.
10. How I was Cured of Rabbit Hunting.
11. The First Mass of Christmas.
12. They killed our President.
13. The Langley Years – 1965 – 1973.
14. My Sister Married a Mad Man.
15. A Real Day's Work.
16. First Post, 1973 – 1976.
17. Tony.
18. Goodbye Dad.
19. Second Post, 1976 – 1990.
20. The Blow-in.
21. Homage to Jack.
22. Third Post, 1990 – 2004.
23. Bye, Bye, Baby.
24. Final Post, 2004 – 2011.
25. A Life.

The illustrations appear at the back of the book.

List of Illustrations.

1. Me around 1957.
2. Dad, blitz clearance around 1945/6.
3. Mum the clippie.
4. Dad and some family.
5. Me on Pat's bike around 1959.
6. Family trip to Blakcpool.
7. Pat & Santa 1950.
8. Dad & Paddy McNicholas, Whit Walks around 1957.
9. Granny Ran around 1955.
10. Me & Pat 1960.
11. Me,, Pat & Neddy 1959.
12. Dad, Kit & Mark.
13. Granny Cunniffe around 1950.
14. Whit Walks 1960.
15. My first communion.
16. Andy Scanlon in Biarritz.
17. Me and Trevor Cook (RIP).
18. Pat & Sean's wedding day 1964.
19. Pat & Sean around 2000.
20. Me on scooter 1969.
21. The guys at my first wedding.
22. Langley RUFC.
23. Tramps Ball 1970.
24. Winners Tramps Ball.
25. Mick O'Rourke.
26. Chase the ace 1980.
27. Terry Fitz and snooker.
28. Mum at 80, 1996.
29. Family portrait, 1996.
30. First BBQ in Ballykilleen.
31. Sutherland High School staff 1989.
32. Ray Riches and trip to France.
33. Crag Vale.
34. Ibiza.

35. First half-marathon.
36. Prizes.
37. Tony around 1959.
38. Cliffs of Moher.
39. Sandy in bath.
40. Danny Pollard (RIP) in the Falcon.
41. The Phantom and me.
42. Our Day Out.
43. 43.
44. Grease.
45. Bugsy Malone.
46. See How they Run.
47. A Midsummer Night's Dream.
48. Dracula Spectacula.
49. The Tempest.
50. Toad of Toad Hall.
51. Headways.
52. Babe 1995.
53. Neall and Joanne's wedding.
54. Friends.
55. Throwing shapes.
56. French cuisine and Neall.
57. The Rose.
58. Lisa & the boys.
59. The twins.

1. Golden Days.

I suppose for me it all began at number 27 Railway Street in the Manchester district of Collyhurst. It was January 1952. The war was over and people were soon to be told they "never had it so good" and I guess that's true of my own experiences. Born in mid-century, a child of the slums, "Hope" was the middle name of every child born at that time. Hope, for a better future, hope, for a better way of living, hope, that we'd seen an end to war. To a greater or lesser extent that's certainly been the case for me. It's definitely true that no one in my generation had it as tough as their parents, just as the next generation will find it just a tad easier for them because of our experience. I suppose that, such is life down the generations!

Anyway back to the Collyhurst of my youth. In the 50's. Railway Street was one of those typical terraced streets made famous in the early 60's by "Coronation Street". Number 27 was a two up two down with a scullery and outside loo backing on to an entry where the dust bins attracted the local rodents. It was where I was born.

I was what people called a jolly baby; chubby with lots of blond curls. My sister hated me with a vengeance. Boys weren't meant to have blond curls and she decided from an early stage to help me to be rid of them.

I suppose this first event in my relatively uneventful life occurred when I was around two although I have no true recollection of it myself. Patsy, my nine year old sister, used to get home from school and collect me and Maura Dowd from the next door neighbours. She would place us in the front room, sometimes called the parlour, and then get on with her chores and her homework.

On this particular occasion she decided it was time to cure me of my feminine curls so that she could be more proud of her masculine brother. Off came the curls without further ado, Maura sat and watched agog. Soon the parlour floor was covered in downy blond curls. Patsy stood back to survey her masterpiece and realised that simply cutting my hair didn't have the desired effect, the blond thatch she had left behind cried out girlie! A change of colour was essential if she were to achieve her goal. So, out came the boot blacking which she liberally smeared all over my pate. After a few minor adjustments with a blunt knife and a final parting created with the knife and a fork she stood back and truly admired her handiwork.

Apart from a few smudges of blacking which had somehow managed to attach themselves to the chubby hands and faces of both Maura and myself the job looked perfect. No one could now confuse her brother with being a girl. For the first time in my life I looked all boy! Now she settled down and got on with her homework whilst Maura and I engaged in the play of toddlers the world over - hitting each other over the head with small blunt objects.

Time passed like a slow cloud. Late afternoon limped into early evening. At this time mam worked at the local pickle factory and dad worked as a driver with a demolition company. Dad was generally the first home. Grimed and dust-shod from his day demolishing what the Nazis had failed to topple. He normally arrived home around six and after checking on the kids he went about his ablutions, made a brew and read the evening news. Mam would arrive around six-thirty. So peace generally reigned in this late afternoon and early evening period. This night as usual dad was home first. He popped his head around the parlour door said hello to Patsy and asked how the babies were. "They're grand", said Patsy proud of her achievements and looking forward to the praise dad would heap on her. "Good, so", said dad and disappeared to wash, brew and read.

Thirty minutes later the peace was shattered. Mam entered like the great white hope that never was. Her first port of call was always the parlour to look in on the little ones and to see if they were O.K.; Annie Dowd or Ned would be calling soon for Maura.

The neighbours thought that my dad must have bludgeoned her as she walked through the door; they were certainly all out on the street within moments of her entering the house wondering what was going on in our house. It had to be murder, they'd all read about it in the "News of the World"; how the wife came home one night and there to meet her as she opened the door was the man that she'd married who had now become a homicidal maniac! The blood curdling screams coming from our house that night convinced the neighbours that they'd be reading about their street in this Sunday's papers.

Mam had taken one look at the babies and her powerful frame for a split second considered fainting but immediately chose fighting. "Paddy", she screamed, "what have ye done to Brendan? Oh my God he's destroyed." By this time dad had spilled his half-filled mug waking from his doze with the paper, thinking, "The bleddy Germans are back". He leapt into the parlour willing to fight and die to protect his youngest but he had no chance against the fury of mum. He was outnumbered, outgunned, outfought and his only defence was in immediate and total capitulation.

What happened that night helped me to understand the meaning of the phrase "Vented her spleen" because mam vented her spleen and anything else that needed venting at my dad.

Patsy came in for some abuse; not enough if you want my opinion, but dad being in charge so to speak, and being an adult fell for the lot. He was tongue lashed to the mast, the stairs and the landing, nothing he could say could assuage mum's wrath. Patsy had early learned to shrink in size and even to disappear when mam went into one of her mighty apoplectic rages. Neighbours, arms folded, stood on doorsteps until they accepted no blood had been spilled. Some even giggled as the cause of the screeching began to circulate, before shaking their heads and muttering "Poor Paddy" and then they went back to their own sculleries and parlours and kitchens and lives.

Mam eventually scrubbed my head until all traces of blacking had been eradicated. Dad was confined to the dog house for the foreseeable future and Patsy was eventually left in no doubt about the death she'd suffer if ever she dared do anything so wicked again.

The strange thing was that my curls never grew back, it was almost as if they knew what Patsy had done it all for. My hair henceforward grew straight and lank. Worse still it eventually turned a dirty brown, probably a legacy of the blacking. Worse still in later years it would thin and I'd have to claim I was growing a tonsure.

I now unequivocally place the responsibility for my hirsute demise squarely on my sister's shoulders. I am sure that had she not slashed off my curls and blackened my locks that I would now be the proud bearer of long blond tresses without a hint of thinning or baldness. My sister has an awful lot to answer for. I suppose that's why I made it my life's ambition to taunt and haunt her for the rest of my natural, or unnatural, childhood. I still miss my golden locks and I'm still losing what little hair I have! Ah me! Story of my life!

2. Feed thy Neighbour.

My father (Patrick Joseph Ramsbottom), Paddy Ran, was the most important influence on my life. He was born in 1918 in a small village called Ballickmoyler near Carlow town in Ireland. He was one of those men who inspired love in others. I believe I can honestly say that I never heard anyone say a bad word about him – except my mother who felt that he drank rather more than he should. He was generous to a fault and would hand over his last shilling if he felt the person asking needed it – this was another reason why my mother scolded him so often.

Dad left home at the age of almost fourteen and was apprenticed to stables in Naas (pronounced Nace). He was allowed home two or three times a year. The object was to turn him into a jockey – he certainly loved horses but at six foot he grew too tall to be a jockey. In those days the only other option that seemed open to him and many more Irish lads and lassies was emigration – sometimes called the curse of Ireland.

England beckoned; he had brothers who had already made the journey, so off he went at the ripe old age of seventeen with dreams of reaching America and becoming a cowboy.

England proved to be good for him and although he always loved Ireland and retained a dream of one day going "home", he learned to love England.

He married my mother on July 22nd. 1936 and settled in Collyhurst, a suburb of Manchester.

I remember him telling me that he had a great wedding without any of the fuss we put into modern day weddings – I was preparing for marriage at the time. He told me that he simply bought a barrel of beer and invited the neighbourhood to share in his good fortune. It was a "great do" he told me.

He was certainly well liked by the neighbours because he always had time for people and always shared his good fortune; much to mum's chagrin at times.

I recall hearing one particular tale about him – there were many tales about him but this one I think really illustrates the philanthropist in him.

It was 1949. Two years before, potatoes of all things, had been added to the list of foods rationed and he'd been working away in Lincolnshire picking the late crop. Late afternoon December 23rd he was returning home to Railway Street in one of the thickest pea-soupers (fog) anyone had ever seen. People born after 1969/70 would not believe how thick these fogs really were! His small duffle-bag was slung over his shoulder carrying a few spuds as well as his spare underwear and socks.

He turned onto Miller Street where the CIS building now stands and crossed over to Dantzig Street intending to call in for a quick one at the Marble Arch or the Angel before finishing his journey.

Now Manchester was still damaged goods after the blitzing it had received during the war and the streets near the centre were a collection of ruins, old mills, factories, warehouses and cold storage facilities. As he glanced down Dantzig Street he noticed, in the gloom and fog, that a truck was unloading sides of beef. The tail gate was under a gas street lamp that illuminated the scene in a kind of thick green phosphorescence. The frozen sides of beef were lined up on the tail gate waiting to be handled into the refrigeration plant. Security should have been very tight because beef, along with other rationed foodstuffs would not be de-rationed until 1954 a full year after sweets were de-rationed.

He had just seen one of the two guys unloading the truck passing into the building struggling under the heavy side of frozen beef. I guess they must have felt secure in the knowledge that no one in their right mind would be out wandering the streets in that fog!

Without faltering in his step and with no need to look around to see if he was being watched dad stepped up, hefted a side of beef onto his prodigious shoulder and marched swiftly away to be lost in the murky gloom of Angel Street within seconds.

He walked just short of a mile to deliver that side of beef to our door without encountering a soul – people tried to stay indoors during the worst of the pea-soupers (thousands died each year breathing in the muck held in that thick, silent vapour).

There were no fridges or freezers in peoples' homes back then so the beef had to go soon. It was expertly divided up, when defrosted sufficiently, and everyone in the immediate neighbourhood had a terrific Christmas dinner that year - courtesy of Paddy.

He was famed for similar deeds; which is not to say he led a life of thievery or criminality. I think that he and the neighbours viewed his actions that night as a charitable act in which he liberated some essential protein for the good of his fellow man! The neighbourhood certainly toasted his health that Christmas and I don't think he had to put his hand in his pocket when he entered the Oddfellows Arms or the Exile of Erin, the Angel or the Marble Arch.

In the year 1961 we were all on holiday in Ireland and Roscommon got to the all Ireland Gaelic Football semi-final against Offally and dad decided to go to the match with Tom Fitzmaurice who had one of the four pubs that marked the crossroads in Cloonfad and, who more importantly had two tickets for the game. They set off late on the Saturday, in Tom's old blue Bedford van, for the game on Sunday at

Ireland's Croke Park stadium in Dublin. They were to return Sunday evening after the game.

The game ended in victory for Offally (one of the counties dad sometimes argued that he came from) but dad and Tom didn't surface that Sunday night. They must have been held up in "match traffic" was the considered opinion of Uncle Mark. "The pub more likely", was mam's estimation!

Around two or three o'clock on the Monday afternoon word reached mum (I have no idea how – I certainly didn't hear the tom-toms), at the small farm in Ballykilleen, that the heroes had returned and were continuing their celebrations in Tom's hostelry. Mum was livid – the shame of it – not only had dad failed to return the night before but now he dallied, for more drink, just a mile and a half away from the house.

It was a beautiful summer's day as I recall and everyone at the farm waited for dad's return and mum's icy welcome home. All of the kids were excited knowing that something big was in the offing.

Still we waited for his return. At four or five o'clock Uncle Mark was despatched to "bring him home". Mark took the bike and that was the last we saw of him until later on. At five or six Tony, who had been across in the bog with the donkey and cart was sent in to "fetch the two of them home". At six or seven Patsy was sent in to find out what had "happened to poor Tony" and to "bring them all home".

Around nine that beautiful summer's evening, along with the rest of the family, I was waiting for dad's return and with him Uncle Mark, Tony and Patsy.

The home place stood at the top of a narrow lane often described as a boreen at the bottom of which stood Delia and John Scahill's home. At the bottom of this boreen was the lane leading into Cloonfad, which couldn't be viewed from Mark's house.

Across the fields we heard them before we saw them. Everyone crowded the dry, white washed, stone wall that bordered the field next to the boreen. Across the field we could see the wall that bordered the Cloonfad Road.

At last they hove into view. Dad and Uncle Mark were stood up in the cart. From our perspective you couldn't see the ass and cart nor could we see Tony driving the cart or Patsy peddling next to the cart on Mark's bike. All we could see were the top half of dad and Mark apparently floating along the stone wall separating the field from the road. They stood with their arms around each others' shoulders belting out The Wild Colonial Boy. It was just like a scene in that quintessentially Irish movie The Quiet Man. The apparent conveyor belt carried them along at an angle to the house to where the road met the lane.

The reaction at the house was mixed to say the least. The kids, myself included, thought this was a great craic. My mother muttered something about the "shame of it" and how she'd "never be able to hold her head up in Cloonfad or the village again" before concealing herself in the cart house that stood opposite the cottage.

Dad and Mark dismounted the cart at the bottom of the boreen and wove their way up to the house, following the cart's progress; still with an arm around each other's shoulder. Eventually they were home. We, the kids, milled about thrilled at the spectacle and excitement generated as the two men entered the house. My mother leapt out of concealment and struck dad a thunderous blow across the head with a switch she had picked up in the cart house.

"God bless all here", I heard dad recite as he crossed the threshold propelled by mother's blow. "So you know where the house is you drunken scut," was mum's rejoinder. Fair play to Kitty, Mark's wife, she did something I had never seen her do before, she got out the emergency bottle of Power's and poured the men a night cap which she handed to them with the words, "Ah now, isn't it only the once an all; the day that's in it? Come on now sit you down and I'll put out the dinner, or what's left of it." And that was it. It seemed to defuse an otherwise explosive situation with mum and dad. For the next hour or two, as we youngsters were sent off to our beds the adults chatted and laughed whilst dad told of his adventures going to and from the match. I listened warm and snug, topped and tailed in the bed, taking great comfort from the familiar murmur oozing from the kitchen. Another night ended in peace and with everyone agreeing there was a tale to tell in the events of the last couple of days!

Dad was like that, he got people laughing and anyone would tell you it was hard to be cross with him for any length of time. He was the most convivial of men especially when he had a drink.

I mentioned that he was always generous. I remember when, as a young surly man of eighteen, he asked me to come out with him one Sunday to do a "bit of a job" in the Stretford district of Manchester. I had been working that summer for MacAlpines on the new M62 motorway, working the summer on a section quite close to the town of Ripponden, consequently I was fairly capable of a decent days work.

A doctor, who had been referred to my dad, wanted a few trees in his front garden pruning. I went with dad although I was still suffering a little from a hangover. The house in question was a big affair standing on the corner of a quiet cul-de-sac. Sure enough the branches of one particular tree hung low over the pavement forcing any pedestrian to take evasive action.

I expected to be sent up the tree and to start trimming. I was after all fit as a fiddle, eighteen years old and used to a little graft! No! Dad wouldn't hear of me climbing and sawing with the huge rip saw he brought along to do the job. I was to make sure passersby weren't inconvenienced, to load those branches I could lift onto the wagon, and to trim smaller branches from the larger ones with a sharp axe so as to make the big ones more manageable. I argued a little with him about how it should be me up there – how hard I argued I don't really recall. I suspect not a lot. Dad did the work and I loitered beneath him doing very little and complaining of boredom. Late afternoon saw the job done and the doctor came along (he wasn't living there at the time) and paid dad £40 for the day's work. Four or five neatly trimmed trees stood swaying testament to his industry. The doctor drove off in his Bentley and dad turned to me and handed me £20 and God forgive me I took it with a murmur of thanks! Dad was generous to a fault at times – like mam said.

He wasn't just generous with money which he held in little value, he was generous of spirit as well. Always willing to lend a hand and never to my knowledge behaving in a hypocritical manner backstabbing people or running people down. He could also be trusted with absolutely anything.

I was a bit of a tearaway in my youth and got up to mischief just as any young man does. Thankfully I didn't get into trouble with the law or dabble in drugs but I was interested in all of the other so called vices. I enjoyed a pint or ten and I loved the women and the craic.

Patsy (my sister) and her husband Sean had three girls (Louise, Joanne and Siobhan). They bought a fine house on Bowness Road, Langley. I often baby-sat for them.

It was a substantial three bed roomed, semi-detached house with lovely gardens back and front where Sean kept a few chickens.

In the summer that I was nineteen I was courting a local girl. Pat, Sean and the girls took a holiday to Ireland to visit Sean's family. Mum, dad and I were to look after the house. One evening I was given the job of checking that everything was alright so I took the opportunity of purloining the back door key and ensuring the bolts were off the door.

Saturday night came along and I ended up in Pat's lovely double bed for a night of illicit bliss with my girl. Around seven-forty-five the next morning we awoke like any normal happily married couple and realised that the front door had just been opened. It was dad checking on the house and he had Daisy our lively and dependable Boxer bitch with him.

My girl and I were out of bed faster than you could blink. We threw the covers back over the bed and snatched up our clothes from off the floor where we had discarded them the night before and in silence we squeezed ourselves behind the curtains that we hadn't closed for fear of alerting people to the fact that there was someone in the house. She was on one side of the large bay window and I was one the other, my bare bum brushing against the cold pane. I was almost whimpering in anticipation of being discovered.

That wonderful dog Daisy raced up the stairs and straight into the bed room where we were, dad following on behind. Daisy of course bounded towards the curtains and started barking, obviously enjoying the game. Dad entered the room. Stood for a moment then called Daisy to him; went out of the room, closing the door, checked the other bed rooms, went down stairs and checked all round before quietly closing the front door and heading off home with the dog obediently walking at his side.

During the time he left the bed room and checked the rest of the house we (my girl and I) became painfully aware that people were walking along the road outside on their way to the early mass at Our Lady's. In embarrassed silence we slunk out from behind the curtains and in clumsy fearful silence dressed, expecting dad to return any moment. During that awful time before he left the house I looked at the curtains and realised that when he looked into the room he would have seen the pair of us silhouetted behind the curtains, she behind the right curtain and me behind the left.

Later that day when I returned home with a heavy heart, I expected the worst. I dreaded the reception I would receive from mum and sure enough it was a truly wicked reception, but no worse than any of the other truly wicked receptions I received when I'd stayed out all night. Dad sat at the drop leaf table reading "Riders of the Purple Sage" and only glanced up to ask if I'd gotten into any trouble. No I muttered. "Good so," he said and returned to his book.

He never mentioned that morning to me, ever. I almost came to the conclusion that perhaps he wasn't aware we were there. Then I recall the morning and know that he did.

My dad could be the soul of discretion. I loved him then for all sorts of mixed up reasons and I love him now and miss him more than I can say.

I can't measure myself against dad and he wouldn't want me to do that. "Be your own man", he'd say. I know I don't have his generosity, I am more parsimonious, in mum's image, but I'd like to think that I inherited some of his generosity of spirit.

To me my dad was a giant in a world of pygmies and me well I'm just the runt of the family.

3. You Never Forget.

I shall always remember the exhilaration and fear of that long ago moment. The moment I cycled alone for the first time.

We left Railway Street when I was four and half, so this must have happened shortly before that.

My dad, who at the time worked on demolition, had got hold of an old wreck of a two-wheeler, which he'd lovingly restored and painted for me. Looking back I suspect that the colour would have given me the colly-wobbles at almost any other time in my life - it was lilac!

For weeks I had pestered him as he returned from work, "Will yer do me bike tonight dad, will yer?" My perseverance eventually paid off because one day the gleaming "new" bike was ready for me to take possession of. Of course it goes without saying that I couldn't ride it, yet!

I spent the weeks following its presentation, standing with my legs straddling the beloved bike, but feet firmly planted on the ground. Stabilisers were a thing of the future, I think, and for now my own legs did the trick of keeping me upright. Riding the thing didn't mean as much to me as just having a bike and so I spent my days giant striding, with the bike between my legs, both feet on the ground, up and down our small street. They were glorious days.

Other kids, less well off than myself, provided a treasure trove of bribes for "just one go". I was discriminating however, in just to whom I would permit a "go". If they could already ride a bike, they didn't stand a chance! I decided this after the very first day.

Tony Berry, who lived just up the street, was one of the toughest kids I knew. He was a little older than I was. His hair was always cropped close to his head; because of "nits" I was informed, and he was always ragged arsed! He was one of the so-called "poor kids" on the street. But when he asked for "a go" on my new bike and peddled off with ease and grace I realised that he was intrinsically richer than I was. His rough, tough experience had made him a sophisticated man of the world to my young eyes. As he rode off on my bike I felt the bitter jealousy of the poor and downtrodden. He didn't get another go on it until I was able to ride it myself and the magnanimity of my own experience permitted me once again to join the human race. For the moment however I was one of the 'Bike Owners Riderless Club' and only those who were as inexperienced as me had the chance of a ride, or should I say a stand!

It was at this time that I can first recall being consumed with the most violent jealousy towards my sister. The fact that she was seven years my senior meant nothing. She could ride a bike, she was a girl! And that made me bitter, twisted and angry. The world was a cruel and vicious place, where girls could ride bikes and boys like me, who were born to ride, could only plant their feet either side and run with it between their legs! The ignominy, the heartache, the unfairness of it all! I can still feel it now.

The relationship between my sister and I was always loving and she took the greatest pleasure in showing off her bike riding skills which, although mediocre, were infinitely more advanced than my own. As she sped past in a blur of wheels, flying ringlets, and fast peddling legs she would shout her words of encouragement, "What's up are Brendan? Can't yer ride yer bike yet?"

I dreamt at the time of the vile accidents which would hospitalise my sister for a very long period, or at least until I could master the riding myself. I didn't know it then but help was close at hand in the form of Bernard Wrigley, who, I think, lived in the pub on the next street or was visiting an aunt or uncle who lived there.

Bernard was six or seven at the time and his voice hadn't yet deepened into the rich baritone that would one day entertain folk clubs around the country, accompanied by his squeezebox. I recently saw an advert for one of his shows where he was appearing with the Oldham Tinkers – the "gravel-voiced Bolton lad" cried the poster. I saw him recently in the movie "Brassed Off" and he hasn't changed too much. He was a smashing lad. I believe that I came to that opinion shortly after he taught me to ride!

Dad was always working and had little time to teach me how to maintain my balance; mam had always so much to do when she got home that showing me how to ride was a low priority; and my sister, well, there was no way I was asking her for help - such was my love for her.

I'm not sure how it came about, but one fine day, as I straddled my bike on New Allen Street, there was Bernard - a big boy, talking to me! "What's up young 'un, can't yer ride it yet?" These words of introduction are with me yet.

"Course a can," I replied with just the right amount of disdain in my voice.

"Go on then, show us," he smiled at me benignly, the wisdom of the Ages in his look.

"Don't wanna, " I mumbled.

"De yer want me ter show yer 'ow to kid?" he asked, still smiling at me.

I considered his offer for a whole split second before total capitulation, "Yes please."

The streets in those days were largely free of traffic, except for the occasional rag and bone cart, so we had the full length of the recently tarred Suddel Street to practice on.

"Right kid, you 'old 'andlebars and put yer feet ont' peddles, I'll 'old seat an' that way yer won't fall off, O. K.?"

"Alright," I grunted, my tongue already protruding, a gesture which was to become a give-away trademark whenever I was concentrating on something.

I found it hard to put my trust in this young god who had decided to look down on me with real pity and so I struggled to not turn my head to make sure that he was indeed holding the saddle. He was, and with a push we were off, Bernard running behind me, his right hand firmly holding the bike steady. Up and down we went, Bernard steadying me and me peddling like billyo.

Suddenly I was aware that Bernard's voice appeared to be coming from a long way off, "Go on, yer doin' great kid." I turned my head and sure enough Bernard was twenty or thirty feet away already and getting further away all the time! I was cycling under my own steam for the very first time in my life. After a panicky wobble I managed to maintain my balance until terminal wobbles set in and I was flung unceremoniously from my lilac bike!

Bernard laughed all the way to where I was lying in a crumpled heap waiting for the pain that invariably followed a fall. His laugh was honest and infectious and before I knew it I was laughing too, being hoisted onto the bike and with words of firm reassurance set on my way again. Within minutes I was riding by myself, free from all external aid, each subsequent fall was merely a hiccup soon to be shaken off. I could ride a bike. I had left forever the army of pedestrians. The wind blew in my face and I was making it blow more strongly, power and wisdom were now mine, from now on I'd be able to help other little kids who couldn't yet ride!

My sister was stood on the corner of our street, talking to Brian Kidd (he later picked up a European cup winners meddle with Manchester United), a glance told me that she had lost one of her holds over me. No longer could she taunt me with her skill and soon I would be more skilful and daring than her - it was good to be alive.

I don't ever recall spending any time with Bernard, again, in fact I don't recall seeing him again until I saw him on television years later although I am aware that he had a fairly successful career as a folk singer (basso profundo). I believe that they moved away somewhere shortly after this episode. I do vaguely remember thanking him. I suppose that I was just a lazy afternoon distraction to him. I helped him to pass a few quiet moments; I doubt he even recalls the event which was so important to me. I shall never forget that afternoon and my gratitude is timeless for the person who taught me to ride my very first bike. To ride whilst others walked!

It's funny how you never forget how to ride a bike once you've been taught. It's even difficult trying to remember what you found so hard about it. All I know is that I can still ride a bike, even though the pleasure it once gave me can never be recaptured. The pleasure I get now is in recalling that long ago moment when I mastered a skill for life with a little help from a bored kid from down "are" way.

4. Early Memories.

My earliest memory is burned into my psyche. It was of being held out above a newspaper in a packed fish and chip restaurant in Blackpool to do my "number two"!

MY mother, God rest her, insisted I was less than twelve months when this happened; to me the memory is as fresh and shameful as if I'd been twenty-one! It's an episode that tells you much about me and a great deal about my mother.

No tales of my childhood memories were as embarrassing or traumatic. The majority were warm and comforting, for example . . . . . .

Christmas time is special for every child and I was no exception.

At that time, in the late 1950's, we'd moved from Railway Street and now occupied 100 Chapley Street, a two up, two down, terraced house in the same district of Manchester, Collyhurst. My dad was a lorry-driver and my mum worked in the local pickle factory; both were Irish immigrants – despite dad's name: Ramsbottom!

The legend on the street sign read "Chapley Street LATE Chapman Street"! I was, as a child unable to make much of this, now as an adult it still perturbs me. Did it mean that Chapman Street suffered death under the Nazi bombing raids? The railway arches and bridges still bore visible signs of wartime strafing! Whatever happened to Chapman Street it was reborn (or born again?) as Chapley Street.

Anyway, as Catholic Christians, the Christmas story was always an integral part of the festival and so it remains for me today. As a child it was the visit of St. Nicholas that excited the most interest in the Christmas period.

Each year his visit brought the simple predictable childish pleasures that were the norm for that era: a good book, some chocolate (it had only recently been de-rationed, 1953), a small game - like marbles, a jig-saw for the rainy days, some nuts and the inevitable, though always welcome, tangerine. Satsumas are definitely a fruit neuveau! Finally there was the "big" present. It was the "big" present in the same way that when you went to the cinema at that time, you went to see the "big" picture. The "big" present was the only unpredictable item in an otherwise pre-determined, though highly welcome selection. You could compare stockings with the kids down the street and everything would be more or less the same except for the "big" present!

One year it was a full cowboy suit complete with Stetson, waistcoat and chaps; another year it was a mediaeval castle with soldiers; and yet another year it was a fabulous second hand two-wheeler bike that Bernard Wrigley taught me to ride.

Everywhere along the dingy terraced streets the "whoops" of red-skins, "hollers" of cowboys as they slapped their bottoms, shouted commands of soldiers, "clang, clang" of trolley buses, "broom, broom" of pedal cars, "wheeow" of aircraft, "rat-tat-tat" of machine gun fire, "boom" of cannons, "chug-chug" of locomotives, "hush-a-bye-baby" of girls with dollies, "bom-bom-bom" of kids with drums, the "swishup" of red-skin arrows hitting their marks and the "aarghs" of kids biting the dust; heralded Christmas morning in those long ago streets.

The whole neighbourhood was alive and fabulously exciting by 08.30 on Christmas morning. I remember it well. Children burst in upon parents between five and six that morning. Parents, who had gone to bed scant hours before having spent their time preparing for Santa. The kids would burst into their room to inform them of the wonderful paraphernalia that Santa had brought and deposited in their kitchens.

The dreams of the previous twelve months had been satisfied completely, surpassed or dashed through the poverty of the times. Even so, joy was for all because all could take pleasure in the honest joy of others. It's hard to be unhappy when there are chirruping children, laughing and giggling outrageously in the streets.

Cries of "look what I got" or "giz-a-go" or "show us", echoed through the terraced streets.

Mums and dads already tired through going to bed late, having filled stockings and then having been woken early, had an hour or two of welcome respite whilst their children plied door to door showing and discovering that year's "big" presents.

Such were the Christmases' of my past. They were special times; times that always bring fond memories to me, even though the presents were not expensive or lavish. They were simple, honest, and hard earned and joyously received.

Christmas morning was only a prelude to the beauty and joy of Christmas day mass at St. Pat's (St. Patrick's, Livesey Street). Having those presents gave you a lot to be thankful for. So to display that you really did deserve them, because you were "a good boy", you went to mass and look everyone, you were pious too!

The eve before Christmas rarely altered throughout those early years. The day would be spent in feverish excitement: last minute shopping, watching mum pluck the once a year turkey (sent over from the family "back home in Ireland") and placing aunt Mollies work of art Christmas cake in pride of place on the table for the day to come.

The turkey from "home" always caused me the odd problem. You just knew that Christmas was imminent when that arrived; brownly parcelled with string and sealing wax four or five days before the "big" day. The opening of the parcel was always a "big" affair and once opened – there it lay, a huge full-feathered and full-headed turkey that had been "gobbling" on a garden in County Mayo only days ago. Mum soon had it strung up; its legs tied together and hung upside down on the back door hook – to let the blood drain to the purpling head! There were no fridges or freezers back then; fresh produce remained fresh in the freezing back sculleries of the endless back to back terraces. There it would hang, daring me to touch it, staring malevolently at me, until Christmas Eve when it would be beheaded, plucked, cleaned, stuffed and unceremoniously thrown into the range to be cooked. It was a truly wonderful sight to see, that great old bird on the back door, even more interesting when shed of its dignifying feathers - at which time it displayed mottled, purpling, cold, pimpled skin.

The smell of the burning feathers, ripe and exotic added to the annual novelty of the occasion.

Late afternoon would find us all, save dad, huddled around the wireless listening to the Christmas edition of the "Clitheroe Kid", or the "Navy Lark" or perhaps one of those wonderful Christmas stories, like O. Henry's "The Gift of the Magi" or Ray Bradbury's "The Gift".

All added to the seriously special nature of the season. Life's rhythms interrupted, in a most pleasing way.

At seven we would be sent protesting to the cold bedroom to get some sleep before Midnight Mass.

Soon it would be Christmas Day!

Dad was always home for mass, smelling deliciously of a last whiskey or brandy. I'd bury my small hand in his and walk closely to him for that extra warmth against the cold, and comfort against the night.

Mass would fly by; the Christmas story once again taking on mystical relevance. Clear and bright images played through my mind like the most recent film I'd seen at the "pictures". I could see the Magi; I stood with the shepherds and looked to the sky; I was fit to burst with love of the infant Jesus, but I was also bursting to know what Santa would bring and it was thus that mass flew by. And then home in the cold, dark, winter-twinkling night and a warm drink before bed.

Dad would have a whiskey and judiciously measure out a portion for Santa. I would oversee the provision of his mince pie and slice of Molly's Christmas cake plus a carrot, for Rudolph of course.

Molly was my dad's sister. She lived in Perth up in Scotland where she was some kind of special nurse. Each year, without fail, at around the same time as the turkey arrived, Molly's beautifully made Christmas cake would arrive tightly wrapped and inside a biscuit tin. It was always cleverly iced and seasonally wrapped in red surround. On the snow-like surface sat Santa, a sleigh complete with reindeer and occasionally a couple of Pixies. The words "Merry Christmas" were smartly etched on the snow-white surface in pink, gold or green letters. Molly's cakes were a wonder to behold and a joy to eat, I've rarely tasted fruitcake since – I think because her cakes had me so badly spoiled as a child.

Between huge brown paper wrapped turkeys and delicious Christmas cakes delivered by post we were the talk and envy of the neighbourhood where post war rationing was still very much a part of the psyche. The early fifties were still hard times for many people in Collyhurst!

If mum was in a particularly good mood she might let Pat and I try a drop of eggnog before marching us off to bed. March us off she would though, generally as soon as Santa's plate was ready.

And so to bed on a brand new Christmas morning; where of course a little boy couldn't possibly sleep.

Toss and turn, turn and toss. Listening for Santa. What would he bring? When would he come? What would be my "big" present? Thoughts guaranteed to keep a little boy awake!

As was common at that time I shared a small double bed, in the back bedroom with my sister Pat. The headboard was squarely placed against the corner opposite the door. The door which in the summer had any number of coats hanging from it; frightening me because as the moonlight caught them they had the appearance of hulking monsters about them; they stood empty sentinel now – all of the coats being placed upon the bed for added winter warmth. The room's one sash window was on my side of the bed against the wall opposite the door.

As I lay, snug as a bug, I gently moved the curtain so that I could look out on the night. Patsy was already dozing, dreaming of her own stocking no doubt! I peered into the endless night sky, listening keenly for a certain sound. I knew that by now Santa would have begun his rounds and that it was only a matter of time before he delivered to Collyhurst.

Stars twinkled in the cold night sky of that long ago Christmas Eve as I searched the Heaven's for sight of a magical sleigh.

Minutes passed and instead of feeling tired I was full of expectant excitement. It was at that moment I heard a wondrous sound. Sleigh bells, and they were very close. I quickly scoped the sky, attempting to look beyond the eves onto the roof. My mind was in a whirl. Santa was here; I'd heard the sleigh bells. My heart pounded in my chest. The anticipation and building excitement was almost too great to bear! Santa was on my roof, oh my! Then the dread set in – if I was awake Santa would know, if I was awake he wouldn't stop, there'd be no presents, no Christmas – it didn't bear thinking about. I had to pretend to be sleeping and I might get away with it. I snuggled down in the cosy bed, pulled up the blankets and overcoats, closed my eyes and before I knew anything about it I had drifted off into a sound and dream filled sleep in which Santa came into my bedroom and let me choose from his sack of "big" presents.

Meanwhile mum and dad had remained downstairs waiting until sure we were asleep before placing the presents in our stockings or thereabouts. Then, making sure to drink the small glass of whiskey, eating the slice of Mollie's cake and taking a god bite out of Rudolph's carrot, they too made their way to bed. The time, I suppose, would have been around two in the morning.

Three, maybe four hours later, they were shaken awake so that I could show them all of the "goodies" Santa had brought. It always struck me as odd somehow that they rarely appeared that excited about my treasure trove, appearing instead to be more concerned about getting me back into bed for a few more hours.

That year my "big" present was the cowboy suit, which I wore and wore out. For a while I was the envy of many of the other kids on the street, especially with my double-holstered Lone Ranger six-guns.

Christmas was a truly wonderful time. I firmly believed in Santa until I was almost nine or ten. I am thankful for my naivety. If you have to hang on to a dream, make it a good one.

Little things made that time very special for me but it wasn't until many years later I realized that the midnight tinkle of sleigh bells that I had heard were produced by the small ornamental bell we had on the mantle at that time.

Dad, part time psychologist he could have been, waited long enough to know that a little boy would be having trouble sleeping and that some incentive might be needed. And so at around one-thirty on those far distant eves of Christmas he would go out into the cold backyard, visit the outdoor loo, perhaps breaking the ice before using it, and then he would stand under our back bedroom window and tinkle our little ornamental bell knowing the effect it would have on his little boy!

I miss Christmas as it was. Midnight mass is now more likely to be at seven or eight in the evening to avoid the drunks. Once upon a time asking, "What time is midnight mass?" would have resulted in guffaws; now! Toddlers now dismiss belief in Santa from a very early age. Presents are more often than not measured in large amounts of money given weeks before Christmas Day. Christmas like birthdays, Mothers days, Fathers days, Easter, and so on, have become indulgent binges of extravagance, where it's not the thought that counts but the amount.

I miss my dad and the simplicity and magic that conspired, with him, to make the early Christmases of my life so special.

5. The Collyhurst Years, early 50's - 1965.

I left Collyhurst sometime around the summer of 1965. By that time we had "flitted" from Chapley Street and crossed the Oldham Road where we lived in a lower maisonette, number 7, Calver Walk.

I had witnessed the coming of electricity on Chapley Street and the move away from cooking on a range to using a gas cooker. Like many of my time I can recall having to break the ice on the outside toilet if you wanted to use it, otherwise you'd subject yourself to splash back or worse! To get that effect now we have to use cling film. I can also remember drawing quite complex designs and pictures on the inside of my bedroom window in the winter time when Jack Frost had coated the inside with a quite thick layer of frost. I must admit that even then I was no artist and his designs were always better than mine!

I recall the house being dreary and dark. The parlour, off the entrance lobby, became my brother Tony's bedroom when he rejoined the family in around 1957 – I can still remember my mother finding his stash of dirty magazines, which he'd hidden in the horn of the old upright gramophone we kept in there!

The kitchen, what we'd call the living room nowadays, was compact. It had a black range, which I don't actually recall being used, apart from making toast and keeping the teapot warm; a settee and a dining table and chairs (all utility items of furniture). Dad replaced the range when I was still quite young with a tiled fire place which was much more modern. Linoleum covered the floor in all of the rooms and the kitchen boasted a mat (it was either hessian or matting, I think). There was a scullery off the kitchen where the new gas cooker and Belfast sink with cold water tap was plumbed in. The two upper bedrooms the kitchen and the parlour had fireplaces but I can only ever remember a fire being lit in the kitchen. Extra warmth in the winter months came from the careful addition of over coats on top of the bedding – duvets were yet to be discovered in Collyhurst and the rest of the UK, and I don't believe that that happened for another twenty years!

Pride of place in the kitchen was the radio, which stood on the table just in front of the window. The radio was certainly the focal point and the whole family would gather round the table to listen to the latest instalment of "Round the Horn", "The Navy Lark", "Hancock's Half Hour "," Beyond our Ken ", " The Clitheroe Kid" or "Billy Bunter". During the day it would be on for "Workers' Playtime", "The Billy Cotton Bandshow", "The News" and of course the "Shipping Forecast" (I loved listening to the names). "Two way family Favourites" was one of the shows we all tried to catch for the banter and latest releases – I used to wonder what "BFPO 40" was, it sounded very exotic to my ears. The radio was the heart of the house; it generated laughter, tears, screams and discussion. "Play for the Day" was one of Pat's favourite shows and became one of mine. Some of the comedy shows would empty the street on a Saturday or Sunday afternoon.

There was panic and shock if and when the huge battery that operated the radio was about to run out and it was quickly despatched to the local Accumulators on Oldham Road where it was traded for a fully charged model. The battery was about the size of a car battery maybe a tad bigger and appeared to be made of glass. It was very heavy and contained deadly acids! I think the shop was on the Oldham side of the old Osborne Cinema, quite close to the Herbalists we'd visit after watching a movie, for a hot Vimto. We had kept my pram, in the backyard, to carry the heavy battery to the shop and every six weeks or so the job usually fell to Patsy and me. She would take me; under sufferance of course. I don't think she ever contrived to leave me there, traded for some more useful battery operated item!

The battery operated radio was replaced the moment the electricity came to Chapley Street. We then got a really posh Bush radio that could pick up Radio Luxembourg and Radio Athlone – heaven for me and Pat and for mam and dad. Of course it also picked up the Home Service (forerunner of Radio 4) and the Light Programme (forerunner of Radios 1, 2 and the some bits of Radio 4). That Bush Radio was still going strong into the 1990's and my brother Tony was still making some use of it up until he became too ill to keep on top of the valve cleaning (they needed blowing with a bicycle pump every so often to stop the crackling). I'm sure that with a little TLC it would still function for years to come – I see models like it regularly on one of the plethora of antique shows modern TV appears to thrive upon!

The Osborne Cinema wasn't the nearest to us, although we probably went there most often. The Rex across the Rochdale Road was the closest but it was considered the local flea pit. I remember, as a birthday treat taking all of my pals and my brand new harmonica there to watch an afternoon showing of, "Davy Crockett – King of the Wild Frontier" and somehow losing my harmonica, which I never got back! The Essoldo was my personal favourite cinema (along Rochdale Road towards Queen's Road, just passed Collyhurst Street). I was sometimes allowed to go there on Saturday's for the matinee (mum didn't believe in going to the cinema during the day especially in summer when all the bugs of the world were in there). At the matinee we could catch up on the latest adventures of Hoppalong Cassidy or Flash Gordon. During the interval they sometimes held competitions: I remember yoyo and hoola-hoop competitions. They were great. The poshest local cinema outside Manchester (the Odeon was the Bees Knees) was the ABC, Miles Platting on Queen's Road. I can remember seeing Cecil B DeMillle's version of "Sampson and Delilah" there with Patsy (It was still doing the rounds in the 50's despite being made in the 40's) and the French short film that won the first Oscar for Foreign short film, "Le Ballon Rouge" (The Red Balloon), was the support feature. Both were brilliant. I used to love those lavish Biblical epics. "Ben Hur", "The Robe" and of course "The Ten Commandments". They were all brilliant.

Of course things were about to change with the advent of television. I can remember every kid for miles around (certainly our street) piling into the front parlour of the Docherty's house for a live broadcast of the series, "Dan Dare Pilot of the Future". We watched enthralled whilst the ten inch square black and white screen flickered though the episode. The Docherty's were the first in the neighbourhood to get a television. We were the first to get a really posh one. Once again my mum plumped for Bush. She purchased a state of the art set from Rumbelows, it was a twenty-one inch (I think) and sat inside a sliding teak slatted wooden door cabinet which was always closed when the television was off. My mother controlled the viewing strictly. We could only watch what she chose to permit us to watch, although she did thaw somewhat over the years. Nevertheless homework always came before the box!

It's funny but the habits I picked up then are still with me, to a certain extent. Mum laid down that the radio could be on during the day and that the telly was for evenings only. Mind you back then there wasn't much on during the day anyway. By the time we got our telly I was far too old for "The Woodentops", "Bill and Ben" and "Jackonory", although I did steal a look at them from time to time.

Soon our evenings swept through the wild west of "Bonanza", "Gunsmoke", "Have Gun Will Travel" (which I think was called 'Palladin' in America), "Cheyenne", "Wagon Train", "Laramie", "Bronco", "Boots and Saddles" (these last two starring Ty Hardin – I loved it that someone could be called Ty), and my personal favourite "Rawhide". I can still remember being frightened to death by an episode when Rowdy Yates and Gill Favor found themselves in an old Indian burial ground where the bodies were offered to the sky on stilts.

Other shows also became staples: "The Avengers", "Danger Man" (a personal favourite of mine and my mum, I can remember watching "Braveheart" the movie twice before I recognised Patrick McGoohan as Longshanks), "The Saint", "The Four Just Men", "No Hiding Place" and "The Human Jungle" with Herbert Lom, all were thrilling in their own magical way.

American cop shows were always that bit slicker than their British counterparts. In our household, as in many others, "77 Sunset Strip", "The Charlie Chan Mysteries", "The Naked City", and "The Roaring Twenties" were firm favourites and later on I wouldn't be able to name a family that didn't tune in to "The Untouchables", "The Fugitive" , and "Perry Mason".

Comedy came into its own on the telly – I said goodbye to old friends like, "The Navy Lark" and instead made time for: "Mister Ed", "Petticoat Junction", "The Huckleberry Hound Show", "The Flintstones", "The Beverley Hillbillies", "I Love Lucy", and many more U.S. shows. Jed Clampett and the clan were firm favourites in almost every household. The best of British comedy provided the laughs with, "Candid Camera", "Steptoe and Son", "The Army Game", and a host of others.

My interest in music was developed watching: "Juke Box Jury" and later "Ready Steady Go". I don't even need to mention programmes like "Coronation Street", "The Good Old Days", "The Black and White Minstrel Show", "Sunday Night at the London

Palladium", and "Opportunity Knocks", which were all terrific at the time and added new dimensions to otherwise quite narrow lives. Collyhurst parents didn't have the spare cash to visit the theatre so these shows offered a glimpse of the good life and provided countless millions with access to entertainment that was only available to moneyed people prior to that time. Three other programmes linger in my memory from way back then, all capturing my interest. Jacques Cousteau introduced me to a lifetime of interest in nature programmes and even today I can't miss an Attenborough special. Finally two U.S sea dramas were absolutely essential viewing for me: "The Voyage to the Bottom of the Sea" with Richard Baseheart and David Hedison and the other one was "Sea Hunt" starring Lloyd Bridges. I loved them all.

I could never underestimate the popularity of comics in those formative years. Every pal I had was hooked on comics and we all had our own personal favourites. Once you grew out of 'The Beano', 'The Dandy' and the 'Topper' (although, truth be told I don't think many of us ever grew out of them) you progressed to either the 'Hotspur', 'Boys Own' or 'The Eagle' – it was the Eagle for me and I loved every page of it and couldn't wait for the next instalment. I remember I used to get one called, 'Look and Learn' (my mum approved of this one, she couldn't see the point in the others) which taught me loads about history, the natural world, technology, wild animals, geography, space and a whole host of other wonderful topics. The adults liked it because it was educational; I liked it because it was fun. I certainly learned a great deal about the world by flicking through its pages. I had quite a collection of 'Look and Learn' – probably all out of date now like much of my knowledge today (that's according to my grandson Declan).

Mum always subscribed to 'The Ireland's Own' and the 'Catholic Digest' which were both great reads in their own way. The 'Ireland's Own' was full of stories and poetry with an Irish slant and the digest had some great jokes in it, usually with a religious slant.

About the time we flitted across the Oldham Road I graduated to hard core comics: 'Superman', 'Spiderman', and my favourite, 'The Fantastic Four'. I had passing affairs with, 'Batman' and 'Iron Man' but always came back to 'Superman' and 'The Fantastic Four'! I wish I had kept those collections. I've seen copies of 'The Eagle' selling for huge amounts. In fact if you had the right issue some of the comic books that I had, they are worth thousands. I had all of 'The Fantastic Four' from the start up until I was about thirteen or fourteen. Then I gave them all away to the 'bring and buy' sale at church! Madness!!!!

I never managed to get them but I always wanted a pair of those x-ray specs that they advertised on the back of the DC comic books. I guess I must have started observing the difference between boys and girls about the time I progressed to DC comics and I thought a pair of the specs would help me no end, because the imagination can only take you so far can't it? I also lusted after a BB rifle with telescopic sight – but a boy can't have everything can he – especially when they were available by mail order from Southern California and not the Collyhurst Co-op or Hugh Faye's?

Whenever I chat with those of my generation and talk comics, radio or TV the mention of one of these can trigger an unbelievable range of emotions and memories. Humming theme tunes or even singing a song: "Gonna tell you a story 'bout a man named Ged, a poor mountaineer barely kept his family fed". Strangely I think the time listening to the radio brought families closer together; the very act of sitting down together to listen and react to the spoken word was just a terrific shared experience. Now I find that some younger adults find it difficult to follow the commentary on a game of football or a radio play! They have to have the visual stimulus of TV. The warmth of those Sunday afternoons with us all chuckling in front of the fire are still etched deeply in my heart listening to Tony Hancock bemoaning the loss of a pint of his precious 'O' Positive or Rhesus Negative!

I think the arrival of television spelled the end of that kids collective era where we all enjoyed cheering and booing the goodies and the baddies together – cheering and booing weren't encouraged in the house – certainly not like they were at the Saturday matinees!

These were my formative years and it would be no exaggeration to say that the sights and sounds I became exposed to had an influence on me and on everyone else of course. I guess they influenced my sense of humour, imparted knowledge without going through the effort of learning, entertained me, made me think and encouraged a love of wild life.

My horizons without the "box" were quite narrow bordered as they were by a handful of streets that I knew well. Chapley Street of course and the street running parallel to ours and sharing our back entry was Slater Street. Suddell Street, and Livesey Street where the church was were all part of my stomping ground. New Allen Street ran at right angles to Chapley Street on the Oldham Road side of the railway arches.   It was on new Allen Street that the Rag and Bone sheds were (an old factory where they sorted through all they picked up on their rounds). If you had anything that might be useable again it was inevitably earmarked for the rag 'n bone man – kids like me were tuned in to listen for his bugle call because if we took anything out to him (old rags, damaged metal wares, in fact anything that might be salvageable or sold on as scrap) we could turn our bundle of rags into a bow and arrow or a whipping top or some other flimsy toy! By the way all toys back then seemed to be made in Hong Kong. The rag 'n bone man would be heard before being seen blowing lustily on his bugle and calling "Rrrrrr booohn" or words to that effect – I might have misheard because even back then I don't think my hearing was perfect!

I remember the Corona man coming once a week and you would take out last week's empties and get this week's supply. Our favourites were: Dandyline and Burdoch, Orange, and Lemonade, with the occasional bottle of Cream Soda. In those days the bubbles used to go up your nose when you swigged straight from the bottle! Bottles were big money way back then and the kids in every street used to do a roaring trade in knocking on doors and asking if they had any bottles they wanted taking back to the 'offy" (off licence) – I think you got 3d return on the average bottle of beer. It kept the streets clear of broken glass and other litter and nowadays we think we invented recycling!

Between my home and the Rochdale Road there was quite a lot of waste ground due to the Manchester Blitz. Several streets had been cleared following the bombing and the area just before Rochdale Road was empty and desolate. On our side of Rochdale Road there were a long series of advertising hoardings reaching down as far as Livesey Street (perhaps a third of a mile). We used to play war games and the like in, on and around them. As I got older and more daring we started climbing them and daring each other to jump down off them onto the Rochdale Road side. They were quite tall but easily climbed from the reverse side. On the Rochdale Road side they were sheer drops, carrying the adverts of the day. They stood where the properties once stood and at their base there was a two or three foot drop where access to the cellars once was. The object was to initially drop from the hoarding, either from the dip in between ads or from the hoarding itself, pushing yourself out so that you landed on the pavement rather than in the cellar space. Once we mastered dropping from the hoardings we would try jumping from them. First in the gaps between the ads (the gaps were maybe two foot lowerr than the actual hoarding) and then from the hoarding itself. This was no mean feat. The hoardings were maybe ten feet proud of the pavement and set back two or three foot from the paved area. You had to at first squat on the dip between hoardings and then jump out and once you mastered that without breaking limbs you squatted on the hoarding itself and jumped out. If you were an absolute lunatic you eventually got to the stage where you could stand on the hoarding and jump out landing parachute fashion on the paved area. I was one of those lunatics and became an adept at taking the jump. Once you were good at that and had no fear, the competition was for two of you start together and sprint climb the rear, jump and then sprint round the back again and beat the other kid to a second jump. We must have been totally insane. I have to think twice now about stepping off a high pavement before I take the plunge! Brrrrr.

I can also vaguely recall pig sties either on New Allen Street or just off it! Here they collected edible waste (potato peel, mouldy bread etc.) from the surrounding neighbourhood. Woe betide you if you were ever caught trying to torture the pigs – I suspect they'd have fed you to them as soon as look at you!

Abbott Street was like a continuation of Chapley Street and it was on Abbott Street that the local non-Catholic elementary school stood, called, funnily enough, 'Abbott Street School'. I mention it because although the school itself didn't feature too much in my life I do recall visiting the play centre on the odd Thursday evening. On Thursday's they turned the school over to educational entertainment for a couple of hours. There were classes for adults and fun things for kids. I vividly remember visiting the magic lantern show there on one Thursday night and being fascinated by the images and commentary which if I remember correctly concerned the recent conquest of Everest. Sherpa Tensing and Sir Edmund Hillary were the first recorded humans to stand on the big mountain's summit in the year after my birth, so in the late 1950's this was still big news and an amazing feat. The Andrex trail (as Mike Harding dubbed the trails leading to the mountain) didn't exist back then. Mike called it the Andrex trail on account of the number of jobbies deposited by the thousands who have visited base camp since it was first climbed. Mike reckons that you don't need a map to find your way to base camp; you simply follow the little mounds marked by millions of sheets of Andrex toilet paper that sit atop the never decaying jobbies! Anyway the slide show and talk must have been excellent, why else would I recall it almost sixty years on? The only other dealings I ever had with Abbott Street school was on the rare occasion St. Pat's went to war with them.

Miss Coffey's corner shop which was a small grocery shop on the corner of Abbott Street facing the school and diagonally across from our house; it was where I used to be sent to fetch a solid loaf. My wages were always the four corners of the loaf, which I was permitted to bite off as a reward for going (the luxuries of life back then). Miss Coffey knew everything that went on in the surrounding streets and she kept almost everything a family might need. She certainly kept everything I needed: lucky bags, mo jo's and black jacks (four for a penny), penny arrow bars, sherbert dips, Bazookas (chewing gum), flying saucers, liquorice sticks, liquorice pipes, liquorice wood (I can't for the life of me remember what these were called but they looked like a twig and you chewed them until they became a soggy mulch – they were lovely and lasted forever). There's a shop in Hebden Bridge that specialises in retro sweets and

I bought one of those sticks there for my grandson, Bradley – he didn't know what to make of it and was very reluctant to put it near his mouth – the sophistication of modern tastes eh? Then there was the penny gobstopper which absolutely filled your mouth, and of course there were toffee cigarettes. Single chewing gum slivers and toffee cigarette packs often came with picture cards to be collected. I must have eaten a lot of toffee cigarettes or chewed a lot of gum because I had whole collections of these picture cards (famous footballers, Olympians, movie stars, trains, ancient soldiers etc. etc.). I saw one of the collections I once had, recently, framed – you would not believe how much they were selling it for. I could have been a millionaire!

Anyway, at the back of Miss Coffey's shop and the houses next to her there was a stretch of waste ground; a croft. It was where houses had once stood until Mr. Hitler knocked them down, making a parking place for the odd truck. It was on this waste ground that the odd battle between the two schools would erupt. I think these battles were a throwback to an earlier period when the enmity felt for Catholics was much greater, but it did surface a couple of times when I was a youngster. I have no idea what triggered these mini wars but I do recall taking a ducker in the head during the second war that I remember. A ducker is what we called stones or off cuts of bricks. I took one right on my parting and the scar is still visible today! These battles mostly consisted of a huge number of Abbott Street kids charging a huge number of St. Pat's kids and then them being charged in turn. Screaming and shouting was the order of the day, "Kill the rat catchers", "Batter the proddy dogs" and then a melee of charging bodies first this way and then that, skirmishes were usually short and as often as not, caught the lads who were at the forefront by surprise before they turned and fled. At the rear of both groups of boys the chancer would throw the odd ducker – just my luck I didn't duck! The rotten thing is you didn't get any shred of sympathy as a result of arriving home with blood gushing from your bonce; instead you got a thick ear for getting involved in silliness and getting blood on your school clothes! As I recall on the two occasions I can remember these battles going on very few people were ever hurt and the battles themselves were mostly about posturing and didn't last too long before the adults came out and drove us all back to our respective schools.

I don't ever remember too much anti Catholic feeling when I was growing up. Oh I'd get the odd shout of "Mick" or "Paddy" or "Rat Catcher" but the kind of hatred that walked the streets of Glasgow and Belfast was something I knew nothing about. In fact, although most of my close friends were school friends, therefore Catholics, gangs would coalesce and function comfortably together to collect bommy wood – wood for the annual Chapley Street bonfire.

Like everyone else I used to get involved in mooching wood from wherever it could be found although strangely I was never into bonfire night. The idea of celebrating the execution of some Guy who had been dead for years by burning his effigy was somehow abhorrent to me. Plus I once witnessed an horrific fireworks accident when the milk bottle containing the rocket slipped and the rocket punched a hole in the face of one of the young lads at the fire before exploding through his cheeks. Ever since then I have been firmly of the opinion that fireworks should only be in the hands of professionals and then I do love a good firework display.

I remember my very first day at school. I was three years old. The details are very hazy but I remember crying a lot and being bribed with sweets before being ushered into a room full of nippers my age and handed over to Mrs. Cleary who won my heart immediately.

I can still recall the location of the room and apart from loads of little 'uns it had a water table (a kind of table with six inch sides holding water in it with boats and other things floating about, I suspect it would be considered dangerous today – by the H & S Gestapo), a sand table (similar to the water table but with sand and various play things in it), all sorts of toys and a great many camp beds for snooze time. Snooze time was some time in the early afternoon when we were all forcibly ushered onto a camp bed and ordered to sleep. I think I enjoyed school from the very beginning.

Mrs. Farrell was the headmistress of the juniors and Mr. Cassidy the head of the seniors. The seniors were across the yard and catered for children from ten up to fourteen. I think Saint Patrick's was an elementary school. I enjoyed my years there. I danced a hornpipe and sang "The Drunken Sailor" at a school pantomime, listened to Eamon Andrews give a talk which I can't recall anything about (Eamon Andrews was the Terry Wogan of his day, he did boxing commentary and hosted "This is Your Life" – a very popular TV show of the era), and got knocked out of the boxing ring by Johnny O'Mara because I'd seen Cassius Clay fight and knew it was all in the footwork. Johnny just ran at me and clobbered me straight out of the ring ending my promising boxing career before it even started! I also won a prize in the Milk Board Essay writing competition when I was about ten. I got a ten shilling postal order as my prize.

Strangely I don't recall too much about any lessons I had whilst at Saint Pats (apart from when we used to listen to and sing along with the radio that was piped into class: 'Bobby Shafto', 'The British Grenadiers' and 'The Skye Boat Song' spring to mind), nor do I recall the names of too many of the teachers. What I do recall vividly is the rodeo that was playtime or dinner time. Juniors and seniors shared a huge tarred play area at dinner time; I think the breaks were staggered. At dinner time the older ones would sneak out the gates or move to the furthest extremities of the playground to fag it or shout over the wall to the girls play area in the convent grounds next door. The rest of us became swirling Dervishes; the play ground ringing out to cries of "Shrugs", or "2, 4, 6, 8 Rally vo". Chains of kids would swirl from one area to another playing Rally vo or British Bulldog. Girls would sing their rhymes whilst playing two, three or four balls against an accommodating wall (with their dresses pushed into their knickers) whilst others skipped in small or big groups, singing out their rhymes to provide a rhythm for the skippers. Under the shed roof marbles were played. Others played 'Tick' or 'Ticky off the ground', racing everywhere to pass on the tick. Some even played hide and seek using the bodies of others to hide behind. Wow it was an absolute whirlwind and all swirling around the odd teacher or dinner lady armed with a whistle or a bell. Very occasionally the cry would be taken up, "Fight, fight" and within moments everyone in the playground would be circling two young men who rarely looked as though they really wanted to fight and who generally looked quite relieved when some teacher would sidle over and throw them apart with a snarl for the rest of us to go back to what you were doing or suffer the consequences. Consequences in those days were swift and generally painful so you went back quickly to what you'd been doing whilst the two combatants went in to lose the fight with Mr Cassidy and his cane! Halcyon days, halcyon days.

From the age of around seven I served daily mass at Saint Patrick's church on Livesey Street and had notions of becoming a missionary priest, until I saw "The Three hundred Spartans" starring Richard Egan, and then I wanted to be a Spartan soldier. My mum nearly died before deciding that she'd kill me instead!

The Whit Walks were one of the highlights of the Parish year; them and the annual Parish trips to the seaside and circus. The C. of E. Parishes walked on Whit Monday and the Catholic Parishes on Whit Friday. I don't think I am being too one sided when I say the Friday walks were huge in comparison to the Monday walks. On the day in question we would be arranged on Livesey Street in front of the church and then with pipe bands and brass bands playing we would march in procession to Albert Square in Manchester and meet up with the thousands from all of the other Parishes of Manchester. My dad would be somewhere close to the front helping to carry one of the huge banners. I remember the colours, the sounds, the atmosphere, the excitement. Saint Michael's was always one that we looked out for. Saint Michael's Parish was in a very poor area called Ancoats but their procession was always one of the most interesting and colourful to watch because so many of them were of Italian extraction or Eastern European. The costumes they wore were much more colourful than anything else you would see on the day. They were exotic. It was always a wonderfully loud and spirited day. Once the final Parishes had reached the town hall we would disperse to make our way home – our parents via the pubs where we'd be treated to crisps and bottles of pop. The crisps in those days had a little blue bag of salt in them and tasted glorious, unlike the pale flimsy and Spartan fare you get in a bag today! Everybody loved everybody on Whit Friday. Whit Monday was good but not a patch on Whit Friday!

Practically everyone would get new clothes for the walks. Last year's Sunday best would become your everyday clothes and your new Whit Monday or Friday clothes became this year's Sunday best. Hardly anyone had to waste time worrying about what to wear when they were going out because you only had your Sunday best or your work clothes and that was it! I think my dad had two or three best white shirts though, because I remember the odd row about whether his collars (which were separate to the shirts) were starched or not and mum complaining she didn't have any 'Dolly Blue' (don't ask) or 'Robin Starch' to do a proper job. "Brendan, pop across to Miss Coffey's and see if she has any."

Sometimes on a Saturday morning I'd be dragged along shopping by my mum and we'd visit Hugh Faye's on Oldham Road (a high class grocer) where she'd buy butter cut from huge circular slabs, thick cut bacon that tasted like bacon, black pudding and loose tea. If I was very lucky we'd pop into Granelli's, which was a couple of shops away from Hugh Faye's and she'd treat me to an ice cream Sundae (Heaven). I don't think I've ever tasted ice cream to touch Granelli's ice cream. They're still in existence although their ice cream today isn't quite what it was – probably due to having to meet some health and safety standard or other. Too much namby-pamby interference by the state nowadays especially in ice cream!

Strangely enough I was always interested in current affairs and rarely missed an opportunity to sit down with mum and dad, or Pat and watch or listen to the news. Looking back the 50's and 60's were eventful times.

Everest and the death of Joseph Stalin, who it turns out probably killed more than his nemesis Adolf Hitler ('53),Roger Bannister cracking the four minute mile ('54), and of course the advent of the King in 1956 – Elvis Presley undoubtedly changed the face of modern music forever. I can't remember anyone who didn't like his sound although mum sometimes complained that she didn't like all that bumping around and the music was all bang-bang – but there again her benchmark was Mario Lanza and Micahel McCormack!

Elvis was certainly an influence on the lives of all those of us around during his reign as king. Music that followed: the Beatles, the Stones et al all paid homage to his influence on their music. Many Brits even tried to emulate his style without ever quite mastering his uniqueness or brilliance: Cliff Richards, Frankie Vaughan, and Billy Fury to name but three from that era. I remember singing "Return to Sender" in the covered area of Saint Pat's playground with practically every boy in my class singing it too and knowing all the words. He was the King.

The 1960's heralded tremendous 'hope' and 'disillusion' in almost equal measure. JFK's inaugural speech moved me even though I was only eight or nine years old, his death (which I will write about elsewhere) killed something in a great many of us. I heard about the assassination before anyone else in the family. We were living by then on Calver Walk, off Butler Street, across the Oldham Road. I must have got home from school and put on the telly to watch Bronco or Crackerjack or one of the other late afternoon shows, when it was interrupted by Gaye Byrne (who went on to host the famous Late Late Show on RTE in Ireland). Gaye Byrne, along with Bill Grundy, was one of the presenters of Granada reports (a local news show usually on after the six o'clock news). He was obviously in shock as was almost everyone who reported on it that night and for several nights to come. I was devastated, we all were. One event that really made an impression on me was the following night (I think it was the Saturday, November 23rd 1963) I was allowed to stay up and watch one of my favourite satirical shows, "That Was the Week That Was" with David Frost and instead of the usual satire and funny quips I seem to recall that they gave over the whole programme to the assassination. One of the key presenters, whose name escapes me now, delivered a very moving speech which had me in tears (tears were never far away during the immediate days following his death) and then, Millicent Martin who was married to Ronnie Carroll, sang, not one of her usual comic songs, but, a tribute to JFK and the loss of hope for the world that his death presaged. I don't know if any awards were given out in those days for outstanding television but that show would have got my vote.

I don't think any other event shook the whole of the world in quite the same way. The deaths of Martin Luther King, RFK, Anwar Saddat, Indira Gandhi, Yitzhak Rabin were all momentous and equally disturbing and earth shattering but none of them hit us with so much force as JFK's loss. I still find it hard to fight back the tears when I think on that time.

Other things happened in the early 60's that weren't as troubling and perhaps influenced all of our lives in ways we can only begin to contemplate. Yuri Gagarin speeded up the space race significantly in 1961 when he became the first cosmonaut to leave the planet. It prompted Kennedy to pledge to place a man on the moon to join the man in the moon before the end of the decade (he wouldn't live to see it happen, but happen it did in 1969). The

Russian's always appeared to be just one step ahead of the Americans in terms of extra terrestrial activities way back then. The Russian Bear didn't make too many friends around the world when they constructed the Berlin wall in the same year that Gagarin parted with gravity. "Ich bin ein Berliner" generated a pride and belief in things to come if we all stuck together against tyranny – today we share "Je suis Charlie" or "Nous sommes Paris", in our confusion, outrage and anger at the Satanic forces arrayed around the world. It is a much darker world than the Collyhurst world of my youth!

We did have some excitement in Britain in 1963 with the Great Train Robbery. I think people were unsure whether to condemn the perpetrators or praise them – the money was after all being shipped for destruction. In a time when so many had so little it was hard to accept that the country had money to literally burn! When caught and sentenced I think people felt that the sentences were disproportionate. Malicious and obvious murderers would soon be getting a slap on the wrist by comparison! I am aware that one of the guards died as a result of his injuries a year or so after the robbery and I wouldn't wish to minimise the suffering that that caused him and his family. Funny, they couldn't bring a charge of murder against the robbers because he'd died over a year after the event, but today they are charging some ancient celebrities with touching people-up, forty years ago – something wrong there I think! I wouldn't want to be in the shoes of some members of those early pop groups who regularly found groupies sat up in bed waiting for them when they returned from a gig! I'm not an expert on this but

I'm guessing that very few of them demanded to see birth certificates in such situations. There is something to be said for the statute of limitations used in the U.S.A., I think. I must admit to feeling a little sorry for one or two of these celebrities who are certainly guilty of what used to be termed "hanky panky" or "touchy feely", but only so long as they didn't go beyond that. If I'm not mistaken it often worked both ways but I've yet to hear of an aging DJ or pop star taking some old girl to court who squeezed his bum or Wilbur in the late 60's!

I mentioned the Parish annual trips to the seaside and the circus. The seaside trips to Southport, Blackpool or St. Anne's involved absolutely everyone. There'd be loads of coaches or 'sharras' as they were called back then. Sharra was short for charabanc. We'd set off at 0800 and travel via Preston, returning around 2100 absolutely exhausted sporting our "kiss me quick" hats or our "HMS Big Boy" sailor caps and carrying huge hordes of rock for future consumption. Later in my life I felt an amazingly strong affinity with the story by Dylan Thomas which is simply entitled, "A Story" all about a coach trip to Porthcall which they of course never reached! Our Parish trips were very much like that only we actually made it to the seaside. The kids enjoyed their donkey rides, visits to the Pleasure Beach (no entry charge back then) or Madame Tussauds. The mums on the beach with their skirts tucked into their knickers like their daughters did when playing two-ball against the wall in the street. Dads' with hankies knotted around their heads and trousers rolled to their knees before gasping for breath and heading off to one of the great many pubs and bars that lined the front. Fish and chips at one of the cafes and calamine lotion to sooth burned backs on the way home. This was the annual trip to the seaside and it seemed to me that practically every member of the parish participated in them.

The trip to the circus was a reward for the altar boys. Some years we'd get to the circus and also a pantomime at the Palace Theatre in Manchester. Ken Dodd was invariably the one you wanted to catch in panto and I don't care what anyone says about him today – he was brilliant back then!

I remember going to see "Robinson Crusoe" at the Palace and Ken Dodd brought the house down with a quip directed at Kenny Lynch who was playing Man Friday. I can't recall the exact context but when Ken Dodd said, "Don't say brown, say Hovis" it left everyone weeping with laughter. I don't think Kenny Lynch who was very popular (he was a regular in the Army Game) thought that the quip was racist or politically incorrect. Laughter and humour were 'incorrect' those days nut nobody knew it – we needed later generations to point that out to us! The "don't say brown, say Hovis" was a quote from a TV advert of the time for Hovis brown bread! You probably can't call it that now!

The circus was something else. Once again we would be picked up by a 'sharra' and taken along Queen's Road to Belle Vue where the zoo was and the Belle Vue Amusement Park (the U. K's. first ever theme park) with the ricketiest wooden bobs in the world (they were later bought by some company in Arizona where I think they are still wowing the crowds today, along with London Bridge). It was the most magical experience I can recall when I was a youngster. The sights, sounds, smells, tastes and excitement of the event was so far removed from everyday life that it was truly thrilling. I loved the trapeze acts with the scantily clad and nubile girls sailing out of reach against the backdrop of the big top. Elephants, tigers, lions, seals, dogs all provided unbelievable demonstrations of skill. I really am glad I got to see all that before they banned them on the grounds of animal cruelty. There may have been some cruelty at some circus grounds but I only ever witnessed a coming together of man or woman and beast involving trust and love on both sides. The acrobats and clowns were always amazing. The whole thing was a full on experience that left a little boy panting with happiness, joy and love of life.

    I can recall going to Belle Vue as an older teenager one New Year's Eve, to the Elizabethan Ballroom, to let in the New Year with thousands of other revellers. I suspect that was in around 1970.

    One year instead of the circus Belle Vue was given over to the Oberammergau Passion Play which was awesome. I returned home wanting to be a priest again and in particular I wanted to give my life for my faith! I hadn't seen "The Three Hundred Spartans" at that point in my life. I don't believe that anyone who has ever witnessed the full performance of their passion play can see it without being seriously moved by it.

When I look back at that time I am more and more impressed with how much culture I was actually exposed to.

At St. Clare's which I attended from September 1963 I was introduced to the ballet, opera (at the Opera House), the Hale Orchestra (at the Free Trade Hall where I later saw Bob Dylan, Elton John and Christy Moore) and to the Faraday lectures. I'm still amazed that I didn't turn out to be brilliant!

I think 1963 was the year I began to have some political thoughts. Martin Luther King's, "I have a dream" speech impressed me no end. Patsy had already told me about the iniquities of apartheid in South Africa and I was shocked to think that something similar existed in the States. Kennedy's death as I've already indicated had an effect on just about the whole world.

Always an avid reader I was already reading William Golding, George Orwell, Aldous Huxley (who died on the same day as JFK) and Graham Greene. I do recall being unbelievably impressed by "The Singer not the Song" written by Audrey Erskine-Lindop – which struck me as very Graham Greenish in style at the time! Patsy was my reading mentor and she would encourage me to read such and such if she thought I was capable of taking it in and then she'd discuss it with me. Everything was leading me towards the writer who influenced my political and spiritual life more than any other writer, John Steinbeck – but I don't believe I read any Steinbeck until later in the decade.

In 1965 on my birthday, January 24th, to be precise Winston S. Churchill passed away. He'd had a series of strokes in the days and weeks before he died – but die he did on my birthday! It kind of took something away from my thirteenth birth year!

I already knew a lot about the great man; some good, some not so good. I knew he'd cocked up in WW1 in some place called the Dardanelles, that he had been willing to use and had urged the use of troops against the working class strikers of the great depression in 1926, and that directly after his "finest hour" following WW2 he was booted out of office by the returning service men and women of a grateful nation. It must have seemed an incredible betrayal to him that he should be so unceremoniously dumped by the nation he'd served during those desperate years.

My own personal leanings were already clearly of a socialist disposition and I was even then reading about and rooting for the Labour Party even though Mr. MacMillan seemed a nice enough chap! I have no doubt, having made my own ongoing study of the events during WW2, that Churchill was the right man to lead us to victory against the Nazis. His belligerent nature, eloquent turn of phrase and bulldog spirit were exactly what this country needed in the face of the Fuehrer's apparently invincible war machine. He was not, however, considered a true friend of the working man and for me the working man has always provided the greatest and truest heroes in any country. Like my Aunt Peggie's husband Gordon Price. An unassuming railway clerk with Welsh antecedents who landed on Sword Beach at 1030 on June 6th 1944 and was in Germany when they eventually capitulated, having spent the whole time chasing the enemy and losing most of his comrades to wounds or death in the meantime. I am extremely proud that recently (he's in his 90's now) he was awarded the Legion d'honneur by a grateful French nation for his contribution to the liberation of France. There's a true hero, the kind of man to sing patriotic songs about and to thank for the life that I have led and all of my generation for that matter. It looks like the descendents of Mr. Churchill are determined to undermine the achievement of these men by honouring Mammon as opposed to man! None more so than Maggie Thatcher ("you can't match her, she's the darling of us all") but that's a story for another chapter in my life, away from the sometimes chaotic but always eventful and generally happy days I spent as a son of Collyhurst.

6. Presidential Exchange.

From the age of three I attended the boys' school (Saint Patrick's), on Suddell Street which was around the corner from the church. Mrs Cleary was my first teacher and I loved her deeply. I can vividly recall the first day when I was delivered to the nursery by my mother – I nearly screamed the school down. I couldn't believe that she would abandon me to these monsters; but abandon me she did, and within minutes I was playing in the sand pit, splashing water in the water tank and racing around the spacious room with all of my new found friends!

Pat, my sister, was seven years older than me and attended the all girls convent school at Saint Patrick's on Livesey Street, which just happens to be the street where Pat was knocked over having left me in the pram outside the shop opposite the convent. She'd been on an errand for mam when I was around eighteen months and she forgot that I was with her. When mum asked how the baby was she panicked and ran back to collect me and got herself knocked over – how she managed that on those traffic free streets I shall never know! That is, as they say, another story.

In 1956 she was a senior girl waiting to move on, having passed her eleventh plus, to Notre Dame Grammar school and in that year the Irish statesman and patriot Eamonn DeValera visited Manchester to officially open the Manchester Irish Social Centre (the M.I.S. club) opposite Queen's Park, in between Collyhurst and Harpurhey.

DeValera was very unpopular in England because of Ireland's neutral stance during WWII when he had been Prime Minister and as Ireland was still in dispute with England regarding the ownership of the northern part of Ireland, Irish ministers could not make official visits to the British Government. In fact relations have only recently permitted Irish Prime Ministers and Presidents to visit England in an official capacity following the normalisation of the situation in the North.

Anyway, DeValera was in Manchester, to demonstrate solidarity with the Manchester Irish by opening their new club. Saint Patrick's school, being named for the patron saint of Ireland and providing a fine education for the sons and daughters of Ireland's sons and daughters, couldn't miss the opportunity to invite Dev, as he was affectionately known, along to meet the senior girls. I don't know whether he met the senior boys or not (me being but a gossoon then), but he certainly met and was introduced to the girls.

It must have been close to summer time because I know that the senior girls, my sister Patsy included, were lined up outside in the gardens of the convent school to be formally presented. All knew that they were being presented to some important dignitary and had been turned out scrubbed and polished, by their proud parents, so as to be acceptable when presented.

The youngsters were lined up in alphabetical order according to their surnames: Ahern's, Brennan's, Coey's, Docherty's and so on, until towards the end of the line stood Patsy, in her pig tails.

Having the surname Ramsbottom always meant being towards the last in line!

The Long Fellow (as opposed to the Big Fellow – the sobriquet of the Irish leader Michael Collin's who was killed during the Irish Civil War) was led along the line of brightly polished girls. He was a tall and angular man who towered above the girls and the nuns who escorted him – the latter brimming over with pride in the occasion. Dev had a word for each girl, he had been a schoolmaster himself before he became a freedom fighter and politician, and he had a lifelong love of mathematics. Slowly but inexorably he was led down the line.

"Mary Nolan, sir", said Sister Ignatius as she introduced the next in line.

"Hello there. Are you a good scholar and do you have a favourite lesson?" the tall man enquired of an open mouthed Mary Nolan.

Mary remembered to courtesy as she had been taught before responding in an explosion of breath, "YesArithmeticMister".

He nodded approvingly and moved on to meet Julia Patterson. Patsy would be next but one.

Soon enough the Long Fellow was staring down at her. He appeared unbelievably tall to her.

"Patricia Ramsbottom, sir" intoned Sister Ignatius.

He appeared to start. "Ramsbottom, now that's an unusual name I think." Patsy's mouth hung open waiting politely, as she's been told to do, for the inevitable question, which was likely to be about her favourite subject – English. He seemed to think for a moment before staring closely at Pat with a penetrating and quizzical look. "You're grandmother wouldn't happen to be Elizabeth Ramsbottom of Ballickmoyler?" he enunciated in clipped and precise tones which had little or no brogue.

Patsy stared up at this giant, suddenly perplexed; he'd gone off script and had questioned her about her very own Granny Ran. "Yes", she mumbled.

"Very good," he returned, "would you ever remember me to her when you next go home and tell her that I said thank you?"

Patsy's mouth closed with a snap, she gulped and nodded vigorously as the long fellow moved on down the remainder of the line to be introduced to Rose Sharkey, Kathleen Tully and Bernadette Vesay.

Patsy's mind was in turmoil. "What was it he asked you Ramsbottom?" demanded Sister Ignatius after his departure. Patsy reminded the nun and admitted she had no idea what he had been on about and didn't know how he knew her granny Ran.

The school day finished as usual at four that afternoon and Patsy skipped her way homewards, pausing to collect the little brat who was her brother from the infants' school.

That night my mother, who was a great de Valera supporter, was glowing in pride and basking in glory. Her daughter had conversed with the great man which, I assume, assured our fame forevermore. Yet even she, our all knowing mother, could throw no light on his cryptic address to Pat. It was a mystery – perhaps even an enigma! We would have to wait until "our father" was home to hear the full story!

Dad of course duly arrived home, having called in at the Odd Fellows for a couple of pints to toast the earlier presence of the Long Fellow on the streets of Manchester. He found himself in a whirlwind of demands and questions. What had Dev been going on about to the girl? How did he know my father's mother – and know her by name if you don't mind?

Once my father began to make sense of the stream of chatter he managed to answer all of the questions, "How should I know what he was on about?"

He, like us, had no idea how the Long Fellow knew his mother. The mystery remained.

Until, later that year when we visited Ballickmoyler and Granny Ran. We were barely in the house that my father had been born in before she was being assailed on all sides by my mother and Patsy demanding to know what de Valera had meant.

As always gran took charge. "Quiet down now and let me finish the tae."

Once she had us all sat down, and ensured we had tea in one hand and a sandwich in the other she calmly asked what in the world we were all so fired up about. Mum told her of Dev's visit and how he had spoken to Patsy in such a personal manner.

Gran sat back and smiled to herself.

"Do ye know anything of the Long Fellow and what he got up to in the war of independence?" she enquired. Mum and dad knew odd bits but Patsy and I knew nothing.

"In early 1919, the Big Fellow (Michael Collins), sprang Dev from Linclon jail, where the British were inclined to keep him. I'm not sure if Collin's did it on purpose but he had Dev dress up as a woman to get him past the road blocks on the way to Manchester and then Liverpool – I don't think Dev ever forgave him for that. Anyway they eventually smuggled him back into Ireland where he went on the run, never staying in the same house for longer than a night or two. Around April 28th or 29th of that year I received a visit from one of the Brennan's – one or two of them were active in the I.R.A. at the time. As you know (to my dad) your brother Jimmy, who was only a gossoon at the time, was a runner for the local brigade commander. Anyway they asked your father and myself if we'd put someone up for the night. It would have been impolite to refuse, so of course we agreed, and so later that same day in the late evening, when all the young ones were in bed, they delivered a hooded figure to the door and whisked him inside and up the stairs to the loft. I didn't know who it was until I took him up the tae. It was then I discovered that it was none other than the Long Fellow, De Valera himself. He was giving out about all the cloak and dagger stuff saying it was all a load of auld malarkey and that he reckoned Collin's was whisking him about the country so that he could have a good laugh at his expense. He went so far as to suggest he might have been happier in Lincoln jail! He was only coddin' of course - I think." She paused and took a drink from her own cup of tea and again she smiled to herself remembering things from the dawn of a nation that we could only ever read about.

"Anyway, he stayed two nights' and disappeared the next evening in the same manner in which he came; off up to Old Leigh or wherever the next safe house would be. He was quite charming when he wasn't giving out about the indignity of sneaking around like some rapscallion and he offered prodigious thanks to your father and myself before he went on his way.

That was the last ever I saw of him until you came home now and told me what he had said to Patsy. Aren't you the honoured little lady (leaning towards Pat who became the Cheshire Cat). So, that's the story; anyone for another cup of tae?" With which she began her usual bustle around the kitchen.

Dad, who had been there at the time (he was born in 1918) was amazed to hear that his own father and mother had harboured one of the most wanted men in the British Empire, after Michael Collins! I know he took a quiet pride in their contribution to the cause because like all true sons' of Erin he relished tales of the Rising and honoured the heroes of those terrifying years. Like many Irish men of the time he marched, as did we all, on the anniversary of Allen, Larkin and O'Brien who'd been hung in Manchester the century before in the cause of Irish Freedom. Their grave in Moston Cemetery was alternately lionised and defiled throughout the passing of the years. Gran's story meant a great deal to him and latterly to myself, when I was old enough to appreciate the hand of history touching us.

Granny Ran was a remarkable lady. Born in 1880 she lived all of her life within the border area of Old Leigh and Ballickmoyler, nestled as they were between the counties of Carlow, Kildare, Offaly and Laois in Southern Ireland. Depending on who was playing football (Gaelic) or hurley dad would oftentimes claim to be from anyone of the these counties.

She married Michael Ramsbottom, a stonemason, and gave up her maiden name of Murphy in 1898 and moved into what I knew as the Ramsbottom's family home in Ballickmoyler. The Ramsbottom's, I am told, settled over in Ireland from Lancashire in the 15th or 16th centuries to avoid religious persecution in England – it's a common name in the four counties. Locally the family were known as the 'Rans' which I discovered was a local pronunciation of wren and taken from the adopted poem of the clan which began "The wren, the wren the king of all birds" (dad would recite the whole thing from time to time, usually when pickled).

Elizabeth Ramsbottom was a powerful woman who operated the doctor's dispensary in Ballickmoyler. She raised eleven children. The old house was next door to the vicar's house, with whom she got on famously.

There wasn't a herb, spice, flower, leaf, mushroom or toadstool that she couldn't name and identify and say whether it had healing properties or not. Local people would visit for poultices and potions to be made up by her and they swore by her efficacy. She even did some of the doctoring when the doctor would be down the country. Bone setting it seems was one of her specialities.

I recall dad telling a wonderful story about Granny Ran which has stuck in my mind over the years.

Dad would visit home as regularly as he could; from once he had left for England, following his failure to become a jockey (he grew to be around six feet tall, which kind of precluded that occupation to him). Anyway, he was home one year, around 1942 when he met a chap in Kelly's Bar (which might have been called Kavanagh's then), Ballickmoyler's only local. The chap was dressed in full cowboy regalia down to the Stetson hat and boots! Dad always loved a good cowboy book or movie. They got talking and the guy, who had been a local, turned out to be in search of a Mrs. Elizabeth Ramsbottom.

It seems that around 1920, Paudie (for that was the name he gave to my father), had been working in the local fields when he caught his leg in a machine. The leg it seems was nearly ripped from him. With robust care and speed they carried him from the field to the dispensary in the hope that the doctor, who ran surgeries there once or twice a week, might be there. He wasn't. The doctor was in fact on the other side of Carlow town delivering a slow burn baby! Even if word could have been gotten to him and he attempted to get back to Ballickmoyler the young man would surely have been long dead from loss of blood.

So it fell to Granny Ran to deal with the casualty which she did in her usual business like way. She cleaned the wound, set the bone, stitched the flesh back together and poulticed everything up in copious dressings. A day or so later the doctor arrived and declared himself 'happy' with her work and that was that.

Paudie had almost died despite her efforts because of the enormous loss of blood he suffered, but he didn't. He made a full recovery and eventually emigrated to America where he had a brother in New Jersey. Returning to Ireland, with his family after many years away, he had made up his mind to visit Gran to offer her his gratitude. He was in no doubt that she had saved his life and his leg, which hardly troubled him – bar leaving him with a distinguished limp!

He was home dressed as a cowboy, as all the Yanks (émigrés) returning home in those days were; whether they worked in the car factories of Detroit, the steel mills of Baltimore, on the Manhattan waterfront or plodding a beat on the streets of New York and New Jersey. It was expected of them to dress so. They helped to maintain the illusion that everyone who went to the States lived the movie star life; practically every movie was a cowboy! And for the few weeks they visited their home place they were lauded. Paudie was the Tom Mix of Ballickmoyler or Old Leigh!

Gran's skill and knowledge were renowned far and wide. Her remedies were valued, and folk requested cures for whatever ailed them for all of her long and eventful life.

Some might say she was privileged to have met Dev, I don't. In fact I'd say the reverse is true, Dev was lucky to have known and met her. She was mother Ireland.

7. Ballykilleen, Cloonfad.

The interminable wait for summer and the chance of going home was like a dull ache to me, a yearning. Summer holidays meant Ireland, Ireland meant Ballykilleen, Ballykilleen meant Padraic and Rita, my cousins. My cousins meant wild and free summers stretching on forever.

The thrill actually began as we left Manchester, boarding the 10.20 p. m. boat train for Holyhead. In those days you could smell the turf fires of Dublin before you could ever see the North Wall. The thrill didn't reach fever pitch until I stepped off the train in Ballyhaunis and into Jim McDonagh's blue, column gear-shift, Ford and took the road to Mark Cunniffe's warm, whitewashed, half-doored, thatched cottage which stood on the brow of the hill above Delia and John Scahill's, with Jack Maddens' home standing silently to the rear.

Every summer was a series of adventures to re-live and new ones waiting to happen. Everything was "the big"; the "big river", the "big cart house", the "big wagon" and the "big tree" on which swung the swing. Everything rang with the peel of adventures to come.

I knew that I'd soon be reacquainting myself with old friends: Aiden, Ger and of course Dimpna and Martha. I knew that some would be pleased to see me whilst others would simply excuse the cheeky English brat who would be wandering the village for what seemed, to them, like forever. Oh those were good days; special days; happy days. Waiting for the bike to come home from the last mass on Sunday and fighting to see who'd get to lick the wrapping on the block of ice-cream. Jumping aboard the wonder of Tom Fitzmaurice's mobile shop or pestering for sweets at Seamus Flood's visits with his mobile shop. It's funny, we might have been miles away, away over the fields tormenting the noble donkey on Reagan's land but we'd always know when the mobile shop was on its way. Perhaps it was the scent of the sweets in the clean, fresh, free summer air. Flying cow pats (these were our early frizzbees), catching wasps, riding the donkey, cowboys and Indians in the furze, fishing with stick and line with bent wire hook, drinking cold tea down in the bog, visiting and tormenting the life out of good, God fearing neighbours. What more could a city boy of nine wish for?

This year was special. Mum, dad and my much older sister Patsy were all at home together. This year I'd have fights with Padraic over who's brother Tony was, we'd visit Salthill and get burned, dad would go off with Tom Fitz to the All Ireland Semi Final and roll home pickled on the Monday following the match, much to mother's shame and the mirth of Mark, Kit and Baby. This year Baby (my mother's sister Mairead – the youngest, hence Baby) would chase us down to John Scahill's, ready to "kill" us for uprooting her rose garden and we'd escape by hiding in the hag, John would later pay me a duck egg for helping (more likely hindering) his haymaking and I'd be as sick as a pup! Oh it was a great summer.

There were many memorable days as there always were. One day, I do recall, that provides a very special memory for me was the day I watched the horse foaling.

I don't know how it came about but on this particular day I was alone. I was rarely alone and I have no idea why I happened to be alone on this day but I was. I was on the far side of the little river that separated Ballykilleen from Culchaboro (I know I've misspelled this but phonetically that's what it's called). It was a glorious summer's day and I lay back in the field opposite Hunt's house out on the Claremorris Road. Slow clouds drifted by in the shape of castles and faeries and faces and other wonderful things as I lay watching. Slowly I became aware of a strange noise. A grunting, a snuffling, a wheezing. I clambered to my feet and realised the sound was coming from the next field. I looked over the limestone wall and saw it was a horse in foal.

She lay panting, lifting her head to look down her body and I realised that there was something poking out of her back end. I looked more closely and realised she was in the act of foaling. I was torn between running off to alert the local farmers and in the magic of the moment. I eventually convinced myself that if the men across the river were half as good as Uncle Mark and Tom Scahill then they would be well aware of the horse's condition and if they weren't present it would be because this was the natural way for it to occur so I stayed to watch.

Eventually the foals head showed and without any ceremony the rest of the birth sac flooded out. The mare was exhausted but she turned her head and bit the sac and helped the struggling foal to free itself. I slowly became aware that I must have been watching for a long time and that the whole world had become silent. In fact it felt like the silence was pressing on my ears. I believe I must have been holding my breath because now I was panting and then the most amazing thing happened. The foal, only minutes old, staggered awkwardly to its feet. They splayed out from its body, its beautifully defined head bobbed rhythmically and it stood staring blindly about for the first time in its life.

For me it was an almost spiritual moment. I was in awe. My heart was pounding and I felt intensely excited. Although a part of me was already thinking it would be great to have the others here with me, yet another part was jealously and selfishly appreciative of the fact that I was alone. It was a day that has stayed with me always. A day to thank God for. One of those beautiful memorable days that makes life so beautiful and meaningful.

Another incredibly memorable day was the day when John Marten Mongen gave me a chew of his tobacco!

We were all off to the bog, somewhere off the Claremorris Road and I was riding with John Marten, Rita and Padraic in the "dunkey and cart". Poor auld Neddy had his work cut out for himself that day! As usual I drove John Marten to distraction with "What's this? Who's that? Where's the other?" and a host of other inconsequential questions. God help him, he had the patience of a saint as did so many of the people who had to deal with me.

John Marten was the family guest and as we'd had lodgers in Manchester I thought nothing more about it. I believe that he lost his family home in a storm, perhaps in the thirties or forties and that he was taken in by the Cunniffe's who provided him with board and a roof over his head in return for his labour.

Talking about lodgers, the most notorious one we ever had was Paddy Cunniffe from Gurteen, my mother's first cousin. He was left one year with the awesome responsibility of looking after my good and faithful dog "Rolf" whom I loved beyond words. On returning to Manchester at the end of that summer we found that Rolf was dead, run over by the milk float, and as Paddy was in charge – it was his fault. The poor man still carries a great burden of guilt over that episode!

Anyway, we were in the cart with John Marten and as usual he was cutting a plug of tobacco and chewing it with obvious pleasure. He could hit a fly on Neddy's ear with one well-aimed splat of spit. Now a skill like that was every young fellows dream so of course I began to badger him until he agreed to cut me off a "chaw".

I sat next to him brimming. Padraic and Rita looked on awe struck and jealous. I was to be a man at last! I considered all the wonderful ways I'd impress friends back in England with my superior spitting ability. I'd be able to knock down a bird in flight or hit any cat or dog in the eye at twenty paces. I popped the blackened knob into my mouth and chewed. Interesting.

I can't say how soon it happened, but it was mighty soon and I can't say whether it began in my stomach, mouth or throat but I do know that it affected all three. The taste was the vilest I'd ever experienced, the gorge rose in me faster than reaction. I physically swooned and if it hadn't been for John Marten I'd have been out of the cart and on my head. Needless to say I soon rid myself of the foul tasting "baccy" and sat in the full and awful knowledge of what it meant to be "green around the gills".

We reached the bog, although I don't recall too much else about that long ago journey or the day that followed it for that matter! What I do recall is that dad and Mark were very impressed and questioned John Marten about how he'd managed to get me to be quiet for so long. I suppose I should be happy that I wasn't force-fed a diet of the revolting stuff on a regular basis after that!

Ah, I miss those days and most of all I miss those people. They brought such joy and happiness to a small boy home for the holidays. Time may be a great healer, and I certainly recovered from my experience that day, but it is also a tyrant that robs us of our youth and worse – of the ones we love!

8. The Kiernan's at number 98.

I recall one year returning from Ireland. It was the same year that Paddy Cunniffe looked after my dog so well that when I returned I had no dog!

The journey back to Manchester was always exciting but anticlimactic. Travelling was always great fun and even better when dad was around. The train journey across Ireland thrilled; the lurching boat that never failed to sicken mum, throbbed with noise, smells and craic; and then the rail journey across Wales and into Northern England with its smuts and clickety-click always felt like it was building to some kind of exciting finale which was ruined when the grey, wet and dark walls on the outskirts of Manchester hove into view. Home again, home again until the next year, or if we were very lucky until Christmas.

Patsy and I would have school to look forward to and I would already be working out how I explained to my friends that I had an older brother who lived in Ireland! Their brothers were always, so it seemed, available to "bash you" if you stepped out of line or picked on them. Mine was a distant threat – but Patsy could throw a scare into most of them and their big brothers' which I was occasionally thankful for.

Anyway this particular year we left the train in Manchester and as usual got a taxi to take us on the short journey home.

Home was 100 Chapley Street (late Chapman Street). It was an unremarkable street in Collyhurst (a suburb of Manchester) which ran parallel to Livesey Street and between which Saint Patrick's boys school was nestled. On the corner of the street opposite our corner was the Catholic Club (which my dad wasn't keen on because he felt they were very cliquey) and next to the Catholic Club lived Mrs. Sweeney and her son Jim (who in later life became the larger than life caretaker of the De La Salle Training College at Hopwood Hall in Middleton).

Mrs. Sweeney remains vaguely in my memory for two reasons: she was the oldest inhabitant on the street living to over one hundred and because I nearly gave her a heart attack. I had just received a good bashing by a gang from Abbott Street school, the local non-Catholic school and had managed to run hell for leather to escape them, pausing to shout "F**k off" before disappearing into the house. I'd have been around eight or nine and I can still vividly recall old Mrs. Sweeney stood on her doorstep physically rock with shock at what she had just heard spill from my mouth! I knew that when mum came home that night I'd be in for it! Language like that was not to be heard aloud on the street and certainly not from the mouths of babes!

Next door to us lived the Kiernan's. They were an old couple whose son had the debatable pleasure of being taken away to the "funny farm" – the yellow van came and took him away to Prestwitch where he'd be locked up and looked after. I don't remember the son, or the taking away of him! I do recall our return home from holiday that year.

The Kiernan family, I believe had lived in Manchester since famine times, which would make the old couple third or fourth generation English. They were a lovely couple, if a little peculiar (according to my mum) and Mrs. Kiernan was a devout gossip. She always reminded me of Old Mother Riley, who was incredibly popular when I was a boy. She wore a shawl and stood on the polished door step with her arms folded willing to talk to anyone who would dawdle as they passed.

Two or three days before we arrived home old Mr. Kiernan had passed away and as was the custom in those days he was laid out, in state so to speak, for all to pay their last respects to him in their front parlour. Their lobby separated our front parlour from theirs. And it was in our front parlour that Paddy Cunniffe had his digs. He had lived and slept in great fear, knowing that the corpse was in the room more or less next to him. Paddy was quite a young man and he told me many years later that the only way he could get a night's sleep was with the drink or at Mrs. Folley's on the next street whose husband did the night shift at Ferranti's. She was an 'accommodating and buxom woman' whose husband didn't understand her womanly needs, according to Paddy!

So we'd arrived back from Ireland. An exhausting, if exciting trip with lots of wonderful memories to keep us going until the next year and as we climbed out of the taxi old Mrs. Kiernan literally dived out of the house and accosted us.

"You must come in and say hello to himself", she shouted to mum and dad. Mum and dad were quick to pick up on the fact that they were being invited in to say hello to a corpse.

The bags were thrown into our lobby and fresh with the travel dust still clinging to us we filed in to number 98 Chapley Street (late Chapman Street). Their lobby was much like ours; dull, dark green and brown gloss paint above a cheap linoleum floor covering. She led us to her parlour where on trestles stood a coffin its lid leaning against the far wall.

I had never seen a corpse before and was terrified and excited at both one and the same time. Quietly we filed into darkened room. It was the custom then to keep the curtains of the house of the deceased closed until after the funeral.

Mum and dad were at the head of the coffin whilst Patsy and I remained towards the narrower end.

Being young my eyes were just about on a level with the edge of the coffin but if I stood just a little on tiptoe I could look along the length of it. It gave me a clear view up his nose. I was intrigued to note that I could see cotton wool up there – had it always been there or was this something they did when you died? Patsy would tell me later. He also had cotton wool protruding from his ears and there were clearly two old pennies resting on his eyes. Filled with dread and excitement I stared at this old man who had been clumping up and down the street with his stick before we had gone away. Such is life I thought in one of those deeply philosophical moments children sometimes have.

Mrs. Kiernan hadn't missed a beat as she showed us into the room. She told us of how quickly he had been struck down and how readily, willingly and easily he had given up the fight. As we all stared at the body, contemplating our own mortality she continued, "Doesn't he look good? He looks just like he's sleeping. Like he's having a nap after a pint o'mild of a Sunday afternoon. He hasn't looked this good in years 'as he?" she opined to mum and dad.

I saw dad lean in close to mum and distinctly heard him whisper to her, "I'd swear he looked a lot better before we left for home!"

Prayers were said, condolences offered and enquiries about the funeral made before we all traipsed next door. Once the front door was closed and we were in the kitchen I saw it was awful hard for dad not to burst out laughing – I think mum's threats restrained him but he couldn't help commenting on how distinctly unwell he looked in the coffin compared to the hale and hearty old man we'd last seen before the holidays.

I don't recall much more about the Kiernans. I remember asking Pat about them years later and she told me that old Mrs. Kiernan had passed away shortly after the old fellow. The way Patsy told me it seemed like that was the polite or expected thing to do back then.

I never did find out anymore about their son but I do know that despite my tears for Rolf and the blame I heaped upon Paddy – he certainly slept better after our return and Mr. Kirenan's funeral.

9. Crossing the Bridge.

I was born and spent my early years in an area of Manchester called Collyhurst. It was, I suppose, a slum area that was being cleared throughout those child hood days. First individual houses and then whole streets were to disappear along with the people who lived in them. I've read many descriptions of those mean terraced houses that people used to live in, with their outside loos and dark satanic mills but this view is in discord with what I recall. The houses were old but comfortable, close together but warm, and full of the finest people you could ever hope to meet. Tough people who spoke their own minds, who cared about their neighbours, who lived life to the full, and who looked forward to nothing more extravagant than a week in Blackpool once a year, where they would sample the high-life from some good value bed and breakfast hotel.

The people who lived in Collyhurst were an ethnically well-mixed bunch. There were of course the born and bred Mancunians, a great many Irish, Poles, Lithuanians, Italians and Ukranians. I attended school with Carls', Janics', Leos, Seans' and Albertos'. These were first generation English and I was just one more thrown into the melting pot. Their parents like mine were hard-working, God fearing and full of ambition for their offspring. They had left their own countries to make a better life, to escape injustice and poverty and they wanted their children to grow up independent, healthy and wise. They had lived through a world war, some of them fighting on the other side, but all had the same desperate dream for their children.

People were always in and out of each other's houses and lives. They shared the highs and lows that living closely brought. Death was a shared experience that brought people together rather than distancing them from each other. It was a great thing if one of the children made it to grammar school and everyone celebrated such good fortune. They were a generous people, ever ready to reach into their own shallow pockets to help someone in trouble. Charity dances were so common at one time they appeared to be in vogue.

I remember vivdly going to the Docherty's house with a million other kids to watch their tiny television, because they had the first one on the street. We'd squeeze into their parlour and watch the minute screen in awe at the live programmes they used to broadcast like.

Kids would organise jumble sales on the brightly donkey stoned front steps of their homes and for a few pence you could purchase relatively unused toys. I recall acquiring a Wyatt Earp gun in this manner, a Ned Buntline special, it's barrel almost as long as my arm - it was useless in any fast draw situation - but it was a beauty! I had one of the fastest draws on the street and I soon reverted to my trusty silver Range Rider six-shooter, caps'n'all.

I used to knock about with any number of lads who were always great fun. We would rummage through the bombed-out houses, as the derelicts were called, in search of treasures left behind by 'flitted' folk. We'd play under the arches at the bottom of the street. We'd make dens on crofts having gathered wood for bonfire night and then we'd defend them against marauding wood barons from other streets. We played alleys for keeps and had raging games of Rallyvo up and down the street. Games of cricket were played with the wickets drawn in chalk against the gable ends of houses or using a lamp post as the wicket. Occasionally we would mount expeditions across Rochdale Road and search Barney's Tip, a vast area of marsh and bog-land separating Collyhurst from Cheetham Hill. Gangs went in and out of fashion and only usually survived as long as the individual feuds that gave birth to them survived, yet gangs were often great fun.

Most of the regular gangs were named after the streets that the members lived on. The Railway Street Gang was probably the most feared locally, two of its members, who were brothers, went on to become professional boxers. The gangs increased in size only when trouble raised its head or when the search for bonfire wood was at its peak!

I was a sometime member of the Chapley Street gang, which was never over successful; probably due to the fact that Chapley Street was such a long street and had so many kids to vie for leadership or to form splinter groups.

The best gangs for fun were the ones you formed with your immediate close friends. These were small cohesive units tied together through friendship, closeness of families and like minds.

I was a member of many such small gangs. Their common features were: secret passwords and secret signs; blood brotherhood;

oaths and threats of torture for giving away secrets; initiation ceremonies; and exotic names. I was a member of the "Death or Glory" gang, the "Dead Enders", the "Back Alley Boys" and the "Demons".

The gang that I remember most about was one formed by a mate of mine called Terry Fitz, he called it the "Kill or be killed Gang". We seemed to have a pre-occupation with violent names, often names associated with death!

Terry decided that those in his gang had to swear an oath, "I promise to defend the secrets of the Kill or be killed Gang with my life or have my thumbs, ears and tongue cut off". We also had to pledge blood brotherhood; this was accomplished by the pricking of our thumbs and the mingling of blood as we recited the oath!

The reason I remember this gang so well is because of the initiation Terry decided on.

The year before, Terry, who was older than the rest of us, had been a member of the Death or Glory gang that had gone in for death defying feats. He decided that the most awesome and frightening of these feats would provide us with an apt initiation.

Carl, Paul, Johnny, Sid and I set off on a day shortly after taking the oath to become initiated into the gang. We didn't have far to travel.

Rochdale Road crossed one of the main railway lines near Osborne Street Baths. Eight sets of tracks passed under the bridge and trains were commonplace; both passenger and freight. As you approached the bridge there were Gents toilets on one side and

Ladies on the other, both on the Collyhurst as opposed to Cheetham Hill side of the bridge. These were the old brick, walk in and turn the corner type that used to abound.

We entered the Gents and Terry hoisted himself up using the urinal for footholds and peered over the top, down onto the rail tracks below. One by one we joined him.

Joining either side of the bridge, which was about twenty feet above the tracks, there was a ledge. At the two extremities there were wide triangular shaped platforms, perfect for us to drop down onto and to group together before the start of the initiation. From the two platforms the ledge reached across to the other side. As it connected with the platforms on either side the ledge was about eighteen inches wide narrowing to about nine inches in the middle section of the bridge. The ledge spanned a distance of between eighty and one-hundred feet.

We all began to wonder what it was Terry wanted us to do. We didn't have to wait long to find out!

"Dere it is," said Terry,"all yer gorra do is cross over to de uvver side."

Stark terror gripped us all and we took sly glances at each other to see who would tell him to "Get lost" and "not be so stupid". My small balls did a version of leapfrog as I looked down at the tracks so far below.

"Well," said Terry with a sickening leer on his face, "yer not chicken are yer?"

"Are we eckes," we groaned.

"It's a bit dangerous in it?" I ventured, fighting hard to sound braver than I felt.

"A bit," answered Terry with determined understatement.

"Wot 'appens if a train goes under while yer on it?" asked Carl.

"Yer just 'ang on till its gone. Look it's dead easy, I've done it loads a times. Yer just pin yer back to the bridges wall an' Bob's yer uncle. It's dead easy."

I didn't like the way he kept saying "Dead".

"Wharrif yer fall, it's a right long way ter bottom?" queried Paul.

"Look are yer goin' ter do it or what?" he asked belligerently, "der yer wanna be in my gang?"

I instinctively knew how to save our bacon, "Let's see you do it then," I demanded. The others looked at me, relief written loud on the grimy expressions which were their faces.

"An' then will you lot?"

"Yerr," we all growled.

"But you gorra show us 'ow first 'aven't yer?" I said feeling ever more confident. I was quite pleased with myself; I felt that I'd boxed him into a corner that he couldn't possibly escape from because no one in his right mind would do what he was proposing.

"Oo'll go next?" he demanded.

Before I could check myself I'd answered, "Me," such was my confidence that he wouldn't do it!

"O.K. cum on then," with which he hoisted himself further over the wall we'd been leaning on and dropped down onto the angular platform below. There was plenty of room on the platform so we all dropped down one after the other. It looked higher and if anything more frightening from this position. The waiting ledge looked very thin and enormously long. The far side of the ledge was incredibly distant.

I found it hard to swallow and even harder to speak or think. I still didn't believe that he would go through with it.

The side of the bridge hid us totally from the busy road and we stood for what seemed a long while. Six boys lost in our own fears and frustrations. Frustration, because I know that we all wanted to say, "No way," but we couldn't. Even Terry, I'm sure didn't want to go through with it. You could tell that his delay was brought on by fearful reluctance. This recognition encouraged us to goad and prompt him into making his move. I suppose that we all hoped that he would balk at the last moment and then the nightmare would be over. Sadly Terry was caught in the same trap as the rest of us and there was no way that he could say "No way"! Eventually he set off, lonely, afraid and foolishly brave. In this same crazy way tens of thousands of young men walked to their deaths from the trenches in the war to end all wars. You had to show your mates you could handle any challenge.

He stepped onto the eighteen-inch ledge. The ledge was now all that lay between him and the deadly tracks below. Pinning his back to the bridge side, the metal wall separating him from the safety of the road, he began to inch his way across. Arms, shoulders and head pressed firmly against the wall, legs moving in a delicate and careful parody of a crab. Left foot inching out, transfer weight onto left foot and then draw right foot along to join it!

"Don't look down," he called back to us without turning his head. He did this more for his own sake than for ours I think. "Yer not supposed ter look down."

We looked down and once again shivered collectively with fear at the prospect of falling so far.

Terry, his head and back still pinned to the bridge's side slowly approached the mid-point where the ledge narrowed to a mere nine inches. He moved more cautiously now, sliding his feet gently along the narrow shelf before committing his weight to move another inch or two. After what seemed forever he passed the middle of the bridge and in so doing seemed to take heart, for he now began to move with purpose and determination reaching the far platform in only half the time it took him to reach the middle. Once on the wider shelf of the platform he pushed himself tightly into the corner, sat down with his knees bunched close to his chin and shouted across, "Right Ramsey, it's your turn".

Such an innocuous invitation to such a heart stopping action!

His words hit me like a sledgehammer, I wasn't ready for this, I couldn't do it, it was too high, too dangerous and I couldn't say, "No way". It was madness!

"Cum on, wot yer waitin' for? It's easy," he goaded.

I prayed for one of the others to ask me not to do it, or to say that they wouldn't do it; that would have given me the opportunity to save at least some face. They wouldn't meet my pleading looks. I knew that they were as nervous and as frightened as I was, but like me they felt trapped by the greater terror of being branded a coward.

"Cum on Ramsey, yer said yer were goin' ter go next so get goin'," shouted Terry from the safety of his perch across the tracks.

His words slapped me in the face. He was of course right. I had said, without any prompting, that I would go next. The fact that I had said it still believing he wouldn't do it didn't make a heap of difference to my plight now. All I knew at that moment in time was that I didn't want to do it at all.

I stepped onto the narrow ledge to put a stop to his taunts. I looked down and stepped straight back up to the others, "Would one of youse lot like ter go first?" I asked trying to sound breezy. They shook their heads, they were closed to me now. In a moment they would turn on me for the coward I was.

"Cum on Ramsey, wot's up wiv yer, der yer want yer mam?" called Terry.

His words hurt and I had no answer for them, because in truth I wished my mum would turn up and save me from this lunacy. Even were I to challenge him to fight, and beat him, I could not escape disgrace - unless I crossed the bridge. If I crossed I could tell him where to go, with my head held high, if we fought and he beat me I'd still have won the greater victory. It was then that I stepped onto the narrow shelf for the second time.

It was a long way down and I pushed myself hard against the side of the bridge as if trying to embed myself in its solid metal safety. I took a first tentative step. So long as I kept my head and my balance I could do it! I took another step away from safety. The ledge was still wide and comparatively safe. The reduction in width was imperceptible, but narrow it did, gradually to a mere nine inches. I took another step and soon found myself well away from my friends approaching the narrowest point of the crossing. The ledge had dwindled and the toes of my shoes were much closer to the edge, the tracks below glistened menacingly up at me. I inched onward, gulping hard breaths to keep down the fear that threatened to gush forth from my body. As I approached the mid-section I became conscious for the first time of the traffic on the other side of the bridge, passing by, indifferent to my predicament. How I wished then that I was on the other side and there in safety I too could be indifferent to my plight. I passed the middle without incident and sensed the ledge widening gradually. It was then that I heard what I most dreaded to hear - a train approaching.

I stole a glance toward Terry, he'd heard it too and was on his feet; I looked across to the others, their eyes were all locked on something that they could see further along the track, around a bend that was beyond my vision, heading our way.

"Cum on," shouted Terry, "there's a train coming. Yer can make it."

I tried to increase my speed towards Terry. The noise was much louder by this time and then I saw it racing towards me following the bend that was about an eighth of a mile away. I knew the moment that I saw it that there was nothing I could do. Unable to run from its path I was a prisoner of painfully slow, slow motion, whilst the train continued to close the gap between us. I stopped moving and tried once again to push myself into the metal sides of the unyielding bridge.

As the train rumbled closer I realised that it was going to pass directly beneath me.

"Oh God please let me live, Oh God please let me live, God please, please God, God, God," my thoughts became an endless stream of God's name repeated over and over and over again.

The train trundled and rumbled underneath me, everything vibrated viciously and me with it! A huge cloud of smoke engulfed me adding further to my misery. Eyes wide open I could see nothing. Disorientation threatened to dislodge me from the precarious ledge, which was my only lifeline to survival.

"Oh God, God, God," the internal cry went on and on and on. The train seemed to take forever to pass below me; I remember I heard the engine whistle, as it emerged on the far side having passed under the bridge. I think hearing the whistle frightened me more than the rumbling and vibrations, it felt like a signal calling me to my doom and that now was the time to fall.

"Oh God, God, God," the litany went on and on and I realised for the first time that it wasn't inside my head any more, I could actually hear myself chanting the mantra. Saying it, not shouting, as though I feared that were I to utter sounds louder than the normal I would be wrenched from my perch!

As if from some long nightmare or from some deadening anaesthetic I emerged, consciousness slowly flowing back into me.

From what seemed a long way off I could hear someone calling out my name.

I opened my eyes wider, white smoke still shrouded me.

"Brendan are yer alright? Brendan are yer alright? The trains gone, are yer O. K. Brendan?"

I recognised Terry's voice, which now seemed much closer to me. I peered to my left and through wisps of residual smoke I saw Terry staring hard at me from the triangular perch where he stood, which was now only a matter of a few feet away.

"Is 'e alright?" I heard Johnny shout from the other side.

"Yer 'e's O. K.," answered Terry.

I'm not sure how I felt, I don't believe that "O. K." summed up my feelings. My heart was still thundering in my chest and I felt as if I was floating, sounds and voices still seemed to echo and be from a long way off.

I completed the crossing slowly and uneventfully, collapsing in relief when I eventually joined Terry on the wide ledge forming the platform.

"Wot were it like? Wot were it like when the train went under yer?"

"I don't know," I answered mechanically. My legs were shaking uncontrollably and my throat felt dry enough to strike matches on. "It were 'orrible! I thought bloody train were goin' ter shake me off. I just closed me eyes and 'oped for the best."

"I thought you were a goner. It went right underneath yer you know?"

"Yerr, a know it did. I nearly wet me pants." We began to giggle, the tension released in snorts of uncontrollable laughter.

"Wot yer laughin' at?" shouted Carl.

"Youse lot, that's wot," shouted Terry, "'cos you're next!"

We both laughed louder.

None of the others did cross the bridge that day and I know that I never ventured across again, from the trackside anyway. The bridge is still there. The toilets are long gone and the hoardings that used to stand next to the bridge have been replaced by a doctor's surgery. The bridge itself has changed subtly. At some point during the last thirty odd years they must have done some work on it.

I still get a thrill whenever I cross it in the car. I think I'd be afraid to look over the side now. Funny how when you're all grown up, that it's not so hard to admit that you are a coward after all.

10. How I Was Cured of Rabbit Hunting.

The summers were always a wonderful time. Although I enjoyed school I couldn't wait for the summer holidays.

On the night we broke up for school my sister and I would be taken down to Victoria Station to catch the 10.20 p. m. boat-train for Holyhead. Arrangements would already have been made by mam and dad for someone to make sure that we made it safe and sound to Ballyhaunis in Co. Mayo, in the West of Ireland. There, our Uncle Mark and Aunty Kit, who would have hired a car to meet us, would be waiting. Only then would the whole summer stretch out for us warm and inviting and wild.

I was ten at the time and the trip that year meant a great deal more to me because I was a little more aware of what was going on. I loved travelling on the boat and the train. Travelling has always been part of the great adventure for me.

The train journey across Ireland was always always fascinating and exciting. I would spend my time watching the bobbing telegraph poles, as they appeared to climb and climb only to suddenly drop to their original level. The Royal Canal paralleled the rail line for much of the journey and it was great sport spotting the anglers, ducks and peaceful cattle drinking, as each made their separate use of the water. I would stand with my head and shoulders pushed through the "Do not lean out" door window of the carriage, gasping for breath and trying to avoid smuts from the engine up ahead. I also enjoyed seeing and reading the names of the stations we passed, these seemed so colourful in comparison to the names of the English towns I knew at that time. Mullingar, Athlone, Roscommon and Castlerea fled by feeding my excitement as if part of some majestic countdown to arrival.

Ballyhaunis, and there to meet us were the familiar and well loved faces of Mark and Kit. Thirty minutes after leaving the train we were stood in the kitchen of their thatched cottage shyly renewing our acquaintance with cousins we hadn't seen for a year.

That summer was long and hot as so many of the summers of my childhood seem to have been. Days were spent roaming the fields, fishing in the sluggish river, riding Neddy the martyred donkey, playing in Maguires big cart-house during those occasional summer showers, watching Uncle Mark mow the hay with rhythmic swings of the cruel looking scythe, rolling in empty barrels, milking cattle (whether invited or not), rounding up the sheep, running in fear from the great mare Rose (who only my big brother Tony could ride), swinging out from the big tree on the big swing and of course hunting rabbits with Padraic.

Padraic and Rita were the two cousins nearest to my age, although both were younger than me. Eileen although only a year or so older pretended to disdain the wilder exuberance of our youth and attached herself firmly to my much older sister Patsy.

Rita was as wild if not wilder than I was. She could run, jump, fight, spit, fish, swing and generally adventure with the best of boys. At night we would curl up together, topped and tailed, the three of us in one of the big double beds in the cottages second bedroom. Eileen and Patsy shared the other bed in the same room, which was filled, with the two beds, an isle the width of the door between us! It was cosy and warm and delicious drifting off to sleep amidst giggles, whispers and threats from the kitchen. Late at night when the others had succumbed to rest I would lie awake listening to the low murmur of voices, which wafted through the bedrooms half open door. Occasional muffled laughter and the not unpleasant aroma of pipe tobacco accompanied me nightly to my sleep.

Mornings were early and full of bustle and then the day, glorious and long lay before us.

That summer Padraic and I set out to become great hunters of rabbits. With grave seriousness we set out to acquire wire and string for snares, we scoured the countryside for signs of rabbit droppings, holes and runs. We questioned the old timers like John Martin Mongen as to how to lay a snare. One day we were ready and early in the morning we set out to capture all unwitting rabbits foolish enough to live near us.

Snares were laid all over Uncle Mark's land and the land adjoining his. We ventured onto the bog-land a mile or so from home and set snares in the gorse and heather where the year before we had played harmless cowboys and Indians, killing all before us.

Having set our snares we sat back and waited for the rabbits that never came, eventually we trudged home praying that tomorrow was already here so that we could count how many we had caught.

The morrow came and the next and the next but no rabbit was foolish enough to pop its head into one of our amateur and clumsy snares. We were crestfallen hunters and so we began to re-discover the joys of toy fighting, split the kipper, and apple stealing. Rabbits and snares were soon forgotten as we began to enjoy the long days that lay before us and soon our hearts and heads were full of the prospect of a trip to the seaside.

Galway on the Atlantic coast has always held a magnetic pull on me and the visit to Salthill was invariably one of the highlights of the holidays. Mam and dad would be over for their two-week break and to fetch Pat and I home.

The arrival of my dad was eagerly anticipated by all of us because with him he brought such fun and zest for life. The whole pace of the house would increase in readiness for his arrival. Suits saved for Sundays would be dusted and sponged, a few bottles of Guinness would find their way to the kitchen, the first question on neighbours' lips was, "When does Paddy arrive?"

The great day was soon upon us. Mam and dad had landed two or three days before. Two cars were hired to ferry the hoards to Galway. Jim McDonagh in his bright red Ford would lead and I'd be in his car!

Jim called for us at eight and of course we'd been ready for an hour or more, watching the approaches for his arrival. Nothing in adult life can match the childish excitement that that journey generated.

The cart road spread out before us until we picked up the newly tarred road in Cloonfad. Fields of barley, wheat, cabbage and potato flew by. Fields full of haystacks drying in the warming sun lay to right and left. Small villages and towns, in name only, sped past us as we approached Galway City, surely one of the smallest yet sweetest cities in the world?

We arrived around ten to be met by thunderstorms of great magnificence. Mum dragged us along, protesting, to Woolworth's where she kitted us out in grey plastic macs for fear of us catching our deaths. The rain soon abated, as all, save mother, knew it would. The sun raised steam from the road and pavement.

We spent the morning touring the shops, not allowed to stop and enjoy the wonderful buskers with their accordions, fiddles, whistles and badhrans.

Lunch was at the Imperial on the main street. We were all expected to behave in a proper manner and to show no one up! Having shown everyone up by making too much noise and complaining loudly about having to sit up straight I joined the others as we headed for the beach, which in my childish mind was the whole reason for being there in the first place!

Galway drew holidaymakers from all over Ireland and Salthill drew all that visited Galway. The beach was thronged with the Irish, Scots, English and of course the tanned, relaxed and exotic Yanks.

Rita and I soon befriended such a couple of Yanks from New Jersey. P. J. and Wayne. They were over for the summer visiting their father's people in Roscommon. Rita and I couldn't get over the idea of someone being called Wayne, it was the second name of our favourite cowboy! We discovered that the P. J. stood for Paddy Joe (the same as my dad) and we had a great day swimming out to the raft and playing wet versions of the "King of the Castle" until I got water in my ear.

I can't remember a time when I wasn't troubled with problems with my left ear and whenever I got water in, it invariably meant a few days of suffering, mostly for those who had to put up with me.

A hurried goodbye was shouted to Wayne and P. J. those close life-long friends of an hour or two. I hurried over to where mother and the other women were ensconced on the beach. I lay down with my troubled ear nearest the ground, going through the ritual that sometimes helped; if I could rid myself of the water fast the pain might be manageable. Rita occupied herself with Padraic and went off in search of new adventures; I spent an hour tapping my head and digging about in the affected ear (doing more damage than good). Luckily the damage this time wasn't too serious and within the hour I felt I'd ejected most of the water and went off in search of rock pools for living treasures, occasionally tilting my head and banging hugely on the other side.

The day wore on, the sun shone and then declined, the men drifted back to the lobsters on the beach, smelling deliciously of the last whiskey and rolling gently the better to distribute the stout they had consumed.

We stopped at a pub for a snack on the way home. The men took the opportunity to top up on stout and the rest of us became quietly alarmed at the way our bodies were glowing. The rest of the journey home would be uncomfortable, the warm glow of our bodies becoming a simmering burn. All who had stayed on the beach suffered to a greater or lesser extent. The hour I'd spent lay on my ear meant that I suffered mostly down my entire right side.

We dropped the men in Cloonfad where they immediately made for Kane's, to compare the stout of home with that of Galway no doubt. The rest of us made for the farm where sure fire remedies were rubbed into tender skin and little ones were unceremoniously packed off to bed! The talk in the kitchen that night concerned itself with the greatness of the day. "When was Galway ever so hot before?" "Did you see the price of such and such at Roaches?" "Isn't it amazing how a blind man learned to play the accordion so well?" "You'd think the men would have enough by now, they've been on it all day!" I drifted off to sleep dreaming dreams as warm as my sunburn of swimming cowboys and Yanks who were Kings of Castles.

It was some days later that Padraic and I remembered, in a rare moment of idleness, our inglorious attempt at hunting and we decided immediately to examine our long forgotten snares to see had we been successful. The fact that it must have been at least three weeks since we'd given them a thought meant little to us.

We set off in great excitement, pausing only long enough to pick up a sack to carry our catch home. We first searched the hedgerow on Mark's land where our first snares had been laid. We found wire that was rusting and empty. Eventually we made our way up to the bog-land over by Mrs. Regan's, the schoolmistresses land. We sought out our ageing snares and still we found nothing. It was then, as we were about to return home, empty-handed, jaded and disillusioned, that we found what we had longed to find.

The wretched rabbit had been snared some time before. Its left hind leg was caught and appeared to be almost severed, hanging by a thread. Such must have been the poor creatures terror and exertions to escape, it had almost torn its own leg off! It lay there now, lifeless, looking very tiny and sad. The lips had shrunk back against its teeth and it appeared to be grinning in horror up at us. The fur likewise was lifeless and dull, matted to its scrawny frame.

We stared in silence, the thrill of discovering our catch stuck somewhere in our throats.

For a long moment we stared; shame, sorrow and anguish welling up within us both. At that moment in time I felt smaller than the smallest rabbit that had ever lived.

After an age we looked at each other and each saw the shame in the other. We wanted to do something but there was nothing we could do. We thought we'd bury it but didn't even have the courage to touch it!

Eventually we kicked it further under the gorse bushes, threw the sack on top and then systematically, without discussing what we were going to do we sought out all of our snares and kicked every last one of them to pieces.

We trudged home under a pall of silence, returning as though from the funeral we felt the creature deserved. Our morose faces and sullenness raised stares and questions when we arrived home but we were both too ashamed to tell any of them the tale.

The rest of that holiday went and I'm sure that I recovered my composure enough to become obnoxiously loud and to enjoy my final few days.

Padraic and I didn't hunt rabbits again that year or ever again and I think like me he's never talked about the sadness and shame we encountered on that day so long ago. Life is tenuous and lessons come in many guises, sometimes they make us better people by teaching us something about the potential for badness within us, sometimes they don't.

11. The First Mass of Christmas

Midnight mass was over and I was to serve the first mass of Christmas over at the Convent.

All of us altar boys looked forward to serving mass at the convent because the nuns always fussed you so much. I suppose it was the mothering instinct in them. Small altar boys, I'm sure, were seen as little priests.

Anyway, the midnight mass was over and I'd just finished putting away the priest's vestments when Sister Agnes came in to walk me over to the Convent.

It was one of those crystal clear nights where every star stood out against the deep velvet blue of the Christmas midnight sky. I looked up, my head fully back, mouth ajar and gaped at the wonder of it all. Sister Agnes nudged me in the direction of the Convent of Good Hope.

Fr. Brannon was to say mass and that was a terrific relief to me because the Cannon (Canon Early) was feared by all and sundry. He had once been known to interrupt the proceedings of the Sunday mass, pick up the huge Tridentine bible, walk down the few steps to the altar boy serving and to bring the book down hard upon the boy's unsuspecting head. All because six-thirty in the morning was a poor time for a boy to be fully awake! This particular action of the Cannon had made a bad impression on me and I lived in mortal fear of falling asleep; one day to be sent to everlasting damnation by a violent blow to the skull with the Holy Bible.

Anyway, the Cannon, thank God, had said the midnight mass and it was Fr. Brannon's duty to say the mass at the Convent. As we entered the silent halls of the motherhouse the loud aroma of eggs and bacon attacked my ten-year-old nostrils.

It was so quiet and peaceful in this female enclave that it always made me feel holy, almost, as though God were somehow tangible in this place. I always felt that I had to whisper and creep about from place to place avoiding any noise that might disturb the sanctity.

Sister Agnes led me through to the small chapel and I prepared myself for the mass.

Few experiences in life have ever approached the spiritual excitement of that long ago night. The angelic singing of the nuns, the deeply rich brogue of Fr. Brannon intoning the Latin liturgy, and the buzzing intentness a boy feels when he's wide awake and five or six hours past his bedtime, helped to make it into one of the most memorable experiences of my life.

Eventually the mass ended. The Convent mass was invariably shorter than the lay mass because the nuns were always busy and needed to be off, about their "good deeds" I supposed.

I cleared away the altar with the help of a nun who must have been approaching her second centenary. She whisked about quietly efficient; I'm sure that she wasn't breathing because she gave no sign of life other than that she was moving about. As a deeply religious young man I knew that the Lord worked in mysterious ways and that if there were such things as miracles then a Convent was the most appropriate place for one. The old nun finished her duties and retired to whatever cupboard they kept her in until the next mass.

Sister Agnes floated into the room where I was removing my cotter and cassock.

This was another miracle to me! The nuns always appeared to float from one place to another, if they had legs I never saw them and I didn't know anyone who had! Oh, my clever older sister insisted that they had legs like anyone else, but still, "seeing was believing" as Thomas said, and I'd never seen them, nor had she!

In the softest voice I've ever heard she invited me to follow her. I didn't dare say anything for fear of the walls falling down; only people who had trained for years could speak so delicately. I crept behind her careful to make no noise in this most silent of homes. From somewhere deep inside the house I heard the quiet response of other nuns at prayer; it was a most gentle and reassuring sound. It made me feel warm and pleasant inside.

Sister Agnes eventually led me into the kitchen, which was white, scrubbed and pristine. She left me in the hands of Sister Paula, a young giggly Irish girl who fed me a man size plate of eggs, bacon, sausage, tomatoes and toast. A pint mug of tea completed this King's feast. It was the perfect end to a perfectly delightful night. Sister Paula giggled as she asked if I'd had enough, "Yough, thunx", I said through a mouthful of egg, toast and tea. She fussed around and made me feel important. This was the way I always felt when I'd served mass at the Convent; it was as though I was every bit as precious as the Cannon! Now there's a wicked thought that's stayed with me through the years.

All good things come to an end and it was soon time for me to take my leave of the pleasant, whispering, humble nuns. I'd a good mile to walk home and some of it passed the bombed out houses of Livesey Street.

We called the houses "bombed out" because they were the derelict slums ready for demolition. They'd started clearing the area years before. I suppose the expression "bombed out" was a hangover from the war, but it had an appeal and attraction to us kids that kept the expression alive.

I left the confines of the Convent and headed off home, I don't think I'd ever been out this late alone before. I was a little frightened but the night was beautiful and the Hindley's and Brady's of this world were still some time away.

I set out in the direction of home keeping myself in the exact centre of the pavement, my eyes straining to maintain the widest peripheral vision possible, nothing was going to take me by surprise! Of course I did not at that time realise that I was attempting to use peripheral vision, as far as I was concerned I was just keeping my eyes "peeled" as any young boy or cavalry scout would.

Weird and wonderful thoughts flowed through my mind. I had always been, a "fanciful youth", as my mother called me.

Tigers stalked me on that bright Christmas night long ago, natives of the Amazon with poisonous blow pipes were lurking if the tigers failed and Nazis with lethal lugers were lying in wait around every corner!

The night was too wonderful to sustain these romantic notions for long. The vastness of the heavens overwhelmed me and raised my spirits. Fresh from not one but two Christmas masses my mind swirled with images of that night two thousand years before. I searched the sky for the star that guided, the one I'd heard so much about, they were all so bright and promising that I'd chosen four or five definites before I had walked to the arches that marked the mid-point of Livesey Street.

The railway arches loomed up and dispelled my thoughts of the guiding star. The new sodium lights picked out the rust spots on the side of the bridge, which in my mind were obviously the remnants of some wartime strafing raid of the Gerries.

Beneath the bridge it was dark and menacing. I consciously moved a little further over onto the far side of the pavement from the inner arch walls. I shifted the small suitcase, which carried my altar clothes, in front of my body so that should anyone jump out to "get me" I'd be able to shove the case at them and make a fast escape. No one jumped out to "get me" and I passed under the bridge safely.

I breathed a sigh of relief on reaching the far side and continued on my way.

I was still about two-thirds of a mile from home and now I had to pass the derelict houses on the Oldham Road end of Livesey Street. These held little fear for me in the daytime because it was in them, with pals, that I spent so much of my playing out time.

They were castles, forts, headquarters, saloons, caves, dens and empties to be wrecked before the wreckers moved in! It was in these empty houses that Johnny, Carl, Paul, Tony and I were Kings, knights, Gerries, desert rats, Hopalong Cassidy, Johnny Ringo, Geronimo and a host of others. We spent all of our wild days roaming and scavenging amongst the debris of those who had left the area before us.

I walked on. As I passed from under the shadow of the arches my mind wandered once more, this time lingering on the presents I hoped to receive later that morning. Would I get the "Winchester" repeating rifle I so desperately needed? Would I get a good book like last year's? I'd received "The Coral Island" the previous Christmas and much of the subsequent year was spent re-enacting the adventures of Ralph, Jack and Peterkin.

As I approached the first of the row of derelict houses I felt myself physically tensing, for whilst I knew they were empty and always found them exciting during the day, at night they held a certain menace and threat which chilled me. The empty sockets of the windows seemed to follow my movements and the gaping mouths of the doors looked as if they waited to swallow me up!

I steeled myself and walked on, once more adjusting my grip on the small suitcase I carried.

I knew these houses well. I'd been born on the next street, Railway Street. It was on these two streets that Bernard Wrigley taught me to ride a two-wheel bicycle, without the aid of stabilisers! These were the streets of my early childhood and I took some comfort from that knowledge. All of my accumulated memories associated with them were warm and loving and good.

I walked on. My eyes strained to the left, searching the gaping holes that once were the windows of these dead homes. I searched for whatever lurked in the darkness within. Nothing happened.

I had passed the first half dozen or so of the terrace when it did happen. There was a loud bang followed by a gruffly uttered oath. I swear to God, I felt the hair on my scalp prickle as though readying itself to stand on end. I may have let out in involuntary yelp of fear, I know that I thought the noises were somehow a threat to me and terror had welled up in my throat ready to be released in a scream. It was then that I took to my heels and I didn't stop until I reached the comparative safety and the lights of Oldham Road.

During that fevered run my ever-fertile imagination had been active. I'd obviously heard a murderer (there had been a murder the year before in Queens Park); it was a kidnapper (I'd read plenty about them); it was some monster from beyond the earth (I'd seen the "Quatermas Experiment" on T. V.); or else it was something worse, something even my fevered imagination couldn't cope with!

I stopped running at the edge of Oldham Road and allowed my breath to catch me up. My rational mind began to assert itself and I eventually came to the conclusion that there was only one plausible explanation for what I had heard.

I had heard a tramp, one of those gentlemen of the road, turning over in the night and cursing his ill luck at knocking something over. It was as simple and as frightening as that!

Tramps were quite commonplace at that time and it was well known that they used the empty shells of the houses for the roof and occasional shelter they provided. The house I had passed was nothing more unusual or dangerous than a "kip" for one of these unfortunates.

I took some solace from this realisation. The tramps were as happy in the old houses as we children were and they were probably more welcome and less malevolent guests.

It's strange but as I stood preparing to cross the road I began to feel that this experience somehow added new meaning to the Christmas story for me. In particular it seemed to give some form of substance to this particular Christmas night. If anything I had been taught about Jesus was true, wasn't it true that he'd been born to be the Saviour of the poorest of the poor? Didn't He come into the world in accommodation not too far removed from the accommodation of the tramp I'd just heard? Wasn't it on just such a night, with a million stars up above, that He chose to come to earth?

The more I pondered these thoughts the more relevance I took from the experience, the more significant this chance encounter seemed to me.

It certainly made me think about the way so many others would be spending that Christmas night. I felt that the tramp was somehow closer to the true meaning and spirit of the season than I could ever be.

I continued on my journey home to the warm house with the surprise presents waiting patiently for the liberation the dawn would bring.

I still get goose pimples when I recall that bump in the night and the curse that accompanied it - without them I don't think that this long ago Christmas would still feel like it happened only yesterday.

12. They killed our President.

I was alone in the house.

Three years earlier we had "flitted" from 100, Chapley Street to 7, Calver Walk which was just off Butler Street on the other side of the Oldham Road. Our new home was a lower maisonette.

The luxury we enjoyed there was unbelievable. I had a bedroom to myself (the box room). The maisonette had under floor central heating, a balcony, a fitted kitchen with all mod cons; mum had even treated us to a new and huge 22 inch black and white "Bush" television with sliding doors that hid the screen when not in use! We had joined the well-healed of society.

We were less than a mile from Chapley Street, which was soon to be demolished as part of the continuing slum clearance programme, so I was very familiar with the area – we were even closer to my favourite place in Manchester – Granelli's.

Granelli's was an ice-cream parlour on Oldham Road. Italians had colonised parts of Collyhurst and a large part of Ancoats around Saint Michael's. The greatest treat I could wish for was one of their special sundaes. I only managed to get one infrequently because, if my memory serves me well, they cost all of a shilling, which was a small king's ransom at that time! So the sundae remained a three or four times a year pleasure, generally following some major event like the Whit Friday walks or my birthday.

Anyway I was alone in the house. Mum was now working at Brooke's Bar on Deansgate; it was a posh cake shop, in Manchester, and she usually got home around six in the evening. Dad was driving for Joe Kennedy's, laying electric cabling all over the North West – he was rarely home before seven or eight at night. Patsy was in the sixth form at the Notre Dame Convent School involved in lots of after school activities, such as smoking, and Tony, who was living with us at this time and sharing the box room with me, had probably stopped for a few beers on the way home.

I usually got home from school (Saint Clare's) around five and occupied myself gainfully watching telly, eating a jam butty and scratching at whatever torturous homework had been set for me that evening.

Life's routines provided the clock that measured our daily lives and life wasn't that bad.

Three years before we had moved into the new house and 1960 wasn't just memorable for that major event. It was truly memorable because a Catholic had become the President of America! John Fitzgerald Kennedy (JFK) had become the thirty-fifth president and not only was he Catholic but he also, like me, had Irish roots. To those who are not Catholic the momentousness of this event would be very hard to describe effectively or to understand. It was a pinnacle of Catholic achievement – to be recognised in this way by the greatest nation on earth, and him Irish too – it was just too much!

I was aware that a Catholic could never become British Prime Minister (sadly this is still true in the 21st century). I knew that only a couple of decades before, Catholics were subject to abuse from certain groups in Manchester when on their way to mass of a Sunday or during the Whit Walks and that the Irish weren't welcome – "No Irish or blacks need apply" was a phrase I had heard often. I knew what it was to be a Mick, a Spud, Rat Catcher even though most of the venom had by this decade diminished. So as a Catholic it was considered to be a wonderful thing that one of us had been elected to such high office – perhaps the world was becoming more tolerant and the "hope" that appeared to be embodied in the new president seemed to infuse the whole world.

This was a good time to be of Irish descent and a Catholic. Then along came the Bay of Pigs and the Cuban Missile Crisis.

British newspapers, always sceptical, were quite openly hostile during the abortive Bay of Pigs affair. I didn't really follow the story but I heard the adults discussing it from time to time. My mum in particular was convinced that the only reason the press were against him was because he was Catholic – "If he were a black heathen they wouldn't be saying what they're saying about him – mark my words!"

The Cuban Missile Crisis was something else. The whole atmosphere of the world altered subtly. Perhaps not so subtly because the likes of a snotty brat, such as I was back then, understood something major was happening in the world.

As with anything I didn't fully understand I sought my clever sister's enlightenment.

"What's a atom bomb Pat?"

"Why do you ask?" she responded.

"Cos' Phil Latowsky, at school, said we're all going to be blown to smithereens by a atom bomb. So what is a atom bomb?"

As always Patsy considered whether she should condescend to impart any knowledge to this horrid sibling who was the Bain of her life. I suspect she saw some mileage in scaring the daylights out of me because she carefully explained not only what an atom bomb was but went on to describe graphically what had happened in Hiroshima and Nagasaki. She then in simple terms pointed out that JFK had given Krushev (the leader of the soviet block or the Ruskies as we always referred to them) an ultimatum (she explained that this was a threat) that if he didn't dismantle and remove all missiles from the island of Cuba, which was only thirty or so miles from America, there would be a war. She then added that it would be an intercontinental ballistic missile war in which the world would cease to exist and that Manchester would probably be the first to go and that there was no point in trying to get away because if the explosion didn't do for you then the fall-out would poison you and kill you, in the most gruesome way, within weeks.

By the end of her explanation my vocabulary had increased massively: minute-men, nuclear weapons, ballistics, intercontinental, fall-out, radiation sickness, vaporisation, epicentre, Armageddon, - I was left in no doubt that I'd be lucky if after a nuclear exchange I was a shadow burned into the pavement outside our house. She mentioned that In Hiroshima they had found peoples' outlines on the ground where the nuclear flash had acted like a camera searing an image of their outline into the ground before vaporising their bodies!

If I tell you that I hardly slept for the rest of the so-called Crisis I would not be exaggerating. My dreams were full of the direst images. I was afraid to close my eyes in case I was vaporised in my sleep: "Matthew, Mark, Luke and John, bless the bed that I lay on, if I die before I wake, I pray to God my soul to take" – how often did I intone these words in my bed?

Then it was over. Kennedy had won. Krushev it seems backed down. The world began to breathe again. The oppressive fear of imminent death was suddenly taken away from everyone. The sense of release was palpable. The papers were full of it, the news on telly was full of it and prayers were being offered in thanksgiving at every church, synagogue and temple across the globe. Manchester was off the hook for a while and I didn't need to dwell on my sad demise any longer although my dreams continued to be affected for year after. Patsy, even then had the makings of a very fine teacher!

So I was alone in the house on this particular Friday night waiting for the rest of the family to get home and occupying myself as usual - up to no good. Happily I didn't have to worry about an imminent nuclear attack; in fact the only thing I was worrying about was whether I'd be let stay up to watch The Human Jungle with Herbert Lom. I'd already been up to mum and dad's room and unscrewed the back of the wardrobe to see if she'd got the Christmas present I had been pestering her for – she hadn't! I knew that I could be the world's greatest scientist if only I got the "Science Lab" that was being advertised on telly since that summer! Perhaps I'd be able to split the atom at home and show the world how nuclear power could be used for peaceful means like boiling the kettle or filling the bath with hot water whilst running a telly in every room of the house.

I was in the kitchen making a brew. I heard the interruption to "Bronco" but continued to spread the jam thickly on the slice of bread. Eventually I went back in to the living room with my cup and butty. Gaye Byrne, was on. It wasn't time for Granada Reports and anyway I wanted to watch "Bronco". I realised he was saying something about President Kennedy, being shot, in some place called Dallas.

The next hour or so was amongst the longest of my short life up to then. I hung on every word. I'd always been interested in the news and history is one of my life long loves – one of my favourite shows back then was "All our Yesterdays". Now it seems JFK was part of my yesterdays.

Mam was first home and she hadn't heard about it. By now we were getting confirmation that he was dead.

To me, to mum and to countless thousands like us, his loss was personal. It was as if a close relative had been taken from us. The shock that gripped us, the disbelief, and the sense of powerlessness was overwhelming. That Sunday evening at seven, after the six o'clock mass, Saint Pat's was filled to overflowing as Canon Early led a concelebrated mass for the repose of the president's soul.

Centre aisle, in front of the gates to the high altar, a coffin draped in the stars and stripes was the focus of all eyes. The outpouring of grief was a tangible thing. This man, who none of us knew, who had little in common with any of us, had in some way touched all of us very deeply – it was also obvious that our shock and our grief was felt by the whole nation. Politician's like MacMillan and Wilson spoke of his loss as though they had lost a personal friend. In fact it felt to me as if the whole world was reacting in much the same way so great was the sense of loss.

I have thought about those days often in the intervening years. I know a great deal more about the man and the president. Despite having had his darker secrets laid bare I still feel that acute sense of loss and I still feel it as a personal loss. I am quite certain that the sense of hope that he brought to the world died with him. The naivety of the post war world, the belief that things would get better and that there would be no return to the dark, dark days, had proved what it was – naive. After his death the world was a darker place where evil people plotted actions that would change our world forever. As if to underscore this descent into the darkness others who offered a similar kind of hope were also taken from us – Martin Luther King, Robert Fitzgerald Kennedy and even in later decades the assassination of Anwar Saddat appeared to take away a more reasonable and modern Islamic response to the dangers facing the world!

To have lived through such times; to remember the event as if it was only yesterday; to acknowledge that his death was an important part of all my yesterdays; his story is intertwined with my own family story and I can never recall that era without hearing and seeing my sister.

I still have an album of Kennedy's key speeches. He was a terrific orator and since him few have expressed themselves so well until the latest American president came along. Barak Obama is the first person since Kennedy to provide that sense of a new beginning and a new hope for mankind as well as being a terrific speaker. Perhaps, should he survive the recession we're all in at the moment, he will live to deliver on his promises and his promise. I certainly hope so because we can all do with a little "hope".

13. The Langley Years, 1965 – 1973.

Some time in 1965 we flitted once again. This time from Collyhurst altogether – the powers that be had long since decided, in their wisdom, that the old terraced houses of traditional Collyhurst must all come down and make way for ultra modern maisonettes and multi storey flats. I don't think it was a particularly good swap or exchange. Families that had lived in the area since the old houses were built were scattered to the four corners of Manchester and beyond. A few chose to remain in the newer housing being built to replace the old but the whole character of the area was subtly changing and not necessarily for the better. Swathes of empty ground strewn with rubble marked where Chapley Street, Slater Street and all the others had once stood. Everything about the area looked tired and decayed, even the newer properties. So like hundreds of others my parents decided to up stakes and make a new life nearer to the countryside! They were both country people after all!

Langley Estate was a newly built overspill estate for the slums of Manchester. Some from Collyhurst moved north to Langley, some moved south to Wythenshaw and some stayed where they were. We went north.

I had never heard of Middleton never mind Langley, although I do have a vague memory of spending a day with a school pal from

Saint Pat's, Carl Nagitis (his dad was a Lithuanian who had settled in England after the war). Carl's dad was a bus conductor or driver at the time and as a treat he used to sometimes take Carl, and on this occasion me, with him if he was on an exotic route. I do remember a half built housing estate and lots of green fields near the terminus where we spent an hour or so. I believe that may well have been an early visit to Langley but I am not completely certain of it.

Anyway sometime in 1965 we moved into 12 Lingmell Close which was just off Lakeland Court shopping arcade. It was a three bed roomed, mid terrace, with gardens' back and front and had an indoor toilet and separate bathroom – it was Heaven! Of course we'd had the indoor facilities at Calver Walk but here it just seemed better and no one lived above us. Outside our front gate was a green – "No ball games allowed" and the whole estate which was largely finished by 1965, although some building continued for the next couple of years in small pockets, was spacey, green and smelled of fresh air. The fields of Bowlee were literally a five minute walk away and would become my stomping ground over the next few years.

My first actual memory of moving to Langley was turning up to register as an altar boy and to volunteer for the early morning mass, which was at 0700 in those days. Things were a tad different to St. Pat's. First you were required to have two cassocks: one black for everyday wear and one red for Sunday's and you had to wear white gloves. I can also recall that one of my first memories of Canon Murphy was when he almost broke my thumb making sure that I crossed them right over left when my hands were joined in prayer – it wasn't easy being an altar boy you know!

Canon Murphy was a fearsome Cork man. He was around six three or four and quite heavily built. I don't think he ever drove a car but he was a regular sight 'put, putting' around the estate on a very small moped. I have some arguments with youngsters who claim the modern Honda 50 or 90 is a moped – they are not. A moped as the name suggests had pedals and when the fuel ran out you could pedal away to finish your journey, the pedals were also used to start the bike's motor running. They are still possible to see on the roads in France. He really was a sight when on his moped!

If the Canon had been a business man he would have been a multi-millionaire. On being assigned to the new estate his first job was to raise the money to build a stone replacement to the wooden church on Wood Street that would become the Catholic Club, beloved of my generation for many reasons. The story of how he set about raising this money is apocryphal. He visited every bank in Middleton and beyond and effectively bullied one of the bank managers to lend against his promise to raise enough to pay for it within ten years. I wouldn't have put it past the Canon to threaten these bankers with Hell and Damnation if they failed to give. Believe me, that if you had met the Canon and he threatened you with Hell and Damnation you would have believed him and loaned him everything you could! The truly amazing thing about this story is that he did raise enough to pay for it and well within the ten years –

an absolutely colossal feat because we're not talking about a minor sum of money!

He did it by badgering his flock to part with all they could and deriding any collection that fell below his expectation. It was considered standard that any youngster starting their first proper job would donate their first week's wages to the church! The names of these innocents were read out at all of the masses on Sunday – the implication being that if your name was never read out you'd somehow shirked your duty! Also whenever you saw him, on his moped visiting parishioners it was rare for him to leave empty handed. "Here Father would you ever say a mass for a special intention," as they parted with the obligatory ten bob note!

I remember when I first watched Marlon Brando in the Godfather wondering if he'd known the Canon because I'm convinced he based his characterisation on him – the Canon was the man who made the original offers you couldn't refuse, although he looked more of a Luco Brazi than a Don Corleone!

In a small way I believe that I did get one over on him although come to think about it I may have hit payback from the Big Guy upstairs for thinking I could outsmart the Canon. At the age of fourteen I applied for a part time evening job during the early summer. The idea was to raise enough money to keep me in cigs when we visited Ireland for the summer break. Mum would have clobbered me if she'd known I was smoking! I got a job working for Paulden's (it later became British Home Stores) going door to door selling central heating. I was paid ten bob per night for three hours work, two nights per week. A chap called Nalley drove us to well established private estates in and around Manchester where he would release three of us (two girls from Quegs – Queen Elizabeth Grammar School) and me to try to sell expensive central heating packages to our unsuspecting victims. I didn't even know what central heating was but I learnt the spiel quickly enough. In those days oil heating was the cheapest but messiest, gas was clean and efficient, as was electric but electric heating was the most expensive. Most people opted for gas. In three weeks working for Nalley I sold eight lots of heating for which I received four pounds when they signed and a further four pounds when the heating was installed. My greatest sale was selling heating to Canon Murphy for the church and the Presbytery (priests' house). I believe the payback came when Paulden's failed to pay me any of the instalment bonuses! It didn't stop the Canon enquiring how much I made on the deal – his prelude to inviting me to donate it to the church (name read out on Sunday), God forgive me but I told him I was still waiting for payment (which in a way I was). I never let on to him that I did make four pounds on the deal. Paulden's made over three thousand pounds on that sale and my share was four pounds! Is it any wonder I grew up with socialist tendencies and didn't make millionaire status?

My first early morning mass was within a week of moving into the new house. I think it was Father Tormey who was presiding and I served with a lad called Kenny Iball (who later joined the army and then went on to drive long haul trucks – I think he lives somewhere in Oxford now). He became my first Langley pal. I do remember having a bit of crush on his older sister who later became a police officer. I could pick them in those days – I don't think that she was ever aware of my existence, although I did get to snog her once when I was about seventeen after a party at a house off Wood Street – I think she might have been drunk at the time!

Father Tormey was a very quiet and quite a shy priest. I used to enjoy serving his mass because it was obvious that he believed absolutely in what he was doing. At the moment of transubstantiation he would sweat and his hands would shake. His faith inspired me and gave me a warm feeling. Mass with Father Tormey was special.

In those days there were three priests living in the presbytery and sharing the workload. The Canon was obviously the main man and Father Kirwin made up the team. Later we would have two priests named Walsh serving at the same time – the younger of the two was always Fr. John, the older was Fr. Pat and then there was Fr. Nosey– he made it his job to try to question all of the young lads of the parish about their impure thoughts and deeds (outside the confessional). Strangely enough I believe Andy and I were the only ones of the crowd I knocked about with that he didn't impose the inquisition upon. Perhaps because he recognised that by then I was too far gone and Andy may have been just too nimble to be caught! I remember we discussed how we'd give him the run around if he ever did button hole us. We even went so far as to rehearse potential conversations:

Fr. Nosey: *Now then do you ever have impure thoughts?*

Me: Yes Fr. Real dirty thoughts.

Fr. Nosey: Tell me all about them.

Me: Well it's mostly after rugby, especially when we play De La Salle Salford and it's been raining heavily. I get home and I just can't stop thinking about how dirty I am and that me mam will kill me.

Fr. Nosey: I don't mean dirty thoughts like that! I mean dirty thoughts about girls.

Me: But girls don't do rugby with us Fr.

The intention would be to get Father Nosey squirming before he got us squirming! I'm not sure I could have carried it off but Andy could display levels of innocence that bordered on insanity and would have led Fr. Nosey to commit the mortal sin of despair! We would try to get him so tied up in knots that he'd eventually give up, because the one thing he didn't appear to be willing to do was be explicit. He never asked "do you masturbate", it would be "do you ever play with yourself"? Our response was always going to be "of course Fr." And when asked to elaborate would eventually get around to saying something along the lines of, "but only when I can't get anyone else to play with me – solitaires a bit hard on your own don't you think?" I seem to recall that Phil did give him a bit of a run around when he sat him down for the chat – Phil just played it innocent and naive. He did look a bit angelic way back then if my memory serves.

Serving on the altar I met friends who became very dear to my heart. Andy Scanlon (see above) who's mum had worked with my mother as a Clippie on the buses during the war (it was a small world way back then) – she once told Andy that my mother broke a chap's nose for using racist remarks to her about her Irishness (I can well believe that of my mum)! She broke his nose by the deft use of the peak of her cap coming down sharply onto the bridge of his nose for simply calling her an "Irish c**t". Not only did his nose break but he also tumbled off the back of the bus wither help! I believe he'd be very careful to whom he might say that to in the future! I also made friends with Brian Kenny who remained a great pal for donkeys years but who has of late become somewhat reclusive, for reasons only he could explain. Brian introduced me to another pal of his who lived on the same street, Rowrah Crescent: Phil Noonan; we would all, soon, become inseparable. More of these later.

I had pals at Saint Clare's but because they tended to live closer to Manchester it became less likely for me make it back that way on a regular basis, therefore my new Langley friends became more and more important. My pals at Clare's did occasionally make it over to 'play' with me on Langley. I say play, it was more like get up to mischief. I do recall a few weekends when Phil Latwosky, Alan Dalghetty, Harry Riley, Spud Murphy and Paul Dale came over and we all visited an old sand quarry that had been used as a rifle range at some point behind The Three Arrows pub in Birch. 'The Great Escape' was everyone's favourite war film at the time so we decided that we should dig escape tunnels in the sand walls of the quarry. Alan went away after our first weekend and designed a whole complex of tunnels we were to make next weekend.

Next weekend we all turned up with digging tools that we'd either pinched from our parents garden sheds or that we'd found discarded on our way to Birch. Alan (the Prof) explained and outlined his plans and we set about with a will. Harry and I were given one of the major digs and everything went swimmingly for quite some time. We did have one or two minor collapses but even these didn't alert us to the obvious danger we were putting ourselves in, so we carried on regardless. Working in turns Harry and I had eventually excavated maybe ten or so feet into our section and we were beginning to bend the tunnel around to meet up with another excavation that hadn't yet progressed that far, when disaster struck. I happened to be the lead monkey when the whole of the roof came down covering both myself and Harry. Harry had been behind me collecting the sand that I was pushing back towards him so that he could push it out of the tunnel. Harry's legs, luckily were sticking out of the tunnel and one of the others spotted him kicking like mad. Phil alerted the others and a mad scramble ensued which luckily (for me) resulted in two sandy boys being rescued from smothercation! I do remember how terrified I was. The roof came down in one clump and I could do nothing but wait and try to keep some air around my mouth so that I could keep on breathing. I was lucky that my hands must have been close to my face when it came down. Somehow the others managed to get hold of my feet and drag me to safety. I believe that put an end to our Langley Mining Enterprise.

Phil and I were always close whilst at school and I often visited his house in Moston. His mum was very good looking and didn't look at all like the mothers of any of my other mates. I remember making fireworks at Phil's which worked a treat and I also remember him introducing me to Zubes – I think his mum worked at the factory or something. With the fireworks we would furtively go to Boggart Hole Clough which was a short walk from his home. Furtively, because we thought the police might arrest us if we were caught with explosives (the police were feared and respected back then). In the park we would strike a light and retire a safe distance to proudly view our handiwork – it's amazing what a bit of sulphur, charcoal and iron filings could do and even more amazing when you added things like magnesium! It was on one of these interludes in the park that I discovered somebody's stash of damp Parade magazines. Parade was a shilling magazine that presented bare chested ladies to the world for their perusal. Phil and I were both very keen on Biology so in the interests of furthering our studies we carefully peeled away soggy page after soggy page to see what wonders lay beyond. Thus a couple of hours of careful study later we returned to the comfort of his lovely home a little more knowledgeable about this world of ours!

Paul Dale and another lad, whose name escapes me now, was the first lad who showed me that you could get served in a pub at the age of fourteen. I was dubious at first but decided to give it a go. I told mum I needed five shillings (25p), which was quite an amount then, to go to the Opera with school. Trips like this were not unusual from St. Clare's. The money was to pay for the Opera, the coach and a shilling (5p) to spend. That Thursday night I got the 121 bus to

Blackley Offices and met up with my two compatriots. We balked at going into the Black Bull, it was too big, and so we found ourselves closer to the ICI buildings where there was a small pub called the Fox Inn (a boxers' pub – it had boxing photographs everywhere) where we, less than confidently, walked up to the bar (it was still fairly quiet – maybe that's why we got away with it) and ordered three pints of mild. We were served, played darts on the Manchester board, had another two pints and left to try our hand at The Grove Inn at Blackley Offices where amazingly we were served again. I say amazingly because this was what we would have called a fairly posh pub. Anyway to cut a long story short I walked home from Blackley (around six or seven miles) having had five pints in total; poked my head around the living room door at eleven o'clock and said I was going straight to bed because I was so tired after a great night at the ballet, sorry the opera. I got into bed and then found that I had to hang on with all my might because the bloody bed started spinning and yawing – it was much worse than a bad crossing of the Irish Sea but it had the same effect. I managed to stagger out of bed, across the landing bumping into everything on the way, and flopping down in front of the big white telephone and placing a direct call for mercy with whoever might be listening. 'Hughey' I shouted but he never replied! Mum was on me like a whirlwind. She cleaned me up, put me to bed and told me I was taking the pledge on the morrow! The pledge was where, as a Catholic you swore off drink – that night I'd have agreed to a lifetime without drink. I did take the pledge but made sure it was the temporary one until I was sixteen – and I stuck to it until that date!

In my fourth year (now Year 10) at St. Clare's I discovered something that would influence the rest of my life more or less and I am not talking about sex!

We had a new geography and history teacher Mr. McGrath. He's probably why I ended up becoming a teacher. He was quite young, about six three or four and he courted and married the smallest female member of staff, Miss Carter who was around five foot nothing. Talk about little and large. They were both lovely – she taught science.

Mr. McGrath imparted knowledge in a fun and enthusiastic manner that was truly infectious. I still love both subjects and in fact reading history remains one of my passions. Anyway Mr. McGrath announced that he was organising an outdoor pursuits holiday and I booked myself onto it. Manchester Education had bought Gyll Head and it's grounds on the banks of Lake Windermere in the Lake District and school's were encouraged to take their motley crews on outward bound week or two week adventures in our case. The centre was staffed with some of the finest teachers it has ever been my pleasure to be taught by and in our two weeks we were introduced to the pleasures of hill walking, camping, rock-climbing, canoeing and orienteering. I was hooked on it all and in later years it led me to offer short outdoor breaks for the children I was by then teaching. Mr. McGrath did the same in fifth year and Eddie Meldrum (a classmate) and I won scholarships to go for two weeks that summer which was absolutely fantastic. We did all of the things we'd done with school plus: abseiling, bivouacking, sea surfing, white water canoeing and a whole host of other exciting things. I recall coming down Sour Milk Gill to the tarn of the same name on a gloriously warm day. We had been rock climbing and bivouacking near Great Gable (I think). We were bushed and dirty. We could see our tents in the valley below; perhaps two or more miles away and some of the lads (we were all lads) wanted to have a dip in the tarn. "In you go" shouted one of our leaders, so about half of us stripped off for a bit for skinny dipping (I didn't know it was called that at the time – it's not something you learned about in Collyhurst or Langley). In we jumped gasping at the coolness of the water. It was absolutely freezing and the only thing that prevented all of us from immediately climbing out again was that no one wanted to be the first to cry 'Uncle'. We splashed each other, shivering and praying someone else would make the first move whilst our leaders sat on the grass laughing fit to burst. It was then that we heard the singing. Angelic it was. I think it might have been something from 'Mary Poppins'. Around forty schoolgirls suddenly hove into view coming down, following the gill as we had done. As they reached the tarn they flopped down and got out their sarnies and started munching whilst watching us slowly turning to blue in the water. Their leaders caught them up and sat chatting to our leaders. Meanwhile we began to enter the first stages of hypothermia. Trying to speak or call out became nigh on impossible because we were shivering so much. We stuck it out as long as we dared and then Eddie (thank God) said,

"Bugger this", and climbed out and we all followed him. Pretend shocked screams and squeals of delight followed our humiliating and naked progress to our sad bundles of clothes. Looking back on it I don't think the girls could have seen much to be shocked about because all of our Willies were inverted and had climbed back up the gap between our legs to escape the cold! The experience didn't put me off camping or the outdoor life which I continued to pursue for much of my life from then on.

I do recall something that happened when I was in third year (Year 9 today) because if it happened today the outcry would be nationally reported!

It seems that we had thieves in the school. This was unheard of in those days. You were given a desk with a lid where you could safely leave your books, pens, sarnies and anything else you cared to store there in the knowledge that no one would touch it. No one had any business looking inside anyone else's desk. Anyway at an assembly we were solemnly warned not to leave anything of value around as there were thieves in the school but not to worry they would soon be caught and dealt with. Within a fortnight of that announcement the whole school was summoned to the hall for a special assembly. Three third years, two from my class, were marched onto the stage each of them carrying a placard emblazoned with the words, "I am a thief".

Jack Dwyer (our Head), Mr. Kusak (deputy head) and several other senior teachers joined them on stage. The whole school was agog, waiting to hear what was to happen. Mr. Dwyer began, "As you know we have had thieves in our school. Shameful! I am pleased to tell you we discovered them red-handed and here they stand before you. When they were caught I called their parents in and told them I must hand them over to the police – their parents begged me not to do that. I then told them I must expel them – their parents begged me not to do that. So I asked their parents what should I do and they agreed that we as a school should handle this ourselves which is what I am about to do." With that he caned the three boys, in front of the whole school, six on each hand and six on the backside. He added, "They will each wear their placard for the rest of the week and then put this whole business behind them."

The three boys, who were quite tough lads, were all weeping by the end of the flogging and they did wear the sandwich boards for the rest of the week but I never heard another word about the incident from anyone in the school, pupils or teachers – it was as Mr. Dwyer said "put. . . behind them". Of the three boys concerned one eventually ended up on the wrong side of the law after leaving school. The other two became stalwart members of society and as far as I am aware never became involved in anything similar ever again. One of them actually became a major business man and a member of the Rotary Club! I don't think they bore scars for life and I don't think that any of them suffered irreversible psychological damage. I think what it actually did was teach them, albeit in a savage manner, a life lesson that indeed was life changing. I am not for one minute suggesting that this is how we should deal with such rascals today – God forbid, because if we did we'd have to be prepared to flog an awful lot more than three boys in any one school! I just present it as something that happened in a different era to the one we inhabit today.

I think the only other incident I would mention from my time at St. Clare's was when Mr. Hitler (I've given him an assumed name to protect his identity) nearly blew up the lab he was teaching in! He was taking a senior class for Chemistry and had got them to the point where Chlorine (CL) became Chlorine Gas (CL2) at which point his equipment decided to explode. Chlorine gas by the way is what was used in WW1 to gas troops in the trenches. I don't think the experiment is permitted in schools today (H & S). Anyway it resulted in the whole school being evacuated for around an hour whilst the fire brigade made the labs and the rest of the school safe for our return. It was one of my favourite maths lessons if I remember correctly! Mr. Hitler was infamous throughout the school. He was one of those ex soldiers who after the war were recruited to teach the new generation. He always carried an eighteen inch baton covered in red leather underneath his right arm, sergeant major style, which he used to great effect if anyone upset him. He was easily upset! I upset him by bumping into him in the playground when I was in second year – two across the bum on a cold day! Ouch. He was mostly infamous in class when teaching Biology. He prided himself that no one who took the subject with him ever failed so at the beginning of a new school year he would sweep into his fourth year 'O' level group asking a question based on that day's lesson. "What is photosynthesis?" The class would pile in behind him, students frantically asking what was it he had said? As you found your place he would arrange his notes on the teacher's desk which sat on a plinth at the front of the lab and then his gown flapping he would sweep to the rear of the room where he would once again ask his question. The members of the class would be desperately trying to track down whatever it was he had said by looking at the index at the back of the textbook. "Foto what? F, ef, ef, ef, ef," at which point he would bring his baton into play. Starting at the back of the class he would stop behind every pupil and say, "Answer?" If the answer wasn't forthcoming the pupil received a sharp rap across the back of the head and then he moved on to the next. By the time he reached the half way point in the class some swot would have worked out the spelling and stumbled across an answer he was willing to accept. His purpose in all of this was to ensure we all got a Biological Dictionary – everyone had one by week two! Effective methodology I think!

I believe Mr. Barber might well have been teaching the Maths lesson I missed – he was a lovely old school teacher who certainly tried to impart some knowledge of the subject to us. Mr. Debonaire was a one of the more senior teachers with something to do with prefects but he was better known for his antics at the teacher's desk. He would place his hand behind the knees of certain, selected, boys and then place his hands on the desk thus causing the young man or young men in question to balance precariously on one leg whilst the other leg rested on Mr. Deboniare's forearms. Mmmmm, it did cause some heated discussion as to whether it was quite normal to do such things! In the end I don't think (or certainly I never heard) that it ever went any further than that. I do recall poor Eddie Meldrum was one of the boys he enjoyed having at the front – Eddie was quite popular with the girls too!

The only other teacher I will mention is Alicia Porter who was our form tutor at times and who taught French. The battles we waged before entering her classroom to see who would sit at the front of the class. This was in the era of the mini skirt and Alicia had the most wonderful pins we'd ever seen. I'd have killed for a place at the front of the class just on the off chance she might cross her legs and sometimes I did!!!!!

I shall leave Saint Clare's there I think although I should perhaps mention the Franciscans who were the parish priests at St. Clare's Church on Victoria Avenue. The Franciscans were a missionary order of priests (Friars) and monks (brothers) and perhaps because missionary life in those days was potentially very dangerous in places like China they seemed to have a love of life and living that isn't always associated with holy orders.

Just before Christmas it was the practice to invite several senior boys to the church to help set up the crib for the Christmas period. The statues of: the baby Jesus, Blessed Virgin, St. Joseph, the three kings, various shepherds as well as assorted cattle, sheep and a donkey were kept in the cellar. It was the boys' jobs to carry them up undamaged where they were made presentable with straw and the like by one of the school's famous Art teachers (St. Clare's had a reputation as one of the best Art schools in the country) into a nativity scene we are all familiar with. In my final year at the school I was one of the senior boys involved and after we had finished our part of the exercise we were invited into the presbytery where bottles of Guinness were handed around. As I was handed a bottle by a priest I felt it overrode my pledge and downed it with gusto (I would be sixteen in a matter of weeks and my pledge not to drink would be ended – also you couldn't really refuse a priest's invitation to have one, could you?). If I remember correctly the reason for the largesse wasn't just to thank us but because one of their own had returned for Christmas from the missions abroad and it was by way of welcoming him into the fold so to speak.

I left St. Clare's with a set of results that were barely enough to win me a place at Cardinal Langley Grammar School in Middleton, where the majority of my Langley pals already attended. All of whom managed to gain lorry loads more GCE's than me!

At the end of Year Ten I worked on the Skelmersdale Estate (see Chapter 14: A Real Day's Work) and at the end of my compulsory schooling I once again found myself working with Kennedy's at the Woodhead Tunnel (one of the longest rail tunnels in Britain). The work this year was much easier and I think my dad kept me away from the more brutal work Kennedy's was involved in. I remember one of the guys seemed to spend all day burning off cuts of the huge electric cables we were laying so that the copper could be extracted and weighed in. I recall lunch times in the local pub where I learned to play various dart games like Killer and Loop and I recall we had a long, long walk back through the eerie tunnel to get back to work. All in all it was a much easier year than the previous year in terms of the demands made upon me. My dad even gave me the opportunity to drive his wagon on some of the deserted country roads.

It was 1968 when I finished at St. Clare's and started at Cardinal Langley. It was also the year I ended my pledge and discovered music.

I ended my pledge on my sixteenth birthday and spent a lovely afternoon being walked around Truffet Park on Langley, barfing up at least three times more than I had drunk. I had obviously learned nothing since the last time I drank – story of my life!

That summer I must have had some free time to myself either before or after going to Ireland. I know I went to France with Andy Scanlon. Cardinal Langley permitted me to join the school's trip to Biarritz because I would be starting there in September.

On Thursday June the sixth I was at Brian Kenny's home on Rowrah Crescent with Phil Noonan. Phil was the smallest of the guys but he was the man with the most spare dosh (money – his dad was a contractor) and he already had a music collection to die for. I had two albums at that time: an Aretha Franklyn LP and one by Geno Washington and the Ram Jam Band. That morning Phil played a track that he'd just acquired called "Your Song" by someone I had never heard of, Elton John. I swear I had an ecstatic reaction – a shiver down my spine – it sounded so good. I know that, that very afternoon I went out and bought the album which I played to death. It was my musical awakening and I became a big fan of Elton.

Now I am not saying that they did this to wind me up but sometime after Phil had played the track several times, one of them asked me what I thought of Kennedy being killed. I thought they were talking about JFK and they knew I had admired him greatly. No they said RFK, Robert Kennedy was assassinated last night. I thought they were teasing me again, because they knew I revered the Kennedy clan for putting Irish Americans on the map. To prove their validity they actually switched on the TV which was still full of the news. I remember feeling totally deflated. Once again the world was doing some kind of backward flip and this guy who appeared as though he might even be a greater president than his dead brother had been, had also been taken from us. All that promise, an end to Vietnam, racial equality, war on crime, a brighter and better world; all taken away by some crazed misfit. Coming so soon after Martin Luther King's assassination in April it just seemed to me that the evil in the world was beginning to hold sway over the good and all of this coming in the same year as the My Lai massacre. I wasn't aware of My Lai at this point even though that had occurred in March. I think the news of My Lai was drip fed to us much later. It's just that the world appeared to be becoming this much darker and sadder place. Good men stepped forward and were mown down, whilst men we trusted over stepped their brief. I think the confidence that we might have had that the new world; the modern world could be a better place took a nose dive in 1968 that it hasn't really recovered from yet. The years that have followed have demonstrated a drift to barbarism, leaders who are deceitful, movements that plague the world and a news media that thinks nothing of destroying individuals and twisting stories to suit agendas we know little about (a media which at the very least is mischievous with facts and often politically motivated). I really do believe that the world today is a much sadder place than it was pre 1968.

After 1968 what did we have to look forward to? Murder in Munich ('72), Genocide in Cambodia ('75), The Tangshan earthquake ('76), the premature death of the King (Elvis, '77), and of course Maggie Thatcher ('79) and that's just in the 1970's! 2001 would underline my fear that the world has kind of spiralled into a dark pit of hopelessness. I know I must be sounding full of doom and gloom but here's the rub – I am still optimistic and I still believe in the inherent goodness of people and I do have hope that the future will somehow be brighter than my fears indicate – if only for my grand children's sake.

Getting back to Langley with Andy, Brian and Phil in the summer of 1968. With a little cash in my pocket I began to discover the joys of good music. After the "Elton John" album, I acquired his first album, "Empty Sky". I was on a voyage of discovery and Phil was my mentor. He introduced me to Tamla which led me onto Junior Walker and the All Stars; soul with Aretha (again); folk with Dylan and the band that saw me through my later teen years The Band! All seemed to be leading the way to The Eagles and country rock. Strangely I never got into one of Phil's favourite sounds The Moody Blues – I don't think he ever forgave me for not admiring them as much as he did! Brian introduced me to James Taylor and

Scanny (Andy) introduced me to the Dubliners although I didn't need much introduction to them!

Music was very much the food of life at that time. Phil had a very wide collection, catering for most tastes. On the nights that we'd end up back at his house in the kitchen with his big portable record player (I think it might have been a Bush!) he was as likely to play folk as well as pop, rock, soul, tamla and country music. He certainly introduced me to an enormous range of music I would just never have come across if not for him. I don't think I really started discovering for myself until I was well into my twenties when Springsteen and Billy Joel became so important to me. Phil grudgingly admits that I introduced him to Billy Joel but as I say that was well into my twenties!

Throughout my teenage years I continued to visit the cinema regularly. I saw my first "X" film – a double bill at the Temple in Cheetham Hill – Boris Karlof in "Corridors of Blood" and Vincent Price in "The Haunted Palace". I thought they were tame even then! My mum had a friend called Theresa who used to work with her at a cake shop called Brooke's on Deansgate before my mum moved to Littlewoods and on to the Bacon counter. Theresa had got a job working for a cinema and she used to get free passes from time to time that she would pass on to my mum for me. I saw, "The Bible", "Cromwell" with Richard Harris, Burt Lancaster in "Elmer Gantry" and the original "Ocean's Eleven". Terrific times. I still go to the cinema and still enjoy it almost as much, although I'd never dream of buying pop corn or anything else; they require a second mortgage nowadays!

For some reason I loved my time at Cardinal Langley, despite the odd hiccough. I already had several good friends there and I met others soon after starting. I could probably fill a book just talking about my time there but I won't. I will mention one person I did meet there whom I met much later in life.

In my lower sixth year I met a new boy to Cardinal Langley, he was doing sciences to my arts. He was called Trevor Cook. The reason we drifted together was because like me and unlike my other pals he was a smoker. Like attracts like as they say. His dad ran the Criterion on Argyle Street in Heywood, which meant that Trev rarely ran out of cigarettes! Anyway, to cut a long story short, he only attended Cardinal Langley for nine months before his dad took on a new pub elsewhere and he moved to another school to take a different set of "A" levels.

I didn't see him again for around thirty years and then I didn't recognise him and he didn't recognise me. He had remained in contact with the business of ale and he opened up a micro brewery in Todmorden, where I moved to in 1987. I believe he opened up the brewery around 1999. Along with the brewery he opened up a small beer house opposite where Morrisons supermarket operates today. The beer house was tastefully called "Bare Arts" because his wife Kath, an artist, paints Picassoeque nudes which are displayed in the window.

Over the years since he opened up the beer house I would call in on occasion with friends who might be staying over – as somewhere different to go. I got on well with him and him with me, though neither of us recognised the other.

Cut to 2012 when Andy and his wife Elaine were staying over. We'd been out for a lovely meal and it was too early to go home and as Andy had never been in Bare Arts we decided to call in and have a couple before heading for home. We got chatting. Andy is a great conversationalist, as was Trevor. Suddenly something clicked inside my head and I looked (stared) hard at Trevor and slowly said, "You're Trevor Cook", which seemed a bit obvious because his name was above the door etc. I clarified what I meant immediately and the scales fell away from his eyes as well as mine. Old pals reunited. It really is a funny old world sometimes.

I enjoyed meeting up with Trevor a few times after we reacquainted ourselves one with the other. I was able to share some photographs I had of the two of us at Cardinal Langley, hanging out! He and Kath were made up with them.

Our renewed friendship sadly wasn't to last because in April 2014 he was diagnosed with Liver Cancer and he was dead before the end of the year. I miss him for all sorts of reasons and funnily enough one of them is because he was such an eccentric, he wore quite loud clothes and sported a very fine range in bow ties! I think his cancer was triggered by an accident he had a couple of years before the diagnosis, when he was run over whilst legitimately crossing the road at a Pelican crossing that was green. He suffered two badly broken legs and was out of action for over a year. I firmly believe that such a trauma can trigger latent cancers!

Back to the late 1960's and Ben Sherman shirts, hipsters, stay-press parallels and later bell bottoms!

Because I smoked I never seemed to have enough money to keep on top of the fashions but I did try. I remember Phil, Brian and myself all acquiring black Jay Tex cardigans because we looked super cool in them! Especially with our stay press parallels and brogues! I have rarely bought any other shoes than brogues and I still find them by far the most handsome of shoes. One pair I had from the age of eighteen or nineteen (Barratt's) and they were still in use when I was forty-five having been soled and healed several times. I'd still be using them but the cobbler told me that he wouldn't be able to repair them again!

I suspect that it was around the autumn of 1968 that we discovered the disco scene in Manchester. At that time there were so many clubs you could go to without it costing a fortune. At the height of the club scene I had membership cards for: Roundtrees Sound, Top of the Town, Tacki's, Spring Gardens, Mr. Smith's and several others. Top of the Town was our favourite club on Corporation Street. I won a copy of Dr. and the Medics "Spirit in the Sky" there, in a yard of ale contest!

I was often so loath to finish the night that I would miss the last bus home which meant it was Shank's pony for me – a walk of around ten miles – that's when the brogues came in handy. There were times when I would walk home from Manchester, leaving at around 0300 and getting home just in time to do my Sunday paper round, before turning up for rugby training!

They were great days for both good dance music and live bands. One of the finest live bands was called, "Burning Soul" and the lead guitarist was a lad from Cardinal Langley. I suppose we were a bit like groupies because we followed them around, but only when they were within walking distance of Langley (e.g. QUEG's).

We all reached the age of consent within six or so months of each other. If I remember correctly Andy was first, followed by me, then Phil and finally Brian (the baby). Obviously we were all well into the opposite sex by then, although I must warn you I am not into kiss and tell. Suffice it to say we all had girl friends who meant a great deal individually to us – vive la difference – as they say. As we reached eighteen we became more civic minded, especially after the "A" levels were out of the way, some doing better than others but all doing moderately well.

Andy stayed on to improve his results. Brian started work with a local hospital where he took his Ordinary National Diploma and went on to get his Higher National. Phil registered at a college in Manchester to take a business degree and I went to De La Salle College to try to become a teacher.

Our civic mindedness led us to seek the help of Father John Walsh, the most approachable of our local priests. We managed to convince him that the young men and women of the parish needed somewhere local to dance and befriend other young people. We wanted to establish an eighteenth plus group in the local Catholic

Club the members of which were totally and utterly against the idea. Youngsters coming into our club making noise and fighting – no!

Fair play to Father John, although he did require a lot of pushing, he managed to negotiate one night a week (Thursday's) where we could have the concert room. I became the club secretary and Phil was the treasurer!!!!! More of that later. I was going out with a girl at the time who had a mate who was a really good D.J., Keith Fane (real name Whalley) who went on to become the match day presenter at Manchester United's Old Trafford. I remember seeing him on TV strutting across the Nou Camp pitch after United won the European Cup and after the trophy had been presented. Something happened in the years that followed which caused him to pull out. Anyway Keith was available and although his usual minimum charge was £10 per night at the time he agreed to £6. It was a terrific hit from the word go. We'd already had the arguments about who could come in and join the club. The members of the club were adamant that they must be practising Catholics, somehow we managed to persuade Father John that it had to be open membership – it was after all the latter half of the twentieth century!

Our early success encouraged us to try out different kinds of night and as myself and Andy, in particular, were getting more and more into folk music we had several Folk Nights. These were unbelievably successful. I remember Joe Walsh, who was the manager of the club at that time, telling me that the takings at the bar had broken club records. I think this went some way to appeasing members, a little, although they still came into the concert room and stood, staring at everyone as they left at the end of a night – just to make sure that we knew they were really in charge.

The folk nights were fabulous for all sorts of reasons: they crossed age boundaries so that the clientele was much more varied than on a disco night; folk was very popular in the late sixties, early seventies; there was a wealth of talent about and not a lot of money needed to change hands in order to get some very fine artists to play.

Mike Harding and his mate Tony Downes headlined on several occasions and we had groups like The Wild Geese from Hopwood College who were magnificent (two of the band went on to perform on Ed Sullivan's coast to coast show in America). Lot of local teachers, like Mike Canavan, dabbled in folk and some were very good, I even got up and gave a moderately good rendition of "Whiskey in the Jar" and "Peggy Gordon". When Thin Lizzie later released "Whiskey in the Jar", I claimed bragging rights that Phil Lynott must have heard me sing it first!

The Eighteen Plus Group lasted about three years before the membership managed to finally close it. I was on holiday in Majorca at the time and when I came back it had been closed for almost two weeks and no one had gone to badger Father John about reopening – I felt fed up of pushing for something and being the one who had to make the promises that were expected of us by the members of the club, so I let it slide. I was really upset when we were closed down. The guys knew I was upset with them and so we tended not to talk too much about the club and in the fullness of time I put it behind me. It wasn't until a year or two later that someone mentioned the accumulated club funds (which I'd assumed had been handed in to Father John). It was a sizeable amount if my memory serves. It was only then that I discovered that Phil (the club treasurer) had sat on it for a good while anticipating its recall but when no one mentioned it to him he started dipping into it to treat himself and other ex members of our committee and associated pals to the odd drinking night out! By the time I became aware of what was going on it had more or less been drunk by them! Story of my life.

I could write tomes about those days. Bunking off school on a Thursday was almost habit forming with myself Phil and Brian. We'd meet up at the bus station in Middleton and someone would say, "Thursday" which was enough to get the three of us and occasionally a couple of others heading back to a frozen house where we would huddle trying to keep warm until it was time to go to our respective homes – in between we would play Tamla or soul and work out slick dance routines to try out at Talk of the Town". To say that two of us became teachers is shocking don't you think?

I worked on the roads during the summers and winters. The summer I left school I had the best road job ever, working for MacAlpine's on the M62 at Windy Gap near Ripponden. I worked on one of the two heavy gangs (I was concreting drainage channels) the other one was the tarmac gang. The tarmac gang was made up almost completely of West Indians and their ganger was the man who got me the start, a townie of my mum's, Tom Fitzmaurice. My gang was a mixed gang of Irish, Poles and English, we got on like a house on fire with the Westies who were as mad for the craic as any of the Irish lads!

My first day was a baptism of fire. Mick Green was a Ballyhaunis man who also knew my father and mother. Tom Fitz introduced me to him and said I wouldn't let the auld man down. "We'll see about that," said Greenie (everyone called the Foreman Greenie). He was a powerfully built man in his forties who suffered fools badly. He was well used to giving orders and having them carried out with hop and a jump. "Come with me," he said. He was a man of few words. I jumped into his open land rover and he sped off to the site offices where there were storage sheds and of course offices. As we arrived a flat back wagon was reversing towards one particular shed, it was carrying hundreds of bags of cement. "Unload that into there," he said and sped off. I saw my life flashing past – it looked like a colossal job and one that might take me the better part of a year to complete!

The driver, an English guy, said, "Come on pal, we'll have this done in no time." I wondered for a moment who he was talking to and then realised it was me. He gave me instructions as to how to take the bags from him off the back of the wagon, walk to the back of the shed and stack them. We started around nine in the morning and it was already a roasting hot day. My shirt came off and on his advice I tried to keep the shirt between my shoulder and the bags, but it didn't stop the cement from blistering my skin. We stuck at it and finished around eleven thirty, I couldn't believe it. "Told you we'd have it done in no time," said my pal the driver. I took my leave of him and started the long walk back to my gang.

I'd walked maybe a half a mile, perhaps three quarters when greenie in his Land Rover screeched to a halt on the newly laid tarmac on the opposite carriageway. He leapt over the mid section and stomped towards me. "Where the feck do you think you're going?" he growled. I must have looked at him with a gormless expression on my face, "I thought I told you to unload that feckin' wagon?"

"I did," I said, "I was just heading back to Mr. Errr," I couldn't remember my ganger's name, "Heading back to my gang."

Greenie thought fast, "Did you close up the shed before ye left it? I don't want to go back there and find it's gone or spoiled now!"

"Yeah, I put a peg in the lock like."

"Okay," he muttered, "McClusky (the name of the ganger man) and the rest if his gang are about half a mile down that way on the left," he said, "get yourself back there quick and don't fecking dawdle or I'll give you what for. I'll be back to you if I'm not satisfied with the way ye left the shed!"

There was no thank you or well done, just that veiled threat. Such was my introduction to working on the road. I loved my time there and met some terrific guys. My ganger man Peter McClusky was quite depressed when I first joined the gang and it took me several days before I found out what was wrong with him. Apparently he'd been best man at his best mates wedding and there'd been some altercation that resulted in the two of them giving battle. Peter had punched his best mate so hard he'd put him into a coma, and one that he didn't wake up from for several days. I'd actually started on the Monday following the wedding so Peter was quite morose for most of the week until his mate woke up and forgave him; then he was a hard task master but a terrific guy. Peter was like me a first generation English lad in his late thirties.

Janich, the Pole, was an older man whose life story was intriguing. He'd fought with the partisans towards the end of the war, even though he was only a teenager. The partisan group he was attached to found themselves sandwiched between the Russians on the one side and the Nazis on the other. Had he been captured by either side it would have been instant execution. He was a lovely chap and was in his broken English constantly asking if we were getting plenty of the "Garamoushkie?" – I think it referred to sex.

I worked seven days a week. Saturday was time and a half, Sunday was double time. In order to qualify to work Sunday you had to turn in on Saturday. It was hard going but I generally managed a full seven days. I remember taking the first girl I married, Julia, to the Hole in the Wall in Manchester for a steak on Friday night and getting her home in time to watch the Andy William's Show (which was very popular at the time). I sat on the couch between her dad and mam and promptly fell asleep. They tried everything to wake me up but couldn't. I did wake around three in the morning, realised I'd missed the last bus from Harpurhey (about eight or nine miles from Langley) and started walking. I got home in time to change clothes jump on my bike, cycle to Oldham for my lift and complete the

Saturday shift. The money was unbelievable; I was clearing over one hundred pounds a week after tax (I got all the tax back when I started college – "Yes," - the only thing the tax man ever gave me). That summer a big gang of us booked a chalet in Towyn near Rhyl and had two of the best weeks I've ever enjoyed on holiday! I spent like it was going out of fashion.

College was terrific. I somehow qualified to get on the Degree course to take an Ordinary Degree in Education (B.Ed) and in my second year began on the degree course. My father had the first of his major heart attacks in between my second and third examination during that year's exam period. I missed a couple as a result and was told I'd have to resit in the summer. At the time it didn't look as though I'd be able to complete another two years so I reverted to the Certificate course which I passed with Distinctions a year later.

That summer I worked with an old friend of the family, Peter Larkin and his partner Des Curley. My parents had known Peter since our time in Collyhurst. Peter and his lovely wife Theresa were from Monaghan, the same county as Patsy's husband Sean – and they were all great friends. I worked for Peter and Des throughout much of my time at college (summers, Easter, Christmas) it was a big help as I didn't qualify for a full grant until my final year when my dad was out of work following his heart attack.

That year, 1973, he was paying me full joiner's rate (I suspect I was paid a little less but I was still very happy) to help build offices for GUS (Great Universal – a catalogue company) in Preston and I was applying for teaching posts. Peter pulled me aside one day and suggested that I stick with him for a year or two, raise enough for a deposit on a house and buy myself a car – I could always go into teaching after that if I still wanted to. I told him that having worked to get the qualifications I felt I needed to see if I could hack it but that if I couldn't would his offer still be open to me. He said it would be so I took my first teaching post at Saint Wilfrid's in Rochdale.

I knew I'd be taking a drop in pay. With Peter I was clearing £79 per week after tax, my first month's pay check as a teacher was £59 and a few pence – after a month's work!!!!!!!!

Had I made the right decision? Perhaps time would tell but that might be a tale for another time.

14. My Sister Married a Mad Man.

My sister married a mad man or so it seemed to me at the time.

I was about twelve and like most twelve year olds I was totally engrossed in my own little world of self gratification and self centeredness. Patsy was at Sedgely Park College training to become the wonderful teacher she became. I think she was nearly finished when she became pregnant!

For years she'd gone out with Paddy McNicholas. A lovely lad from Castlebar in the County Mayo. Paddy had secured my mother's vote but it seems Patsy needed just a tad more excitement than Paddy could provide. Anyway after courting Paddy for several years she "finished" with him and took up with a "wild one" (my mother's words).

Sean had left Castelblaney in County Monaghan to join the Irish Guards and he had only recently rejoined civvy street. He was "mad for the craic" in those days and he provided the excitement Patsy needed. She was always "wild", so it seems they were suited.

Before her death (much too young at 65 in 2011 – RIP) she confided to me that she set out to hold on to him, something none of his other conquests had managed to do. She realised early he was the man for her and no one else would do.

I was oblivious to much of what was going on because as I have already suggested I was totally focussed on my little world and no other world mattered! As a consequence the first I knew about things was when the arguments started between Patsy and mam! For several weeks the peace of the house was shattered. Patsy was the proverbial "demon from Hell". Patsy had announced she was marrying Sean and that was it – no discussion – it was going to happen. Dad, saint that he was, quietly refereed these occasionally violent bouts which usually ended in tears from Patsy and my mother clenching her tongue between her teeth (something she was renowned for doing during heated debates).

Sanity of course, eventually, prevailed and the day of the wedding was set for Friday, November 6th 1964.

Patsy and Sean were duly married and dad managed to ensure that the peace was kept for the rest of the day. Mum gave a frosty welcome to Sean and the pair moved in to the house where we lived on the Langley estate: 12 Lingmell Close.

In so far as it didn't really affect me I thought, 'well that's it. Pat's married.'

I have struggled to try to remember whether they went away for a few days or not but for the life of me I can't. But I do recall vividly what happened on the first Monday, after the wedding, as Sean got ready to go to work.

Lingmell Close as the name suggests was closed to traffic. In fact outside number 12 was a large green. The top end of the close was in the form of an "L" shape with parking at the bottom of the "L". Then there was a lawned green through to Hellvellyn Drive (all of the streets, closes, drives and avenues were named after places in the Lake District on Langley).

On that Monday morning I was still in bed when pandemonium broke out. My mother was screaming, Patsy was hysterically laughing, dad had long been gone to work and Sean was tripping over himself trying to pull on his clothes and get out of the house. Parked in the dead centre of the green was a lorry with four or five guys hanging over the sides and out the doors wolf whistling, yahooing, offering words of encouragement to Sean, saying "How are ya mam?" to my mother, and generally "lowering the tone" of the neighbourhood (mum's phrase).

Eventually a sheepish Sean emerged from the house, calling apologies to mum, blowing kisses to Pat and trying hard not to laugh too loudly as he joined his pals. No sooner was he aboard than the juggernaut leapt across the green and out onto Hellvellyn taking Sean to tarmac some corner of Manchester not yet covered in the black stuff!

Mum considered "flitting" because she'd never be able to live with the shame "he'd" brought to the house. Dad, regretted not being home for it – "it sounded like a great craic altogether" and Patsy and Sean immediately started to save up to buy their own home on Bowness Road, which they did within a very few years via a period of sane time away from my mum in a ground floor flat on Searness Road, but not before they had three wonderful little girls: Louise, Joanne and Siobhan.

In the late 1970's they flirted with the idea of emigrating to Australia and got so far as passing the interviews and booking passage before the girls rebelled and said the only place they'd be willing to emigrate to was Ireland. It was thus that in 1978 they packed up everything they owned and moved back to County Monaghan and built their own place in Killycrum, near Castleblaney.

Patsy was my only sister. She was the clever one in the family. I know she was a terrific teacher because I had the privilege of working with her whilst completing one of my own teaching practices and I have heard countless ex students telling me how good she was. She was my conscience, my adviser and my sounding board. She could always be counted on to bring me down to earth when I waxed lyrical. I miss our heart to hearts and knowing that she's no longer there for me to seek advice from is almost too hard to bear. I miss her every day and I try to ensure that I remember her daily in my prayers. She is more often than not the last and the first person I think of daily. Until she was gone I didn't realise how much she actually meant to me. She will always be in my thoughts.

I know that Patsy had no regrets about her life, because I asked her before she was so sadly taken from us. Sean provided her with a wonderful home, beautiful children and more than that he gave them a way of life that many would aspire to. They were happily married for forty odd years and I know that Patsy wouldn't have changed a one of those years for all the tea in china – and Patsy liked her tea – ask anyone who knew her!

15. A Real Days Work.

The summer I was fourteen I got a job selling central heating door to door. I worked for ten shillings (50p) a night and was promised eight pounds commission on anything I sold. It was four pounds on signing and the other four on completion (I only ever received signing fees!). I was actually quite successful and managed eight signings in five nights of work over a three or four week period! I say that I was quite successful because I managed to get one of the shrewdest men I have ever had the pleasure to know to sign a contract, Canon Murphy of Our Lady's, Langley. I was terrified of meeting him for months afterwards for fear that he'd demand that I donate the commission I hadn't received to the church! If he'd been anything but a priest he would have been a millionaire because he definitely had the Midas touch! He paid off the loan on the church and the local secondary school in less than twelve years, having first obtained the loan from the bank which never loaned to the clergy!

The following year I was to try my hand at real work. Whatever money I earned would provide spends for the annual holiday to Ireland.

My father that time was working for a firm of contractors called Regan's, pronounced Raygan's. He was a driver with a fearsome reputation as a powerful worker.

He took me down to All Saint's in Manchester, where the firm used to pick up its road crews, on the first Monday of my summer holidays, at six-thirty in the morning. As we approached the pickup point he told me to climb out of the wagon, walk around the corner and line up with the men I'd see there. He explained that none of the men appreciated favouritism and that it would be better for me if they didn't know who I was initially. I think that he was making it easy for me to quit if I felt that I couldn't handle it!

I followed his advice and walked around the corner to discover hundreds of men standing or sitting on the steps of All Saints Church. Some were in groups talking loudly about the craic the night before, some were holding confidential and quiet conversations, others were sat reading the morning papers marking off the day's betting, and still others were standing or sitting as if alone in the throng of work hardened men.

I took my place with them and said a silent prayer to help me through the day. I shrank within myself not daring to enter into conversation with any of them, my heart pounding. They all appeared to be Irish and their brogues lilted over me in a welcome and familiar way, although even this did not set me at my ease.

At around six-forty-five things began to happen. The wagons, which had been parked some way off, started up and drove to the edge of the steps. Men began to uncoil themselves from their groups or their thoughts. They all stood and the air of expectancy was almost tangible. A group of older, rugged looking individuals peeled themselves away and began walking along the lines of men nodding to this one and shouting to another. As a man was thus marked he would make his way to a wagon and climb aboard. In this manner the vast majority of men were selected and joined their comrades aboard one or other of the armada of trucks.

At the end of the procedure I was one of about fourteen left unselected, standing, trying to appear unconcerned and yet attempting to look like I was able for any work they had available. I was extremely conscious of myself; it was like being one of the last selected to play soccer during a games lesson at school. Insecurity and shame played dirty tricks on my facial colouring. I felt abandoned and very lonely.

As if from a great distance I heard my father's voice calling to someone called Maher suggesting he give the young lad the start. It was a moment before I realised that the man called Maher was signalling to me to climb aboard one of the wagons. As cool as I could I walked towards the truck and climbed aboard, thankful for the anonymity afforded by the ten or so men already aboard. I stared shame faced at those who remained on the steps and I almost shouted "sorry" to them. They were all probably better able to face the type of work expected than I was.

The wagon lurched to a start and the men aboard staggered against each other, some swearing loudly.

"Jaysus, it's a great day to be working," said the man next to me, clinging to the trucks side panel.

"Yeah," I replied lamely.

"Where are ye from?" he asked.

"Manchester," I replied struggling to relax.

"Have ye worked with Raygan's before?"

"No".

"Who were ye with before?"

"No one." I broke the first rule that my father had given me, "Crack on you've done this kind of thing before," he'd said.

"So this is your first day of diggin' is it?"

"Yeah," I replied whilst praying that the bottom of the truck would open up and let me drop through it.

"Well ye'v picked a right team to fix yerself up with. They'll work ye 'till ye drop, and that's no lie."

"Will ye stop frightening the boy Quinn, can't ye see he's terrified," cut in a big man standing next to Quinn. "Don't pay no heed to this auld omadawn. What's yer name boy?"

"Brendan," I stuttered. The big fellow had certainly hit my state right on the head; I was terrified.

"Well now that's a fine name now but do you have another one to go with it?" asked the big fellow.

"Ramsbottom", I stuttered.

"Well now dere's a ting. His first name is as Irish as they come, his second is pure John Bull. Now ye wouldn't happen to be Paddy Ramsbottom's son would ye?"

I was troubled because I knew my dad wanted me to stand on my own two feet and not be plagued by any comparisons with him. Try as I might I could not say that I wasn't his son, "I am," I mumbled.

"Well now then don't you worry none Brendan, no one here is going to bite you and if they do they'll answer to me. Stick close to me and I'll see you alright. The names Tom Hogan," as he said this the big fellow pushed huge work grimed and calloused hand towards me. I took it limply and he pumped my arm up and down. "Maher's an auld bastard," he said, "but he'd shit in his socks before he'd upset me, so just do as I advise and you'll be sound." My hand felt tiny in his paw.

We were travelling for a good forty-five minutes, heading west along the East Lancs. Road towards Liverpool. We were to work on a new estate called Skelmersdale. The estate wasn't too far from Wigan, which we passed through.

Wigan was on its Wake's and I don't believe I have ever passed through a place so utterly quiet and deserted. I didn't know what the Wake's were at that time and it seemed to me that the whole town had been abandoned, perhaps for some nuclear test! It reminded me of one of those cowboy towns where the tumbleweed blows across the main street.

Eventually the wagon halted and unloaded the crew. We met up with others who had been deposited earlier. Shovels, picks, grafts, sledgehammers and bars were handed out to the assembled men. The brew boy, a gnarled and world-weary Dubliner, took the orders for dinner. My dad had given me two pounds and said, "Have what the others are having." So I ordered a pound of steak and paid the man my seven and six pence. Then it was down to work!

Eight o'clock on a fine summer's morning in what was to become Skelmersdale saw my baptism of fire into the world of work.

I was given a shovel and Tom gestured that I should follow him. He carried a graft. I'd never seen or heard of one before, although I knew that to graft was to work hard. The graft was similar to the shovel though with a straighter handle and the blade was much longer, perhaps twelve inches in length, nine inches or so at the top tapering to about four inches at the working end.

We made our way to the trenches that had already been begun the previous week. There appeared to be miles of trenches to my untrained eye. They were three feet wide at the top and four feet deep. We were preparing the way for heavy-duty electric cables.

Pairs of men aligned themselves along the engineer marked area ready to excavate the next section.

Tom motioned for me to stand in front of him and facing him, "Now then, I'll break it up and you throw it out. O.K.?"

"O.K.," I answered feeling anything but O.K.

Tom drove hard down into the earth with the graft and broke up one huge clod after another. I bent to the task of shovelling up the broken dirt and heaving it to my left. After a little while Tom showed me how to dig using my knee for added leverage. I would place the shovel in front of the dirt and then push the handle through my right hand with my knee until I had scooped a full enough load to throw out.

By brew time, at ten o'clock, my hands were blistered, my back was aching, my shoulders felt heavy, my knee was throbbing and the back of my hand was bruised and painful. The tea was strong and thick, ready to be scooped out of a stainless steel bucket by the cabin. It was good tea and I wolfed the few sandwiches mum had given to me.

Brew time was all too soon over and at ten-twenty we were back at the digging. The longest two hours and forty minutes of my life lay before dinnertime. Somehow I managed to last out, with the help of Tom. He talked incessantly, cracking jokes, telling me where he knew my dad from, where he was from, where he lived and what he thought about life in general. I listened and laughed and dug. It all washed over me as if I were in some kind of a dream (I think the SAS call it survival mode). My body was making so much noise, screaming at me to stop, that I hardly heard much of what was said; I certainly can't remember anything at all that Tom actually said on that first day!

Lunchtime arrived and I sat outside to the rear of the cabin. The brew boy brought my steak wrapped up in two huge slices of bread. My hands were so swollen and sore that it actually hurt to hold the giant sandwich. I sat there and stared at the steak and thought, "I can't go on! I can't do this for another four or five hours! I'm going to die! Every part of my body hurts and I just can't go on!" The tears, unbidden, welled up from somewhere just under the surface and I cried, I sobbed, I sniffed, tears wetting the great sandwich I held in shaking hands. Through my sniffs I managed a bite and realised how ravenous I was. I delayed further tears whilst I attacked the food, slurping more of the delicious tea to wash it down. That brew boy was as fine as any chef who has fed me since! By the time I was finished some of the other fellows were emerging from the cabin. I wiped my eyes and pretended I'd been sleeping.

The men were involved in some kind of debate about how strong one of them was. The one they were arguing about was known as Donegal, he was a truly magnificent specimen of a man. He was about six-six with shoulders so broad that he'd have to turn to enter most doors. Donegal sat by the cabin smiling quietly to himself taking no part in the debate. Quinn shouted to him to show the others what he could do. Effortlessly he stood up to his full height and with great forbearance said, "Ah now! What is it you want me to do?"

"Pick up Hogan there, on the shovel," shouted Quinn, "he's about the nearest in size to yourself though not as broad!"

"If it will keep you happy then," said Donegal. He always spoke very correctly and very quietly. He stooped and picked up a shovel.

He stepped from the cabin, went to the other men and placed the shovel head carefully on the ground. With a nod of his head he invited Tom to stand on the blade. Tom did so and once again Donegal stooped to the shovel.

I watched with baited breath, as did most of the others. Quinn was the only one looking about him to ensure that all were watching to witness the feat. Unbelievably Donegal straightened up, his right hand pushing down on the handle, his left hand close to the blade. He stood up straight and Tom, who had placed his hand on Donegal's head for balance, now let go. Donegal was now standing erect with Hogan standing erect on the end of the shovel. What happened next was even more unbelievable because Donegal then bent his arms raising Hogan higher still until he was almost held at chest height. Donegal appeared to be quite relaxed; he certainly did not seem to be straining himself.

Unconsciously I had climbed to my feet and stood now with the others - awestruck, my own aches and pains forgotten for the moment. Just then Maher, the Ganger man, called a halt to the entertainment by stepping up and shouting, "Alright now, let's get back to it, they'll not dig themselves ye know. Put him down and stop the blatherin' Donegal!" And that was that, a moment passed.

Tom jumped down and winked at Donegal and me; the others had already started back to the trenches.

I'd left it too late to runaway. I suspect that if I had known where I was I would have run even then but Wigan and Skelmersdale were names I think I'd heard for the first time that day!

Tom rested a huge paw on my shoulder and said, "What do you think of that then?"

I shuffled along by his side feeling insignificant and very insecure. How could I hold my head up with real men like these? "It was good," I stuttered lamely.

Before I knew it we were back in the trench and my body was going through the motions whilst my mind screamed and cried out for release and escape. As though through some dim tunnel the rest of the day went and I have little recollection of anything more about it.

Six o'clock in the evening must have arrived and the backbreaking toil ceased for that day. I was out the next day and that was hard. In fact that first week was harder than anything I can remember. I had never known hardship and pain like it. The next week wasn't quite so bad and the third saw me something of a veteran.

I had and continue to have the greatest of respect and admiration for those men I worked with and all of the others like them. Unlike me they continued to build Skelmersdale, the motorways, the bridges and tunnels whilst I continued my education. They worked in all weathers, all seasons and often with little thanks, appreciation or remuneration. Many of them lived in digs where they could only return after nine-thirty at night. They often left their wages with the landlord of their local because he was the only one they could trust. He became their trusted banker. They lived hard and often died young. They were the very best of men. Certainly better than many of those who were born with the silver spoon in their mouths like me! They helped to bring the man out in me, if only for a short while and I thank them for that.

During my time with them I received five pounds a day and two pounds ten shillings for Saturday mornings; twenty-seven pounds and ten shillings per week! It was a king's ransom. Twenty pounds I gave to my mam, the rest was for the holidays. I managed to kid Maher that I could handle the work until just a few days before we went to Ireland. He sacked two of us that day, me and a new lad fresh over from Ireland, I was supposed to be showing him the ropes – so the poor lad had no chance. "Feck off Ramsbottom and take that no good heap of horse shite with ye," were Maher's parting words to me. I didn't mind but I felt for poor auld Padraic who was just starting out.

My best mate Brian also got a summer job that year for the first time, at a bakery in Manchester called Duncan and Fosters. He worked similar hours to me for seven pounds ten shillings per week, which was a good average wage at that time. I told him on the eve of our first pay day that if he was going to earn real money he'd have to do a real day's work. I know that I did.

16. First Post, 1973-1976.

Saint Wilfrid's R.C Junior High School was in the Whitworth area of Rochdale, near the Oxford public house on Whitworth Road. Holstein Avenue, I think it was on.

As I mentioned earlier I was working for Peter Larkin as a third fixing joiner helping to build offices for GUS (Great Universal Catalogue) in Preston when I applied for my first teaching post.

I sent in a general application to the Manchester pool and heard nothing until I already had a job.

Saint Wilfrid's was my first specific application. I was interviewed at Saint Patrick's presbytery, in Rochdale, I took that as a good omen. There were five applicants being interviewed including a nun from Birmingham. I somehow bluffed my way through and was offered the job: English with some Drama. Afterwards John O'Loughlin (the Head), Frank Barber (his Deputy) and Peter Hill (Head of English) took me to a pub in the centre of Rochdale (I think it was The Grapes) to celebrate with a pint. Once in the pub Mr. O'Loughlin told me I had already gotten him into trouble. Didn't take me long, I was thinking! Seemingly he'd practically promised the job to the nun from Birmingham because her mother, a Rochdalian, was very ill and she needed to be closer to home. I felt extremely guilty but also very chuffed – my first real job. Now I had to discover if I had what it took to become a teacher – I had my doubts.

On my first day I was presented with my teacher's kit: a register, box of chalk, board duster, acme thunderer whistle and a tawse. I since discovered the tawse was the Lochgelly Strap 3. Strap 3 because it had three tails to it; I never used it! I only wish I still had it because it would be a real museum item now – strange to think parts of my early career are now consigned to museums!

I don't think I actually taught at Saint Wilfrid's, I believe I did more learning – if anything I was merely a facilitator. It was a wonderful school where the youngsters were keen and willing. I tackled elements of English grammar that I never felt capable of tackling again throughout my career. If I had to find appropriate terms to describe the school at that time I would be forced to use words like: happy, successful, enjoyable, warm, cosy, friendly et al.

My colleagues were a wonderful mix of the eccentric to the profoundly academic and representative of all four corners of the British Isles. Three were from Northern Ireland and had been to De La Salle before me: Liam, Richard and Patrick (Paddy who went on to marry a French girl and who then lived and taught in France – he was a French teacher after all). Others were older and wiser: Mildred Sutcliffe who ran the tuck shop, Peter Green (English), Mike Henstock (School Counsellor), Kevin (PE), Colin the geographer, Ed and Paul the art teachers, Kevin Marsh who was a youngster like me teaching History, and a host of others. I also recall a Polish chap, whose name I just can't bring to mind, who used to brush his teeth at every break time and lunch time.

In my first year there I used to bus it in. It was an awful journey, involving three buses. I remember I read Spike Milligan's "Puckoon" whilst travelling to school and the other passengers must have thought me insane or at least slightly tapped because at first my shoulders would start to shake uncontrollably, then I would make some stifled squeals whilst trying to control myself, then I would guffaw and finally the tears would run down my cheeks. I would be totally helpless for several minutes and I could sense my companions nudging each other and 'tutting' at the show I was making of myself. "Puckoon" is still the funniest book I ever read, though Tom Sharpe's "Wilt" is a very close second and probably better written.

Mildred would give me a lift to Castleton where I could get the number 17 to Middleton when school finished, which saved me a little time on the interminable journey home. I got married at the end of my first year at Saint Wilfrid's and we moved into a quasi-semi on Caldecott Road in Blackley. I think Kev Marsh might have started at Wilfrid's in my second year there because he started giving me lifts from Victoria Avenue, but Kev was rarely on time. I bought a racing bike from Billy Goulding who was one of our close pals on Langley and started cycling to school each day. It was a round trip of thirty miles and I managed it until shortly before leaving Saint Wilfrid's at Christmas in 1976.

Once I got married and realised that a teacher's salary was not the best financial foundation in the world (£59 per month didn't quite cut it), even though following the Burnham Committee Report my salary doubled in my second full year, I looked for ways to top up my income. I had continued to work behind bars since my college days. I worked at the Catholic Club on Langley for Joe Walsh and when all of the staff went on strike for a better deal he took the opportunity to sack us all! Julia, my wife, and I took jobs at the Red Lion near Blackley Offices – we had a terrific time there. It still wasn't enough to make ends meet so I applied for a part time job at Buckley Hall Detention Centre (now a women's prison in Rochdale). I'd be working behind bars again! Ron Shooter was the Education Officer there and he and I got on like a house on fire. I was soon doing three nights a week teaching: English, Social Studies and Art (I couldn't draw a card never mind paint anything!). So for two or three years I was working full time at school, three nights a week at Buckley Hall and three nights a week at the Red Lion with Sunday's all to myself. During long breaks like Chirstmas, Easter and of course the summer holidays I worked for Peter Larkin, if he could find something for me.

If you wanted to make ends meet, have a nice home and perhaps save up for a holiday you had to be prepared to work for it. Luckily there was plenty of work way back then.

I said I never used the tawse in all my time at Saint Wilfrid's but I do remember once using corporal punishment on two wags. Wilfrid's was a middle school and handled children from first to third year (Year 7 to Year 9 nowadays). I had responsibility for the second year rugby team and one lunch time going out for training these two rascals called to me as I jog-walked to the field, "Hey, Rams Arse". Now if they had left it at that and pretended not to be looking my way when I turned to see who was calling, it would have been okay. However, as I turned the pair of them, with hands cupped around their mouths to amplify the sound, once again hailed me with, "Rams Arse". I had no alternative but to be seen to act, my little rugby squad were watching for any sign of weakness. "My room quarter past one," I called out to them and carried on with the training session.

At one fifteen I got back to my classroom and the two boys were sat in the cloakroom waiting for their sentence. They did look sheepish. I told them they were stupid. Stupid for shouting out a silly insult like that and stupid for getting caught. I think they realised that I would have let them get away had they used their nouse! So they, like I, knew it had to be dealt with. "Right, what do I do? Take you down to Mr. O'Loughlin and let him thrash you whilst informing your parents?" I asked myself rather than them.

"Aw sir can't YOU smack us. Don't tell me mam, she'll kill me," one of them ventured.

"Well I don't want you dead," I said, "what I if I give you a couple and you help me with the rugby training for a couple of weeks?"

"Yeah, right sir, thanks sir," their gratitude was pitiful.

I didn't use the strap – I'd had too much pain with one of them in the past myself. "Touch your toes," I said and gave them a couple of cursory slaps on the behind with the flat of my hand (I'd be arrested nowadays and called some highly disturbing names) but it hurt me as much as the two boys – my hand was tingling for ages afterwards. They were incredibly grateful and sure enough they joined me for rugby training for the rest of the year and became class enforcers for me. I'd walk into class to the echo of one of them threatening the others with, "Shut it he's here." It would still be ringing round the room as I made my entrance.

I never did use the strap although corporal punishment would be something I would have to be prepared to use in my next but one job! I hasten to add that the reason teacher's were presented with a tawse was because it was expected that discipline in your class would be kept by the judicious use of the three tailed wonder. I don't believe it was ever needed in a class room situation, though I wouldn't discount the value of its use against stupidity and bullying. I didn't need it because my children realised I liked them and they in turn began to like me; when a child likes you they don't want to upset you, especially when you let them know that you feel personally let down by some of their behaviour. I suppose I've just expressed one of the fundamentals of my teaching style.

I was a wild child and I have often wondered how I managed to stay out of trouble: like taking drugs or getting involved in criminal activities etc. I can honestly say that I have never taken drugs although they were readily available at times in my life. I believe that it boils down quite simply to the fact that I didn't want my parents upset and I knew they would be if I got in trouble with the law. I wouldn't be able to hold my head up in their presence if I let them down like that. So it's love of parents, not necessarily being a goody two shoes that keeps you out of trouble – I applied the same (twisted) logic to my charges and it generally appears to have worked, I think – they'd probably tell you something different.

The two and half years I spent at Saint Wilfrid's were extremely happy. I think most schools were happy places at that time, although I have heard the odd nightmare tale regarding the savagery meted out in some schools during those early years of my career.

Mr. O'Loughlin obviously became aware that I was applying for promotions at other schools. He pulled me aside, which I thought was really nice of him, and asked if I would give it another year and that then he would surely have something for me. I was tempted but felt it was unfair that just because he and his board of governors felt that promotion should only come after you'd served an apprenticeship of four or five years. I was ready for some responsibility and so applied to the Sutherland High School in Heywood where I would spend the next fourteen years of my teaching life and there I would begin to learn about the craft of teaching.

My interview at Sutherland High School (Suthie) was in early November, just after the Autumn half term. Unexpectedly my father passed away whilst on Holiday in Ireland with my mum on October 20th 1975. It was an extremely traumatic time for me. On returning to school everyone was very gentle and understanding with me, including the children who were amazing. My interview was on the Thursday of the first week back. I think some people thought I'd give it a miss because of what had happened but I knew that my dad would have wanted me to carry on as near to usual as possible, so I went and got the job!

Leaving Wilfrid's was hard. I had made good friends with the staff, the children were absolutely fantastic and a great many parents were quite put out that I was leaving. I was showered with presents (mostly expensive pens, some of which I still have though most were pinched within a few weeks of starting at Suthie – not by the children I hasten to add – they were taken by someone attending a night class from the teachers cloakroom). The staff at Wilfrid's had a whip round and presented me with £100 which was a King's ransom at the time – I was overwhelmed. Funnily enough I never received a leaving present form any of my other schools, certainly from staff, even though I always contributed to the staff leaving fund. There were extenuating circumstances for this by the way – it's not that they all hated me – I think!

I took my leave on the last day of the Autumn term 1975 ready to start the next phase of my teaching career at Suthie in January 1976.

My life seemed blessed during this period. I enjoyed my work. I was earning, just about, enough to make ends meet and still manage a continental holiday. I was marrying the girl I hoped would be my wife for the rest of my life and the world seemed full of promise.

My first year teaching didn't unnecessarily alter life at home with my mum and dad. Dad had recovered somewhat from his major heart attack and had even got a job at Chadderton Cemetery. He came home one night and said to me that he had a smashing new job with loads of responsibility – he was over hundreds of men! Mam gave him a hard time if she caught him smoking and he wasn't supposed to drink much. Dad, as full of mischief as ever, treated the business as a bit of a game with mum – so he continued to smoke (secretly) and generally had one or two more drinks than she was aware of when they went out (which wasn't too often – his pay had fallen sharply). I coughed up more than I wanted to in keep but anything I earned on top of my salary was mine so that was okay because of my part time jobs.

During the week I still palled around with Phil, Brian and Andy. We'd try to get to the Catholic Club most Thursday nights – strange how Thursdays seem to recur as important days for me. In the club we were still looked on with suspicion by members and in particular the committee because of our time running the Eighteenth Plus Group.

We had some cracking times, playing snooker (I was never particularly good), Noonan, considering how short he was and remains was a much better player than me although I'd never have admitted that at the time. We played a lot of darts and younger lads ingratiated themselves with us. Peter Russell and Pete Stockdale became regular pals in the club. Peter Russell was a fine darts and snooker player although he suffered from some form of infirmity which caused his arm to lock during a darts game on occasion. There was nothing physically wrong with him it was some kind of mental block he had. He would line up the dart, his hand would bob up and down prior to release and then when he must release he couldn't let go of the dart. It caused a lot of laughter and not a little consternation if you were his partner and playing a game for money!!!

Saturday and Sunday afternoons were our time in the club. We'd meet up mob handed. Brian, Phil, Mick O'Rourke, Dave Carling, Peter Russell, Pete Stockdale, Billy Goulding, Graham Fairhurst and occasionally Malcolm Tyner plus sundry others and of course myself. We would push two or three tables together and play chase the ace or bastard brag. In an afternoon the most you might lose, on an ordinary day, was about 90p (on average you'd manage three games at 30p per game for your three lives) but you could win a lot more than that if you managed to win a hand. I can't possibly do justice to how funny some of those long ago afternoons were. A drink with good mates, a laugh, and set the world to rights – it was what life should have been all about.

I was working two nights a week in the club at this time along with Julia (my wife to be) and Phil. Brian occasionally did a shift at the Britannia Inn (the Brit.) in Middleton for Mick Gallagher who eventually took over from the fearsome Bridie.

Friday nights Julia and I would go to the cinema, to a club or for a few drinks in Middleton.

I remember watching "Bonnie and Clyde" at the ABC Victoria Avenue and at the end of the movie everyone in the cinema was speechless and filed out more or less in silence – the only other film that had a similar level of violence at around that time was "The Wild Bunch" which we saw at the college cinema club. I can also remember watching "The Sting" at the Palace Cinema in Middleton and at the end everyone remained seated for a long moment before someone started clapping and before you knew it the whole cinema was clapping – I hadn't witnessed people applauding a film since Hopalong Cassidy or the Lone Ranger at the Saturday Matinee when I was a nipper.

My bachelor night was a pub crawl around Middleton with all the guys. This demonstrates how stupid I was and to an extent remain. I took out my wallet containing all of my holiday money as well as the money for the night out. I recall parts of the night vividly. Singing the Black Velvet Band and Whiskey in the Jar in the yard of the Hare and Hounds where Mike Dillon's dad had the licence. We visited the Ring 'o Bells, The Old Boar's Head, the Assheton Arms, and two or three others before finishing the night in the Brit where Bridie had a great reception for us. Shaking her walking stick at me and telling me to, "Keep the noise down Ramsbottom or your barred!" It was all tongue in cheek by the way. Bridie loved me because she loved my dad, like everyone else.

On our way home that night we staggered up Wood Street, some of the houses had already been cleared because I seem to recall we were off the main road with some waste land between us and the roadside. Graham, who was always on top in the fashion stakes, was wearing a very expensive pair of platform soled shoes. Somehow Mick O'Rourke got one of these precious shoes that Graham had been bragging about all night (they were going to be the next big thing!) and of course we started playing rugby with it. Graham was our rugby coach. We'd formed Langley Rugby Union Football club as an offshoot of the Eighteenth Plus Group. Mick who had gone to Bishop Marshal School hadn't played rugby at school but took to it like a duck to water and became the undisputed captain of the squad. Anyway Graham was having a hard time limping after us and threatening us all with dire prognostications if we didn't return the shoe to him immediately. At which point Mick converted the shoe straight under the wheels of the 121 bus heading to Manchester as it passed us on Wood Street. That Graham didn't cry still amazes me to this day. I think like the rest of us he was too shocked initially to react. After our initial shock and horror someone started laughing and that started everyone off. Graham was dismissed by Mick with a "You soft git". Graham picked up his mangled fashion item and stormed off home? We carried on up Wood Street.

At some point before we reached Our Ladies Church where I was to tie the knot in the morning someone shouted, "Pile on" and everyone grabbed me and threw me into the privets that fronted many of the houses. This continued with different people being selected for this special treatment until we reached Millbeck Road where Scanny and the O'Rourkes lived. A last super pile on was called for and I was physically manhandled over the privet fence and left to my own devices. I extricated myself as best I could and eventually made it home with Phil (my best man), Brian and Andy where I discovered my wallet was missing. Panic ensued.

God was smiling down that night because the very first place we looked was where I had last been catapulted through the fence. It had somehow got trapped in the bushes, thank God. I retrieved it and we all went back to the house where my mum, God bless her, gave everyone a good shot of Jameson's finest Irish Whiskey and then fired them off so that I could get to bed – I had a big day tomorrow in case they'd forgotten!

The wedding was a great day by all accounts. I know it began for me at around 1130 in the Gay Gordon with a pint to steady the nerves! It's difficult to recall everything when it centres around you so much. Father John Walsh officiated; Julia had agreed that any children would be brought up in the faith. Mick Carr was at the church door playing the pipes – it was lovely – I never got to ask him was it a lament he played?

The reception was held at the Middleton Conservative Club (the only place we could get and possibly the last place I would have wanted it to be at). Phil delivered a speech which was so memorable I cannot recall a word of it or even if he actually delivered it. Keith Fane did the honours in the evening and Julia and I left at around ten o'clock that night to catch a flight to Majorca. I'd had such a terrific day that I managed to puke out of the cab window as it sped towards the airport! Julia was not impressed. Story of my life!

I worked hard to make our new home on Caldecott as nice as possible. I had a stone fire place fitted and put beams up in the living room to turn the house into a cottage style property. It looked lovely. I remember Uncle Stephen, my mother's brother, telling me I was a great man altogether being able to do what I was doing. In time I fitted new windows back and front (the front windows were bay windows) with a bit of help from Peter Russell and his dad Tommy. Julia's dad, Sid, was a plumber and he put in a new avocado suite in the bathroom as a wedding present and then charged us £100 for fitting it! My mum and dad contributed a state of the art King sized bed. Everything seemed hunky dory!

I was soon working three or four nights a week and during every holiday when I could get work. I continued playing rugby. We used to meet up with the old gang on a Friday night in Middleton and we got out on occasion to a club or a special do. Julia worked for the Hospital Board and their Christmas do's were generally excellent. I remember trips to Salford Rugby Club to see Tony Christie and the Dubliners (at different times), the Golden Garter in Wythenshaw to see Freddie and the Dreamers, and disco cruises on the Royal Iris on the Mersey. They were great days and the future seemed to promise better to come.

We were the lucky generation. Foreign holidays were something our parents never even dreamed of. Julia and I went to Ibiza (before it was spoiled) in 1970. I remember we travelled with Blue Sky on a Comet jet – the first time I'd ever flown. A few weeks before we were due to go the hotel we were to stay at (the Pina Playa) was all over the news – half built, building site, food terrible, noise day and night, pool a mess, and black outs on a regular basis.

The TV advised us to see our travel agent which we duly did. We were offered another hotel though they couldn't guarantee the resort or the island. We discussed it and decided that all we wanted was somewhere to come home to and crash after a day in the sun and at £69 each we thought we'd stick with the Pina Playa. It was one of the few good decisions I ever made.

The hotel, which later became a five star, was fantastic, the food was superb, the accommodation outstanding, the pool brilliant and although there were a few black outs, they affected the whole resort not just our hotel, as we'd been led to believe. We became friends with two girls from Birmingham and through them made firm friends with two Spanish lads who looked after the pool and its bar. They took us all over and made sure we paid for very little. At that time the hotel workers were working for an absolute pittance and so when they went clubbing they only paid (Spanish prices as opposed to tourist prices) for their drinks – entrance was always gratis. They took us to the biggest club, at the time, in San Antonio – the Flamenco. The floor show was something straight out of Sunday Night at the London Palladium – it was breathtaking. I remember seeing Los Lobos (probably got the name wrong) who had a European hit with one of the songs they sang that night, "Guantanamera" (it was originally a Cuban song – recognise Guantanamo from the title?). I think when it was released in the UK it was re-titled "Quanta la Mera". I made the mistake that night of buying a round when both of the Spanish lads were dancing with the girls from Brummy. I nearly died at the price I was charged and the guys were quite annoyed with me for doing it behind their backs – they knew I'd be ripped off! Those two lads gave us a very special holiday and all for a few shots of Johnny Walker Red Label which they worshipped! I was quite taken with the Cuba Libres myself!

The next year we visited Majorca for the first time. Palma Nova. Again we had some fraught times in the lead up to the trip. I recall that for some reason (I think it may have been a mini recession in the building trade) Peter Larkin couldn't use me! I was on my own, looking for decent paid work, with a holiday already booked and waiting to be paid for.

I managed to get a couple of shifts at a Co-operative Bakery in Manchester at £12 a night shift (a pound an hour, which was excellent money then). I absolutely detested it. I was partnered with a Pakistani guy who just wouldn't talk even though he had good English (I think it was a coping mechanism for him). He just got on with the job and kept chatter down to instructions and few of them were required. The work was easy, basically stacking loaves of one type or another onto racks that you then helped load onto delivery trucks. The work was spasmodic; you'd be busy for twenty minutes then have to wait for twenty minutes until the next task was required. It was mind bogglingly boring. At the end of each shift I felt like opening my veins and of course I just couldn't get into the habit of sleeping during the day! I quit after two nights and left the work to the winos and tramps who were the usual night crew enlisted to work with my mate, the talkative Asian.

Julia went mad with me for jacking in the opportunity to earn £12 a night! I told her if she wanted to earn £12 a night she could go in my place but that I wasn't going back!

I heard that a contractor called Paddy McGoldrix was taking men on so I made my way to the Ben Brierley near Moston

Cemetery where he hired from and was duly given the start! When I asked him how much he'd be paying he told me £4.50 per day. This was less than I was used to at this time – I'd earned £5 a day with Kennedy's when I was fifteen and didn't know one end of the shovel from the other, but I agreed to the price because it was the best available at the time.

The work was brutal. He was building a sewage plant – ironically it turned out to be the one between Todmorden and Hebden Bridge which later in my life I would pass with regularity, living as I do in Todmorden. On the Thursday, pay day, McGoldrix delivered the pay slips to the site and the ganger gave them out at lunch time. I looked at mine and found I'd been paid £4.00 and hour! I collared the ganger and asked him, "What's this?"

"What's what?" he fired back.

"Mr McGoldrix said I was on £4.50 a day."

"And what have you got?"

"£4".

"Well then that's the rate. Come on back to work."

I sat back down and informed him I'd wait and talk to Mr. McGoldrix about this. I sat there from lunch to six when he arrived with the van to take us home.

"What the feck are you doing sat on your arse?" he asked as he jumped out of the van.

I reminded him of our conversation on Monday morning and he belligerently said, "Well four's all you're getting."

So I said thank you but no thank you. I informed him that if on Monday he had told me it was £4 per day that would have been okay – not good, but okay – but I didn't work for men whose word was no good! He didn't like that and I thought for a moment he might dump me in this dreadful site on the other side of the world! Thankfully he dropped me off and didn't speak another word to me. When times are hard some employers can pick and choose what they pay out and who they take on, taking advantage of the hard times. It was an important lesson for me and although my experience isn't exhaustive I've met few entrepreneurs I would truly trust during my life time.

Julia went mad. Anyone who knows her will know what I mean. She had an acid tongue and could strike you dead at twelve paces if she felt you were out of kilter with what she thought. £4 per day was better than £0 per day as far as she was concerned and try as I might I couldn't convince her that there was a principle at stake here – there's a holiday at steak was all she could say!

Friday I searched for work, I even toyed with the idea of going back to the bakery but only momentarily. Nothing turned up. Saturday I contacted everyone I knew in the building game and some my dad knew. Nothing turned up. I suspect Julia and I had words on the Saturday night – we occasionally did, because on the Sunday I went to the Catholic Club, met up with the guys, played darts, chase the ace and maybe even had a game of snooker and then went home for dinner.

I had just about finished dinner when Phil's dad Dennis Noonan knocked on the front door and spoke to my mum. He wanted to speak to me but he wouldn't come in. I thought it must be something to do with Phil so I went out and sat in the car next to him. I hadn't a clue what was coming.

"Are you working at the moment Brendan?" he enquired after a little introductory chit chat.

I don't think I stopped to think but just answered, "Yes, I'm out with Paddy McGoldrix working on a sewage plant somewhere out in Yorkshire".

There was a bit more chatter about the type of work and whether I was enjoying it or not when he asked, "What's he paying you?"

"£5.50 a day", I volunteered.

He thought for a moment and then explained that his one employee Mick Leonard was going back to Limerick (Dennis was also a Limerick man) and would I consider filling in for him whilst he was away. We'd already covered the fact that I had a holiday to go on in about four or five week's time.

"I'll give you £6 per day," he said.

My heart leaped in my chest and I almost said deal straight away but some devilish streak in me whispered: 'Play it cool'.

"That's really good of you Mr. Noonan but I don't like to let anyone down and Mr. McGoldrix was good enough to give me the start so. . . . ."

"Alright," he said, "I'll give you £6.50 a day. What do you say?"

What could I say? I reluctantly agreed to leave Mr. McGoldrix's service and start with Mr. Noonan in the morning. I went from £4 per day to £6.50 per day in the blink of an eye. I felt a little deceitful about what I'd done but only a little because I knew that the average rate, even then, was £8 to £10 per day, so I figured we were both getting a bargain.

Most of the work we were doing was in Ashton-Under-Lyne near Oldham and the first thing that struck me was that he seemed to go all around the houses to get there. I learned later from Mick Leonard (his employee) who became a good friend of mine, that he'd had a car accident years before whilst making a right turn and he would drive two or three miles out of his way ever since to avoid a right turn! Takes all sorts eh? Sadly both men are gone to God now – Mick in a terrible car accident and much before his time.

One of the jobs we had whilst I was out with him was concreting the foundations and ground floor of an old folk's home. We completed the foundations with few problems and made ready for the big day when we'd lay the floors. There were just the two of us. The big day arrived and Dennis told me he had twenty-six cube of concrete ordered – it was an enormous amount! As we arrived on site two of the wagons were already there so we set to work with a vengeance. Almost immediately there was a setback.

Dennis bent to pick something up and cried out. He couldn't straighten his back. He suffered occasional attacks of sciatica and he was having a bad one now. He gave me instructions to get the easy stuff down. This meant guiding the concrete shutes over the floor space that was accessible from the road. I started whilst Dennis was helped into the tea cabin. I managed to get the first two trucks emptied and had started raking the concrete into position and then vibrating it so that it filed every space available. Two more trucks arrived and sat waiting there like a slow threat. Dennis, fair play to him, struggled out of the cabin and he had rigged up a float on the end of a brush handle so that he could float finish the concrete from a standing position.

The spaces that could be reached from the road side were soon filled and the rest of the concrete had to be banjoed into place - shovelled into space. The trucks tipped their loads onto the pavement and by this time Dennis had managed to get one of the guys who worked for another contractor to lend a hand. He stayed by the tipped concrete and helped me fill the barrow which I then had to wheel over a maze of planks to where it needed to be.

All day the trucks arrived. Seven of them I believe. No time for breaks, eat your sarnies where you stood, shovel and wheel, shovel and wheel. We usually finished and eased off at around 1730, leaving sometime closer to six. On this day we were still at it at 2100. I got home around ten-thirty well and truly goosed. It was the hardest day's work I ever did and one of the longest.

"I'll see you straight for that," was what he said on the way home. He never paid me any extra although he did take me back on for two or three extra weeks when I came back from Majorca, which he didn't need to do – Mick Leonard was a powerful worker and Dennis didn't need anyone else. I enjoyed a very easy two weeks working on a housing project somewhere in Hattersley, filling and driving a drot (a vehicle with a flip up front for carrying any building materials) with cinders and swanning around the site. Life of Riley.

I seem to recall it was a beautiful summer and I was able to top up the lovely tan I'd got in Majorca.

Needless to say Julia was happy and when she was happy the world was a nice place.

Majorca was fantastic, made all the more enjoyable because we could afford to go on many of the excursions: the Caves of Drach, the pearl factory, the barbeque and loads of other fabulous experiences. We met two lovely people there that year: Janice and Michael Bond who have remained friends and in contact with me ever since. We spent a holiday at their home in Mamhead near Dawlish in Devon the following year. As always it was a terrific break and the memories helped to keep me going for another eventful year. They had the most wonderful property standing in its own walled garden with the longest private greenhouse I've ever seen in an ordinary home, where they grew tomatoes.

Michael was in the furniture business. The manufacturing side of it and worked in a local factory part owned by him and I believe his father. Janice's father was an hotelier with an hotel in Dawlish. He took us out on his motor launch one evening trawling for mackerel – we gave up on the trawling and started fishing. I caught a big Bass which he offered to cook for me back at the hotel.

In those days I wasn't a fish lover so I presented him with the fish and told him thanks but no thanks! This, by the way, is my only fishing tale – I enjoyed the experience on the boat but subsequent attempts at sitting on river banks fishing left me cold!

Michael had friends in the Royal Navy and had attended a couple of fancy dinners at a Royal Naval establishment in Portsmouth. At one of these special affairs a friend had offered him a bottle of whisky.

It had a fascinating back story. During the Second World War an American Colonel happened to be in North Africa as Rommel was pushed back. More importantly he happened to be in the right place when the Allies liberated 23 million litres of alcohol that the Germans had stockpiled. The quick thinking Colonel arranged a bank loan back home and purchased all 23 million litres at 10 cents a litre. He then arranged for it to be shipped to Italy at another 10 cents a litre. There were no bottle plants running anywhere in Europe following the destruction of the war but in Italy there were lots and lots of glass blowers desperate for any kind of work so he put them to work blowing litre bottles for less than 10 cents per bottle! By this time the 23 million litres had become considerably less than 23 million litres due to spillage, spoilage and pilferage! He still had a huge amount of liquor in all its variations: gin, brandy, rum, vodka, whisky etc., which he now began to sell to a very thirsty Europe at 10 dollars a bottle, especially to his fellow Americans who had money to spare and then some. The vast majority was drunk within moments of purchase – Europe was a very thirsty place. Some bottles, however, managed to remain intact. He'd gone to the trouble of having them labelled with a potted history of how they came to be and a few canny service personnel saw the potential in them. Michael bought a bottle labelled Third Reich Whisky – with its potted history – every bottle was unique because every bottle had been hand blown by Italian artisans. My contribution to this wonderful tale was, "Shall we crack it open then?" Michael pointed out to this Philistine that he was holding a piece of history which although he had parted with £25 for said bottle would in time become worth more as fewer and fewer remained. "Anyway," he said, "if we did open it we might find that it's turned to vinegar and once opened its worthless!" So I never got to taste the Third Reich's Whisky but I've often wondered if Michael still has the bottle intact. I must ask him next time I speak to him. For a short while I felt like one of the Eriskay islanders having discovered the wreck of the S. S. Politician and its cargo of whisky immortalised in the movie "Whisky Galore".

    One of the highlights of our visit to Devon was a trip to the Northcott Theatre at the University of Exeter where we saw a production of "Everyman" the ancient morality play – I was particularly taken by the performance of God! He was Inspiring. We arrived in the city early in the afternoon and spent a most enjoyable period visiting the cathedral and then the book shops. I bought a hard backed copy of "Bob Dylan's, Writings and Drawings" which although quite dog-eared now is still part of my huge collection of books (don't tell my wife)!

I am really pleased that I kept in touch with Michael and Janice they are a lovely couple. Michael, I'm afraid, like many in the manufacturing industry hit hard times and if I understand things correctly he has been bankrupted a couple of times and now I hear he's not in the best of health. However he and Janice are still plodding on and give every indication that life is still the joy it always was. Nice people.

Good friends are hard to find and holding on to good friends isn't always easy but I'm proud to say that although I don't see all of the guys that I grew up with too often these days we are all still in contact and we climb out of our personal castles for the odd birthday or retirement celebration. Thankfully most of us have made it to the twilight years relatively unscathed.

Way back in the 1970's as I was approaching my final year at De La Salle, two old pals decided that they might want to try teaching and joined the college. Brian Kenny and Phil Noonan signed up. Brian had worked at a hospital and obtained his higher awards as I mentioned earlier and Phil had dropped out of Business College following a health scare with an ulcer that was to dog him for the next few years. Both of them began their studies as I was preparing to leave and earn a living for the first time in my life – I'd obviously worked before but never in a permanent job! I was desperate to discover whether I had what it took to make it as a teacher. Patsy my sister was already well established and by all accounts a brilliant teacher.

I was lucky enough to be placed at her school for my first Teaching Practice. She taught at the Assumption RC Juniors at that time. I did quite well, so well in fact that the head asked the college if I might be spared to go on their annual trip to Staithes in Yorkshire. Julia came with me and we had the most wonderful week staying on an old army camp. It was wet and miserable most of the time but the enchantment of Staithes is such that you barely notice the weather. I've been back many times and it remains a beautiful, windswept and wild place created for photographic opportunities! I especially remember the "Cod and Lobster" pub which is still there, although its modern carnation is a poor one in comparison to the one I recall through my rose tinted specks!

Brian became a very fine teacher and worked initially at St. Dominic Savio's on Alkrington prior to moving on to our old alma mater, Cardinal Langley following a reorganisation and the closure of Dominic's.

Phil's ulcer interceded just prior to his final exams at De La Salle and he dropped out once again. His mother put up with him for ever such a long time until one day she threw him out of the house and told him not to come back until he had a job because he wasn't going to be allowed to slob about at home anymore! I believe that he took his first job to spite his mum – it was as a glorified lift boy at Littlewoods in Manchester. I believe it was the making of him. First of all he got used to getting up early, earning a wage and taking a pride in a job well done. Sometime later that first year he was chatting to one of the early morning delivery drivers (from Tibbut and Britten, I believe) who happened to mention they were looking for a transport manager, but he added sadly, the applicant had to have a couple of GCE's, Phil quietly wondered if nine 'O' levels might be enough. Needless to say he got the job and has rarely looked back since. He's made a good life for himself, with a lovely wife (Pat) and two fine sons.

Andy Scanlon went his own way. He was always the hardest working of all the guys when at school and I am sure this continued into his working life. He signed up with Taylor Woodrow Construction when he left school and took the qualifications to become a Quantity Surveyor (that's the guy who tells you how many bricks you need to do a job and how much it will cost you in terms of materials and labour). Later on he worked for Rochdale Council's Surveying Department and finally he moved once again into the private sphere working now as a loss adjuster. A loss adjuster makes his money looking at an insurance claim and working out whether anything can be saved for the insurer – a claim of a million pounds might become a payout of £750,000 once a loss adjuster has looked at the claim. I think there were times when he made money hand over fist and he took on some major jobs but one thing I do know is that whatever he did he always did it to the very best of his ability. Whoever he worked for got their money's worth with Andy.

In those early days of the seventies he wore his heart on his sleeve and he had it broken a time or two until he met Elaine and settled down into married bliss to have two lovely children: Natalie (my God daughter) and Andrew Jnr. whom I helped, in a little way, to achieve good pass grades at GCSE in English and English Literature when my mate Mike Coffey (Head of English at Cardinal Langley) had predicted fail grades following his mock exams! Obviously I have never made anything of this to Mike!!!!!

Andy has remained a very close friend for all of our working lives and he still remains the closest and most approachable of all the old gang. We've even had holidays together – but that's maybe for another time.

There was another guy who was at De La Salle at the time as me, Danny Pollard. Danny, like Mick O'Rourke had attended Bishop Marshall and I think he joined the college the year after me. He was courting a lovely girl, Monica Lyons and as happens she got pregnant before he completed his course. He would have made a terrific teacher – I believe one of his sons (young Danny) has completed the journey he started all those years ago. Anyway, Danny dropped out and worked for Spar, eventually moving into management where he was very successful – so successful he went on to set up his own supermarket in Perth in Western Australia when Monica and the family emigrated to make a better life for themselves – he might have been with Tesco at the time he made the move.

Danny and Monica had the best parties. They started married life in a cottage flat on Langley and their parties were legend. I remember that late on we would sometimes see who could place the Guinness bottle furthest. Each person would start with two empty bottles of Guinness and in the position of a press up would attempt to reach as far as they could before releasing one of them and getting back into the start position without collapsing. The one who placed their bottle furthest won. Danny was one of the strongest men I knew and he had a long reach. I would manage to place it pretty far and he would beat me by an inch. I would then beat him by a whisker and he would beat me by an inch. In the meantime Mick O'Rourke would never give in and would keep trying until his palms were bleeding and blistered. Danny always won!

He and I completed our induction to Prestwich rugby club on the same day. He was also a terrific rugby player. I think on the day in question we had been playing in a seven's competition. The two of us were escorted into the bar after our baths and sat side by side at one end of the bar. We were to complete the Cardinal Puff initiation. This was a beer swilling initiation, one of many variations. The object was to drink three pints whilst performing a simple repetitious ceremony.

The first pint was placed in front of you and using the index fingers of both hands you touched your forehead and said, "I salute Cardinal Puff for the first time". You then tapped your forehead once simultaneously, followed by eyes, the nose, the mouth, the underside of the chin and then the top of the bar and the overhang of the bar. At which point you picked up the pint and tapped that lightly on the bar once then proceeded to drink the pint without taking it away from your mouth (you could take a few gulps though). After this you repeated the performance only this time everything was done twice: "I salute Cardinal Puff for the second time". On reaching the pint you tapped it twice clearly on the bar and in two distinct movements you drank the pint. On the third occasion you had to say, "I salute Cardinal Puff for the third and last time," then everything was done three times! However if you made the slightest of errors you had to start back at the very beginning. Obviously you were not permitted to drink just three pints and finish – errors were always spotted, even when there weren't any! We made it to the equivalent of our ninth pint (this is in a very short space of time by the way). Danny began before me – I think they were going to permit us to finish because we were on our final "Puff". As far as I am aware Danny did everything perfectly. He picked up the pint and carefully tapped it on the bar three times. He took his first clear drink and took the glass away. He took his second clear drink and took the glass away. Finally he lifted the glass to his mouth, tilted his head back to drink and just kept going. He went straight over backwards off the stool. Somehow he managed to lose the glass before coming into contact with the clubhouse floor! In my inebriated state I thought, "Hmm. I've won."

I was allowed to go through the ceremony for the third and last time although I am fairly sure that I cocked up a couple of times. Like Danny I got to my third and final mouthful. As I emptied the pot I knew it wasn't going to stay down and without missing a beat I immediately re-filled the glass with my last pint and if my memory serves me well I even put the head back on it!!!!!!!!!!! I can't recall much of the rest of that day but Danny and I survived to play together again.

Sadly Danny was the first of the guys to pass away. In the years since Cardinal Puff he had emigrated and become a very successful business man in Australia. He never forgot his routes however and whilst attending a business conference around Saint Patrick's Day he stumbled on steps down to his hotel bathroom and landed badly banging his head so fiercely it took his life. I still find it hard to believe such a big, full of life guy could be snuffed out like that. I know he is still missed by everyone who knew him.

I attended a memorial service for him at Our Lady's on Langley and though I'd done really well to hold everything in until they played 'Danny Boy' – then I just fell apart. Danny Pollard (1951 – 2004; RIP).

As 1976 dawned I began another chapter in my life at the Sutherland High School which once I had been appointed I discovered was the toughest school in Rochdale according to many of the wags I knew! I don't think I ever found it like that, although it was very, very different to St. Wilfrid's.

17. Tony.

Tony, my older brother, was evacuated to Ireland during the Second World War. He was only a baby and my mother took him over to leave him with her mother until the end of the war.

By the time the war ended grandmother had become very attached to the child and begged that he be permitted to remain with her, "Just a while longer, until England is sorted out again and everything is back to normal". She got her way and before anyone realised it Tony was attending school and it became increasingly difficult to insist he be moved back into post war England.

The years' flew by, grandmother eventually died and Tony finished school. He was now old enough to make his way in the world and to decide where he should live. He decided to give England a try. So at the age of fifteen he joined his parents and the rest of the family for the first time since the war, I was just five years old.

Never one to be idle he got himself a job straight away and found himself working for Murphy's, one of the toughest firms of contractors in Manchester at that time; in fact many of the men, from the West of Ireland, were Gaelic only speakers.

Tony was born for the hard work and he took it in his stride, working alongside men of twenty, thirty and forty; establishing a reputation for hard work, hard living and recklessness.

The rows at home were all to do with staying out late and drinking although there was one cracking row when mother found some dirty magazines shoved deep down inside the horn of the upright gramophone in the parlour where Tony slept. Tony always gave as good as he got and he continued to live life the way he found it.

One night following a whole series of nights during which mum had threatened him to be home before midnight, he arrived home at one or two in the morning and found the front door locked.

He knocked and shouted and then he banged. Eventually he shoved his fist through the glazed upper section of the door and let himself in. He was in a rarely pickled state and didn't appreciate the danger of mother shouting for dad to go down and sort him out!

Dad, patiently suffering, went downstairs, where Tony was smiling and staggering in the friendliest of ways. "Hit him," my mother shouted down to dad and my dad did. He slapped Tony with his open palm; Tony hit the wall and slithered down it oblivious to everything that was happening. Whether he was knocked out by the slap or whether he was just over tired we'll never know, but mum came running down the stairs in twos screaming at dad for not knowing his own strength and for being a big bully and killing the boy. Tony slumbered on blissfully unaware, dad shook his head and went back to bed whilst mother ministered to her errant boy's needs.

Tony rarely learnt from such experiences. If anything he became more rebellious, occasionally staying out all night but that was the first and the last time that dad ever slapped him. Mum would fume at him whenever she had the opportunity and Tony would stay away as long as the money lasted out.

For a good few years Tony brought colour, excitement and wild arguments into the house. I loved him and I hated him. I hated him mostly because one Sunday afternoon he came home a bit the worse for the beer and sat on my favourite repeating Winchester rifle snapping it in two! He was however mostly out of the house and he and I rarely met except for the odd weekend when he might not be working.

On his way home from work one night he fell in with the wrong crowd. There were two or three fellows lying in wait for him in the middle Yates's on Oldham Street. One was a Scottish guy who was a sometime drinking partner of Tony's. They wouldn't hear of Tony going home too early and they plied him with strong liquor.

Tony drank the famous "Blobs" that night for the first time. A "Blob" was a hot Australian white wine with copious amounts of sugar in it – the original alco-pop. They were strong, sweet and fast acting. Before very long Tony had had to hit his Scottish friend for being too lively and this had caused the Scots lad to hit one of their other friends because he didn't dare hit Tony. Although Tony wasn't very tall, he had a knockout left and a dynamite right, drunk or sober, and he had been known to stretch men much bigger than himself!

The night wore on and the friends fell in and out with each other on more than the one occasion. Tony found the "Blobs" very pleasing and didn't realise that he was rapidly reaching that standing-up-falling-down stage that heavy drinking sometimes visits upon a man.

The night ended and they were ejected from whatever watering hole they had made their last stand in. The friends separated and went their own way. Tony began the two-mile stagger along Oldham Road to home.

It was six the next morning when Tony awoke and he wasn't in bed. He lay for a long moment trying to piece together something of the previous night. It was a cool spring morning and he found himself shivering. He looked around him and noted the fact that he was lay on a bare concrete floor, broken factory windows looked down onto the empty streets below. He was three stories up in a derelict factory just off Oldham Road. He was lay on his left side and his left leg and arm were still asleep, he rolled onto his back and was immediately aware of the chasm that was the ground next to him. He had slept all night next to an open lift shaft; a full roll to his right would have taken him over the edge and into an even greater oblivion!

Even in his groggy, cold, hung-over state he realised how close he had come to meeting his end. He began to shiver again and it wasn't just with the cold this time. His hands began shaking uncontrollably. He got up and made his way out of the potential death trap and along to Gino's. Gino was an Italian who ran an Espresso Bar opposite the Daily Express building. Gino's bar, as Tony knew, was open earlier and later than any other coffee bar in Manchester.

Tony made his unkempt way there now, snatches of the night coming to him as if part of a news-reel. Gino had swept up and cleaned the tables and was organising the place for the arrival of his first early morning customers. The bar would be busy by half-past six! Tony staggered in.

"Hey Tony, you look like shit!" called an amused Gino. He was used to seeing men coming in to him in the mornings still suffering from the excesses of beer drunk the previous night. "You been out on the tiles again eh? Iss no good for you. Don' you mama tell you about dis things?"

"She does Gino, now leave off there's a good fellow. I feel bad. I need one of your specials," Tony finished and looked pleadingly at Gino.

Gino was popular with the early morning brigade, not just because he brewed good coffee but because you could also rely on him to provide a luxurious hair of the dog. Although highly illegal in England, Gino had maintained one of his country's most exquisite traditions, the provision of strong cognac first thing in the morning. Newspaper men coming off the night shift, detectives going home after a tough night and young navvies trying to come to terms with the night before were amongst Gino's most loyal and regular clientele.

He poured Tony a large Italian brandy and a cup of piping hot espresso coffee to chase it. Tony's hands shook profusely although he didn't spill a drop. The brandy disappeared in one huge mouthful and the shakes began to subside almost at once.

"You're a civilized man Gino," exclaimed a now warm and recovering Tony.

"Italian's always bin civilized Tony, You Irish and Inglish are the barbarians."

Tony drank the welcoming coffee and, with real thanks to Gino, he set off for work. He was feeling better by the minute!

It was a rare day indeed when Tony or one of his friends took a day off work because of the beer. They might occasionally start work and not return to it after lunch if they became embroiled in a "session" as these things were called! Men like Tony and the men he worked with then were a rare breed. They knew their worth in terms of their ability to work, they were paid well, by and large, and the camaraderie that they found in each other's company was wondrous to behold. They were certainly larger than life characters.

Tony looked as though he would live the rest of his life in Manchester. Apart from the rows with mum about coming home at a sensible hour he seemed happy enough.

He began palling around with a fellow called Vinny Mac. Vinny's brother Paddy was courting Patsy, our sister. Anyway, Vinny worked with Tony, but dissatisfied with is physique he had obtained some barbells and used to work out regularly at his digs. His landlady was terrified that the weight of the equipment would break through the floor one night and crush them all to death whilst they listened to the radio.

Vince soon filled out. The workouts didn't do much for his height but he certainly broadened and became much more muscular – a kind of short Charles Atlas. The two were inseparable and the temper of one was as fiery as the other. They swung from one scrape to another keeping largely out of serious trouble until one weekend when they fell foul of the barrow boys.

It wasn't long after Vince's accident. They had been travelling by bus one evening and as they approached the stop Vince had stepped off the moving bus, something he'd done a thousand times before, and he stepped straight into a lamppost. He was knocked out for a short while and both of his eyes were blackened, but apart from that there was no serious damage anyone was aware of to him or to the lamp post. Accidents of this type seemed commonplace for the Macs', his older brother Paddy, Patsy's boyfriend, stepped off a moving bus, in a state of inebriation, shortly after this episode and left the soles of his shoes on the pavement; like Vince he suffered no other ill effects!

Sometime after this accident, Vince's eyes were still a little dark, the pair of them jumped off another moving bus outside the St. Vincent Public House on Oldham Road, it's now called St. Vincent's House. They were intent on grabbing a couple of beers before going home and dressing up for the Friday night dance. They ordered their beer from Hunt, the softly spoken Irish landlord, and drank the work from their dry tongues. They were just starting the second pint when two big English lads came in; Tony knew one of them was the son of one of the Tibb Street barrow boys.

The barrow boys as their name suggests, ran the street barrows around Manchester but more than this they were a semi-organised group of individuals who could acquire or do anything or anybody that needed doing. They lived their lives largely outside of the inconvenience of the law. Before off course gambling was legalised the barrow boys took and covered the off course bets. They were like a criminal fraternity who always helped each other out; cross one and you crossed them all. Most people rightly feared them and few would knowingly stand up to them.

The two lads who entered the pub that night were about the same age as Vince and Tony, who were about nineteen at that time. Vince and Tony were drinking when the others walked straight to them in the empty pub, "Yer in are place," said the larger of the two to Tony. Tony knew this one, he was called Frank Leach and he had a mean reputation for a young fellow.

Tony nearly spilled his drink, "What?" Vince looked at Tony.

Hunt moved closer to the group and asked, "Now then gentlemen, what I can I get you?"

The four at the bar ignored him.

"I said yer in are place," repeated Frank, the threat in his voice inescapable.

"What do you mean?" asked Tony, "How can I be in your place?"

"That's where we always stand, innit Norbert? So push off lads."

"Or else?" enquired Vince.

"Or else we'll be forced to push you off," interrupted Frank's pal Norbert.

Tony and Vince very deliberately put down their drinks and stood up to their full height, which enabled the other two men to tower over them. They must have looked easy meat to the barrow boys.

Hunt hurried over again, "Now then boys there'll be no fighting in this house. If ye'v an argument take it out back and settle it like the gentlemen ye are."

"Suits us Paddy," said Frank, although Hunt's name wasn't Paddy! He winked and smiled at his mate, "Shall we join our Mick friends out the back Norbert?"

"Yeah why not? I'd love to join are Mick friends out the back," answered Norbert, "Pull us two pints a mild Paddy we'll 'ave 'em in a minute."

Tony and Vince were at a loss. They'd been in plenty of scrapes before and quite a few fights but this one seemed so silly. It was obvious that the two lads they were going to fight had come in to the pub expressly to find someone to teach a lesson to, but for what reason Vince and Tony couldn't figure out. Even though they couldn't figure out the reason for the challenge they felt obliged to humour Frank and Norbert.

They made their way into the pubs back yard where there was plenty of room for physical discussion.

It was a fairly straightforward and one might say mundane fight until Norbert, who was receiving a particularly blunt and persuasive argument from Vince, pulled out a set of brass knuckle-dusters. Vince saw red and began to severely chastise Norbert. Tony realised that something had upset Vince and stepped up the punishment he had been meeting out to Frank. They punched, kicked and butted until both Frank and Norbert were a fairly bloody heap on the floor. Happy, smiling, as bloody as the two on the floor, Tony and Vince, their arms around each other's shoulders, re-entered the pub and finished their drinks. Having finished their beers they drank Frank and Norbert's and advised Hunt that the two in the yard would pay for the beer when they were able to stand and with that they were off home, looking forward to the night.

They had a great night, the battle soon dismissed as but another event in eventful lives.

It wasn't until the following week that the rumours started circulating.

Two barrow boys had been viciously beaten up without any reason and the ones who did it were going to pay. The ones who did it were dead men!

The news eventually reached Vince and Tony. They believed that the barrow boys would kill; they'd heard rumours about certain men who had crossed them in the past and who had since disappeared. Trying to reason with them they knew would be like trying to reason with an oncoming train – hoping that the truth and sound arguments would encourage it to stop before it hit you!

There seemed no other course open to Vince and Tony, they must either wait and see what would happen or hope that they'd get some kind of chance to run!

Everyone they spoke to who knew the barrow boys painted a dark and forbidding picture. "If they mean to get you they will, and nothing you say will stop them from doing what they want!" was the loudest message coming across to them. It began to appear to them that they had no other option than to run.

And run they did! South. They headed for London one warm June day, intent on working and laying low for a while. They changed their names. Tony called himself Arthur Griffiths for quite some time during this period, after the Irish patriot and first President of the Irish Free State.

Vince didn't stay away long he returned to Manchester, eventually settling down. He married raised a family and made a good life for himself.

Tony remained in the south, eventually making his way to High Wycombe where he too eventually settled down, a little. He married and raised two sons. For a good many years he continued to be a "firebrand", he was nicknamed "The Hoddy" in deference to his skill as a hod carrier. Of course as he now approaches the twilight of his years he has quietened down a lot.

I go down to visit with him from time to time. I still love to sit and listen to him talking about those wild, wild days of his youth long into the night. His stories are colourful and exciting. He is a man who has never been afraid to take life and shake it by the throat. I don't suppose he'll ever change totally and I don't think I'd want him to change that much.

18. Goodbye Dad.

It was almost as though he'd planned it!

Mum was a very highly-strung woman and if it had occurred at their home in England she would have fallen apart.

They had been home a week, at mum's home-place, staying with Uncle Mark in Ballykilleen; a place where we had all spent the most wonderful times in the past. They had been out the night before to Kanes in Cloonfad and by all accounts they'd had a great time. Dad as usual was the life and soul of the gathering. Although he didn't drink as much these days, he had a few, as they say. They were home and in bed by one-thirty, which is early by anyone's standards and at five dad let out a loud moan and died. The earth didn't stop rotating, there was no cataclysmic or world shattering event, no radio or television announcements - yet the world that day became a poorer, emptier place for his passing.

I was at home preparing to go to work when my sister's husband Sean phoned and said, "Son I've bad news for you." Of course I knew before he said another word and it felt like an icy hand gripped my heart and squeezed it. I made arrangements to go over to my sister's house so that we could organise our journey home; I phoned school and told them I'd be off that day (the Friday before October half-term); and then picked up the breakfast dishes, took them into the kitchen and started washing them.

As I washed, great spasms of grief shook my whole being and I cried as I don't believe I have ever cried before or since. It was a gloomy morning in late October and I could see my own anguished reflection in the kitchen window as I wallowed in pity for myself. It was then I heard his voice as plain as day, "What the thump are you crying about? Didn't I tell you I was happy to go? And isn't it better like this than with her alone in England? She'd never have survived the shock. And haven't I died in the country I loved?" To this day I swear I heard his voice and as always it calmed and soothed me. I knew what he said to be true.

I recalled three years earlier when he'd had that first massive heart attack and I sat by his bedside in the hospital. He woke in the early hours from the morphine-induced sleep. I of course, ever the dutiful son, was asleep. In my sleep I must have sensed him stirring because I woke and he said, "Do you think this is it son?"

"Think it's what dad?" said I.

"The end son?"

I cracked ignorant and told him I had no idea what was wrong with him and he wasn't to be silly he'd be right as rain soon.

"If it is," said he, "I'm happy. I've lived the life of three men and if I go today, tomorrow, next week or next year, I'm happy to go."

His words came flowing back to me at that moment and they comforted me. I heard myself repeating mantra-like the words "That's right, stop being stupid!" and before long I was in control. I finished the pots and went off to Pat's. We flew home later that day and journeyed across Ireland by train, poignantly reminding ourselves of all those past happy journeys with mam and dad when summers stretched endlessly before us. Our journey on this occasion was melancholy and tearful. We travelled across an Ireland that was in the grips of the Tied Herrema I.R.A. kidnapping; the whole world watching the siege in Monasterevin, County Kildare.

Dad was laid out in his best suit on the bed where he'd died, his huge hands clasping the rosary in the way he'd clasped his hands when napping in life. He had been laid out by my uncle Paddy Cunniffe, who later told me that because dad's shoulders were so broad he'd had to rip the jacket straight up the back seam to get it on.

Tony, my older brother arrived, and our family was now complete and yet incomplete.

Tony and I approached Uncle Mark and asked if we'd be allowed to dig dad's grave. Cloonfad had no official gravedigger. Graves were usually opened by friends and relatives. Mark looked terribly uncomfortable and drew us outside, after dad he was the man we both loved more than any other. "I'm afraid ye can't do that," he said, "Pat Hett and Willie Mahon have already been to me and asked for the privilege and it would be awful upsetting for them if they didn't get to do it." He studied our faces to see if we appreciated the etiquette of the situation. Both of us nodded stupidly and muttered apologies for asking and saying that of course that was all right. Mark hugged us both to him and whispered, "It's an awful thing to lose a father and it's an awful thing to lose a friend." We loved him more at that moment than ever before.

Dad was buried in the pretty little cemetery overlooking Cloonfad. Everyone from miles around the parish turned out and filled the church to capacity. I delivered one of the readings and was shocked at how many were present, especially as dad was a Carlow man and this wasn't his home place.

The day was as dismal as I've ever seen. It lashed it down with rain so we weren't able to carry the casket from the church to the graveyard. Instead we walked behind the hearse like drowned rats. In retrospect it was probably just as well because the casket was so heavy I'd never have been able to carry it the distance and that would have been a terrible shame to bear!

Kitty, Mark's wife, said it was a good sign when the heavens opened at a funeral because it meant that the angels and all the saints shared in your grief for the passing. Paddy Cunniffe suggested that it was wet because they were spilling a drop for dad in welcome. The implication being that dad would have joined in!

Pat Hett (R.I.P.) and Willie Mahon had done an incredible job in the rocky Mayo earth. They had dug the deepest grave I've ever seen.

We laid dad to rest and I swear the whole town had traipsed to the cemetery with us. It was raining so heavily and it had turned so bitterly cold that I took their presence as a real mark of respect for a man they only could have known as an occasional visitor to their hometown. We said the prayers and trekked the short distance to Kanes where fair-play to mam (she was never fond of encouraging one to drink) she stood at the bar, a thing she never did, and said, "The drinks are on Paddy." God, how he would have loved that moment and even though he wasn't present he was felt in everyone's company.

He had been a larger than life man and the hole he had left was larger than that left by most. We drank to his memory. Tales were told of his wild days. Stories, some of them true told of incredible strength, tremendous stamina, powerful days and years of hard, hard work, legendary drinking sessions and a generosity that ennobled him amongst men of all types. Mam often said she wished she had a shilling for every pound he'd given away to those who asked it of him because she'd be a rich woman, and he surely did have difficulty in refusing anyone.

We had a memorial service for him at Our Lady's, Langley the following Thursday when we came back to England. Our Lady's is a powerful big church and again I was called upon to do the same reading. I was almost struck dumb when I turned to face the congregation. The church was so full they were standing at the back and partly along the aisles. There had to be approaching a thousand people there to celebrate the life of this ordinary extraordinary man, my dad. Although full of his loss this sight filled me with pride and I nearly wept through the whole reading.

His long ago words from a hospital bed come back to me often and I still visit with him regularly in my dreams where he's as full of life and fun as he always was. Waking I am still touched by a momentary anguish to realise that I have been dreaming, dreams that have not diminished him for me in thirty-five years.

I firmly believe that if a man had an ambition in life it couldn't be greater than having the courage and the belief to be able to say, "I've lived the life of three men and if I go today, tomorrow, next week or next year, I'm happy to go."

I'm a big man now, over six feet and heavy for my size but I'll never be as big a man as my dad.

19. Second Post, 1976 – 1990.

The Sutherland High School (Suthie), on Sutherland Road Heywood was the second school I taught at and here I did learn something about teaching rather than facilitating. I also learned things about myself as a teacher. I learned early on that "A" level teaching wasn't for me – I didn't have the necessary self discipline to prepare sufficiently and to reduce the work to an understandable level for the student – I suppose I was after all only a few years older than the students in my care. I did become quite good at delivering "A" level General Studies - in time.

I was appointed as second in charge of English. A promotion. Suthie was a much bigger school in every way than St. Wilfrid's. St. Wilfrid's had a clientele of around three to four hundred, Suthie's clientele was nearer nine hundred. The staff at Suthie was very big and it would take a long time to get to know everyone and even then some would remain quite remote and occasionally aloof from me.

My immediate team leader was Ray Riches (Head of English). He was a lean, mean, teaching machine very popular with most of the student body and the staff. He was intelligent, sporty, witty and quite welcoming. On the team were Bob Shannon; a really nice, very intelligent guy who had some difficulties with discipline. Eileen Fray, who was to become one of the finest teachers I have ever worked with, Eileen was classically educated and she was one of the most conscientious and hard working teachers I ever witnessed. Later Anne Attfield (I think she was called Malone when she joined the staff later marrying Robin Attfield, manager of the Hearing Impaired Unit) would join the team and like Eileen she took my breath away in relation to the amount of work she was prepared to put in. I occasionally worried about their health and well being because they worked so hard. Viv Ling completed the early team and Viv was a lovely straight forward girl with a similar background to me, I think, certainly in relation to where she hailed from. The final member of the team also worked in special needs, Marilyn Whitehead (RIP). Marilyn was a lovely lady in the truest sense of the word – she was a man's woman and enjoyed the company of strong men or men whom she felt carried themselves like men. She gave the impression she was dipsy and scatty but Marilyn was a fine teacher and one who cared deeply about the children in her care – she was one who would go the extra mile for them! The English team at Suthie was definitely one of the best teams in the school in terms of pushing the boundaries of results and achievements. Much was down to the astute selection of team members by Ray and a great deal to the conscientious and very hard work of profoundly good teachers like Eileen. When Ray became a deputy head at the school Phil Bell, one of the nicest guys you'd ever meet, became head of the department.

The school was led by Lillian Hindley who was married to a vicar. She was a lovely lady whom I believe the consensus felt would have made a fantastic head in a girl's grammar school. On my appointment she had two deputies (I'd only ever heard of schools with one deputy) Ross Gavin and John Mackareth. Ross was very much the pastoral person whilst John was the academic. Both offered a great deal to the school, although John left at the end of my second year to take up a headship elsewhere – I would have liked to have worked under him (that's about the best tribute I'd ever pay to a colleague moving into management and there aren't too many I'd say it about).

I was impressed that the school had its fair share of eccentrics. I've always loved the eccentrics; they made life that bit more interesting and exciting and none more so than the Head of Humanities, Bryan Edwards. Bryan was and is a legend. He had introduced a form of wok experience to the school by the time I joined it in 1976, something that other schools wouldn't begin to emulate until the eighties when the government finally caught on to the idea that it might be useful for young people to learn about and experience a little of what working life might be all about - talk about teaching someone how to suck eggs! Bryan was streets ahead and led the school onwards to all sorts of national awards including being the first school in Rochdale to be recognised as Investors in People. He was a star man but he was also a nightmare to work with at times.

Bryan's experience had taught him that most teachers looked down their noses at Social Studies and RE, for which he had responsibility so he invested very heavily in paper lessons. In the event that one of his staff was taken ill (a fairly regular occurrence at times) or that he wasn't allocated enough staff to deliver his curriculum; he had a million lessons on spirit duplicated paper. Once

I got to know Bryan I was amazed that he wasn't permanently high on the liquid solvent he obviously spent hours in the company of! I used to think of it as spirit destructive paper because if I was unlucky enough to be available for a cover Bryan would descend upon me with three or four hundred sheets of this stuff (still freshly ponging of the solvent), thrust them into my hands and tell me, "Get them to do this first, then read this bit to them, get them to copy this out, then answer the questions on this sheet, if they finish that ask them to draw the tabernacle of David and if they finish all of that tell them to start on the questions on sheet seventeen which they can finish next lesson." At which point he would disappear having spotted his next victim for a cover lesson! In the fullness of time he realised that I didn't mind engaging the students in discussion about the subject matter he was throwing at them and that I didn't like the paper chase. He was very magnanimous in accepting this and once he realised I was actually willing to question the students and see if they understood the work, he was happy to let me get on with it – he still gave me the duplicated sheets but now with the words, "Just in case," preceding any other instructions.

    I remember him accosting me in the corridor outside one of his suite of rooms one lunch time. He probably had a cover lesson for me that afternoon! He had a group of youngsters in the room who sounded like they were practising for some kind of gaol break – the noise was pounding. Bryan pulled the door to the room towards him and continued addressing me without a break in his pitch. He couldn't see what I could see and I couldn't get a word in edgeways for quite a while. In the meantime one of his youngsters had followed him to the door and as Bryan pulled it towards him the youngster tried to hold it open – as a consequence I could see the youngsters ten fingers wriggling in the gap between the door and jamb whilst Bryan lent his weight against the door to keep it pulled too. The decibel level rose exponentially as the youngster began screaming. Bryan oblivious to all of this carried on instructing me about that afternoon's lesson! The youngster did survive by the way and without any of the expected broken bones that I had feared!

Bryan was a one of the gems of the system. I'm not sure the school or some of the students in the school ever realised how special he was. He was also a very good tennis player and he still (in his eighties) plays a good standard of table-tennis.

Of course successive governments, since that time, have done their level best to eradicate the eccentrics and to people the profession with grey automatons. Automatons that: toe the party line, submerge themselves in preparation, delivery, assessment and meeting targets. I know that there are still magnificent teachers out there (more than anyone would guess) but a great many of them are being ground down by systems that don't respect their humanity, that want them to be seen to shed blood, and who have filled management with people who only see targets, who are dedicated to pleasuring Offstead Inspectors, manipulating pay to set staff member against staff member by differentiating pay on some kind of modern payment by results merry-go-round linked to staff assessments! There are dangers here and some of them are exposed from time to time of Heads who practice subtle forms of nepotism within their institutions or worse!

When I started writing this book I mentioned that I conceived the initial idea at a time when I was involved in a very mild form of industrial action. Part of that action, way back then, was to protest against Maggie's government that seemed hung up on the fact that some teachers were not very good and that some were lazy. To get at these parasites to the profession they did what governments always do they used the sledge hammer to crack the nut. All teachers were made to dance to the government fiddle just so they could sort out the ones who were in it only for the holidays and the job for life! Luckily I was there when our unions were a force to be reckoned with – now all of the hard work done before I became a teacher and whilst I was a teacher is being dismantled by subsequent governments determined to get results for the least possible amount spent and never mind the human tragedies left in the wake of such progress. I wonder would (subversives) like Bryan survive in this day and age? Sadly I doubt it and as a result I think our children – yours and mine miss out.

At Suthie we prided ourselves on turning out productive, caring, and capable young adults who have proved their worth in a thousand different capacities and in the far corners of this big old world. Exams are one measure of academic ability but they say little about the human qualities of loyalty, responsibility, open-mindedness, curiosity, humility, dependability and a host of other facets that make up the person. Due to modern society's acceptance of what successive governments deem success at school we are losing a whole generation of youngsters who may not be the brightest sparks in the firmament (we can't all be young Einstein's) but who are nonetheless more than capable of becoming competent and capable leaders in their own communities. I am privileged to have seen over and over again how in times of crisis individuals who left school without any qualifications can move mountains when the so called professionals have let the rest of us down!

End of tirade for the moment – but I think you get the idea that I am highly sympathetic to young teachers today who can't rely on a strong union to protect them or who are led by managers who work without their best interests at heart or a government that gives a hollow hoot for any of its workforce, teaching or otherwise.

Again I repeat I am of that very lucky generation. The teaching profession I joined in 1973 was great fun and happiness was not a dirty word to describe experiences at school for both students and staff. I'm sure that the expression "schooldays are the best days of your life" was coined for that period and if it wasn't it should have been! Academic studies were pursued but they weren't the, be all and the end all, other achievements were valued equally as much, if not more so. I miss those days when naivety wasn't looked down on from a great height!

In my first year at Suthie I was attached to McDonald House and during our pre sports day when we were selecting the best of the house to represent us during sports day I was full of enthusiasm and encouragement. Eventually as the morning wore on the house moved onto the Javelin. Now I had broken a school record in Javelin and was appalled at the lack f knowledge displayed in throwing one. In my usual big headed manner I announced that I would show them all how to throw one before we moved in to the 100m! I was at the time suffering from a nasty cough exacerbated by the fact that in those days I was a twenty a day man! In a most nonchalant fashion I prepared to throw one, intending to bask in the awe and admiration of the rest of the house. I did my text book run up, hampered somewhat by the fact that I was still in my ordinary clothes. I let fly. It wasn't my best effort but it easily out distance the best that anyone in the house had thrown but as I released it I felt a kind of twang and thought 'Oh dear, a muscle pulled!' We moved on to the 100m. I had two stop watches which I used by holding them above head height to time the first two past the post. After the first race or two I found it increasingly difficult to hold them up at all. I was beginning to feel unwell. My breathing had become a bit ragged; luckily lunch time arrived before I collapsed.

    I managed to make it back to the staff room under my own steam where I sat down and began gasping for breath, plus I couldn't bear to place my back against the seat I was sitting on. At some point Ross Gavin was walking through, probably on his way to lunch, when he caught sight of me. I could tell from his expression that I must have looked dreadful. I was by now pumping sweat, unable to speak fluently and barely able to catch my breath. Fair play to Ross he had me out of the school in his car and at Bury General before you could say, "Are you feeling alright?"

Once in A&E I was placed in a cubicle where I continued to fight for breath and where I was also conscious of great pain in my back. I seemed to be alone in the cubicle for ever such a long time (it was probably moments) when a young Irish doctor came in and examined me. By now I knew I was having a heart attack or worse! Following a cursory examination he jumped up and said, "Right we'll get you admitted," and with that he began to leave the cubicle. "Doc. . ., doc. . ., doctor, wh. . ., wh. . . , whas wrong with me?" "Ah sure it's nothing," he replied, "just a collapsed lung," and then he vacated the booth. I sat absolutely aghast and feeling extremely sorry for myself. A collapsed lung, Oh my God, that's got to be worse than a heart attack! Seemingly to doctors a pneumothorax (collapsed lung) is quite common place and not usually life threatening. Of course I knew nothing of that never having heard of one before.

Anyway, I was whisked off to a ward, where a suitably relaxed and fairly arrogant Registrar named Doctor (Mr) Lally eventually arrived, cut a small hole in the left side of my chest (I've since claimed it as a bullet wound) and inserted a tube to re-inflate the lung using an underwater seal. I think this happened on a Tuesday.

I was still in hospital that weekend when the guys came to see me. Now somehow the tubing that Dr. Lally had fitted had become blocked, my fear and the pain involved had kept me more or less sleepless since admission. On Saturday morning around 1130 two junior doctors, whom I shall call Mutt and Jeff arrived to re-fit a new tube. I was given a shot of valium which along with my sleep deprived state, acute exhaustion and the terrific pain I had, pushed me over the edge and into some kind of mindless state of euphoria where I was neither awake nor asleep. Mutt and Jeff somehow managed on their third or fourth attempt to complete the procedure, by then I didn't care I just wanted a bullet to put me to sleep! Mutt and Jeff were bunglers par excellence and delivered oodles of pain in their key stone capers! About 1330 the guys arrived to see how I was getting on, carrying a six pack of Guinness (no draught cans back then) and three copies of Playboy! Graham Fairhurst (he of the platform shoe fame) took one look at me and decided I was on my way out. He found a phone and contacted Julia to tell her she needed to get here soon otherwise she'd miss me checking out! Julia was scheduled to arrive that evening. As the visit drew on I picked up strength and the effects of the drugs started to diminish and I suspect it became evident to everyone I was actually going to survive the afternoon.

 I thank God that I have never had to go through that again. Mutt and Jeff's repair job apparently held up and I was released the next weekend. The summer holiday had started on the Thursday prior to my release. So I could look forward to a long hot summer; what a way to finish my first two terms at Suthie! The summer of '76 was wonderful.

 Anyway my new job got off to a fairly good start. I had to take the top GCE English group and introduce the new CSE English course to the school. I also had to do a little bit of drama teaching and found myself timetabled in cupboards off one of the dining rooms with an interesting mixture of the ROSLA (Raising of the School Leaving Age) kids including David B******.

The school leaving age was raised from 15 to 16 in 1972 and for the next few years there were youngsters at school who really didn't want to be there. They took ROSLA personally – "Why me?" was the cry. The immediate years after ROSLA were quite tough in secondary schools throughout the country because up until then most secondary pupils opted to leave at 15 and only those who knew they could do well and who wanted to take exams stayed on beyond that age. As a result exams were fairly new to an awful lot of schools – that is setting them for the whole of a leaving year group! Some youngsters voted with their feet and stayed away, some came in under duress and let everyone know they didn't want to be there, some made the best of it knowing they couldn't buck the system.

David and his classmates were in Year 10 (fourth years then) and all they wanted t do was kill time or if they had to, kill you! Although I'd bluffed my way through a bit of drama at St. Wilfrid's this was a different kettle of fish and the students were much older and looked it. David practically had a beard, he was six two or more and everyone in the school including a great many teachers were terrified of him.

I remember looking at what texts the school had to offer because practical drama wasn't really an option when pursued in a cupboard. My own knowledge of drama at the time was actually quite limited – I'd seen a few plays whilst at school, mostly Shakespeare, I'd been to the ballet and opera but nothing I'd seen on stage seemed appropriate for this group of grumpy youngsters who were all set to blame me for the fact they had to stay on. I looked at 'Lady Windermere's Fan', 'Hobson's Choice' and then I found a text that I found interesting in that I thought it might appeal to teenagers who struck me as potential delinquents. I settled on Aristophanes, "Lysistrata". I was still quite young and easily misled!

My reasoning was quite perverse. I felt that as young people becoming aware of their sexuality they might become engaged in something where women used sexuality to get their men to do their bidding and give up war. Few of the class were what I would term fluent readers but somehow we staggered through the text and somehow they began to like me and we very soon gelled. The whole class turned out to be a terrific group of young people, I'm not sure how much they understood of the text but they trusted me enough to get through it and apparently to enjoy it – we did not attempt to act it out and I swear that if I had suggested acting to one or two of the girls in the class they would have acted the Harridan to me! I'm not sure if any of them had an acting bone in their bodies – the powers that be (senior management) only appeared to be concerned that they were contained and not disruptive. I think when they saw how the students got on with me it impressed them no end.

David was given to long disappearances. At some point towards the end of Year 10 he began one of these long stints away – I believe (if the other students were to be believed) that he joined a fair that had been in the area and gone off to become a tattoo artist. The only thing David seemed really interested in was drawing – but he didn't get on with the members of the Art Department. He did some very interesting sketches for "Lysistrata" that I managed to destroy, without upsetting David I might add, after each lesson. I don't think Mrs. Hindley would have liked to see toga clad men and semi-naked women cavorting about with what appeared to be broom sticks pushing the men's togas out in front!

David did return to school at some point in Year 11 and proceeded to tattoo every boy in his year group. He was placed on a reduced time table so as not to upset or frighten too many teachers. For some reason he was quite happy to rejoin his drama class and another (I might have taken the same group for Social Studies – thanks Bryan) class I took. By the time he rejoined the school I was an acting Head of Year and had to deliver some assemblies so I got to work on David and one or two of the other toughest boys in the school and the outcome was an assembly in which three of the hardest, toughest lads ever to attend Sutherland performed the "Mahna Mahna . . . m" song/tune, from the Muppet Show in front of the year group I had responsibility for. It went down an absolute storm – the deputies and other senior staff sneaked in and couldn't believe I'd got these very significant young men to do it. My year group were in stitches as well as in awe – it did my reputation a great deal of good among the student body – I think their reasoning was that if someone like David was willing to do something like that for me, I couldn't be all bad! For the life of me I can't recall the theme of the assembly or worse than that I can't think of any theme that might have been supported by it! Oh my!

I suspect that class helped in my next promotion because before the end of my first two terms I had been approached and asked if I would take on the role of acting Head of Year whilst Mervyn Lee (one of the other 'few' senior people I would have been happy to serve with at any time) and Ian Geary took a year out of school to obtain their degrees. The school was moving away from the House system as its pastoral arm, to the year system and I was excited to be amongst the first to help establish the system. Pat Kearney (Art) was given the second acting role.

At the end of my first full year, having served as a Head of Year in an acting capacity I was fortunate to be given the role permanently, after an interview of course. Mervyn was coming back to the school as a deputy head and Ian as a Head of Year (they had both been housemasters). I believe that Pat and I were watched very carefully during the course of the year and I think that in particular they looked at how we made us of corporal punishment. I remember John Mackareth (deputy) having a quiet word with me early on and saying, "Always question whether corporal punishment is the right course of action because if it isn't each stroke will knock that child further away from the person they should see as the most approachable in a school." I took on board his advice and always questioned the use of punishment. I certainly never in the whole of my teaching career ever felt the need to punish a student for any misdemeanour during one of my lessons but I had a hell of a job convincing some colleagues that thrashing someone because they'd forgotten their homework or gym shoes or for talking in class was an improper use of the tool. I'd had enough of that when I was at school. As a consequence some colleagues must have felt I was soft and favoured the students too much – they may have been right! I think the judgement of senior management at the end of the year was that Pat had over used it – even though I'd be fairly sure John had the same advice for him as for me.

I did make use of corporal punishment and made sure that my year group knew when and why it would be used. Thinking back to my own days at school – we never felt aggrieved if we felt the punishment was just retribution. So I tried to base my decisions on that principle. In assemblies the boys were warned that smoking would always result in the slipper (I had a size twelve pump which I kept in my desk draw – it was a huge thing that made a terrible sound when I'd crack it against my office desk to show them what it was like). I said that as a smoker I knew that no slipper would stop them from smoking, because it hadn't stopped me, but that if each stroke knocked them fifty yards further away from where Years 7, 8 and 9 pupils could see them, then I was happy. I didn't want them smoking where the youngsters would be influenced by them – I also pointed out that it was a filthy habit that was very hard to kick once you were earning and able to pay for a twenty a day habit!

The dreaded slipper was also used to deal with bullying and I am sorry if this upsets some of the modern day thinking on how to handle the persistent bully but encouraging the bully to fear you and the consequences of his actions did work and did protect a great many youngsters. I know in an ideal world we would sit down and analyse what was going on and try to get the bully to empathise and eventually to break bread with whoever they were bullying – but in the real world you have commitments that impinge on your ability to deal with such issues effectively in a sophisticated modern manner and time appropriate manner. Thus when faced with three or four eleven year olds who had been handing money over to fifteen year olds because they feared for their lives it was easier, more efficient and expedient to make the fifteen year olds fear what would happen to them if they continued down that road – so I, and others, clobbered them and threatened them with worse to come if they ever so much as looked at the youngsters they had been bullying again!

What can I say – it was system that worked by and large. Most youngsters are intelligent enough to way up if the consequences of an action are worth it and I honestly believe that most felt that physical punishment, especially if delivered after a dire warning, just wasn't worth courting. Just like most of the youngsters who grew up in that system, myself included, chose not to tell teachers to "F*** off" or worse, because they/we weighed up the consequences and it just wasn't worth getting the strap, cane or slipper for mouthing off in that manner. Pupils telling teachers to "Go f*** themselves" or striking out and hitting teachers has only become a problem since the consequences became acceptable to youngsters! I rest my case – but I also add that you can't turn the clock back!

What irks me now is that the consequences of an action might not be addressed for a full week or two. For example: a youngster is terrorised by an older student. The older student's parents are invited to come in, perhaps following a short period of exclusion (more often internal exclusion now) or perhaps not. An appointment is made. The parents of the older student fail to show. Another appointment is made. This time they show up and because they are kept waiting they enter the meeting in belligerent mood. Their son denies everything and according to them he's an angel at home who attends Sunday school regularly and always volunteers for Children in Need. The fact that the teachers concerned know he is a rat bag of the first order, are in difficulties, because they can't tell the parents that they're lying through their teeth. Plus because it happened almost two weeks ago the little boy concerned has nearly forgotten about it and isn't quite so sure that he feared for his very life when the older thug threatened to rip out his throat and do something nasty down his neck! It's all dealt with in a limp and unsatisfactory manner, resulting in the young thug leaving the head's/head of year's office with a wry smirk that says, "Got away with it again!" The little one later that year begs his parents to let him move to the other academy down the road where he believes he'll live in less fear!

    The solution to this kind of thing is never going to be easy but I would certainly suggest that when youngsters are involved and they are frightened justice needs to be swift, predictable and commensurate with the offence given.

    It's easy in hindsight to pontificate on such matters but I hope that any youngsters who came to me felt they had my ear, my sympathy and my support when they were in distress. I recall threatening one really bad apple with serious action if he ever so much as looked at the first years again. 'Gus' Geary (Ian Geary) became a Head of Year when he returned having got his degree and he was with me when we both gave this vicious young bully the heavy word. I believe we succeeded in putting the fear of God into him and he never bothered our first years again to our knowledge, although he did do time shortly after leaving school for attacking a milk man on his Friday night collection and hitting him over the head with a brick before robbing him. I'm not sure we could have prevented that although I do think we would have tried if we could have foreseen it! We could certainly have warned the police about him as we could have for the at least one of the two pupils who became murderers that I came into contact with at Sutherland.

Ian was a top guy. He was feared and loved in equal measure. A real man's man. I think his first love was always rugby union which kept him going even following his retirement from teaching. Again he was one of those eccentrics (in the nicest possible sense of the word) who didn't care too much for authority other than his own. He told it like it was and didn't appear to care if he occasionally gave offense to those senior to him, if he felt they were talking rubbish. He did respect some more than others and he would fight hard for young teachers if he felt they were getting a hard time from management. I think I got on pretty well with Ian.

George Naylor and Harry Wilde were Heads of Year in the lower school rotating second and third year. Both were terrific guys.

I learnt a great deal from George but I think George wasn't too keen on me – I was the young upstart with a lot to learn, suggesting this and that at meetings instead of keeping my head down and getting on with things. I think George felt aggrieved that my ideas meant more work for all of the other Heads of Year and he much preferred the status quo.

Harry was lovely. He just got on with whatever he was asked to do and hardly ever complained about anything. Both Harry and George had made up the original Heads of House, a title and job they retained as the school moved over to the Year system. One of Harry's traditional 'jobs' was to book the Christmas movie(s) – sometimes one for the lower school and a different one for the upper school. I recall one year. I was attending the funeral of Andy Scanlon's dad (RIP) on the day it happened and around 1300 hours I rang school to enquire how things were going and to ask whether I should try to get back before the end of the day. Ross Gavin told me that I needn't worry about trying to get back in because they'd sorted out the strike by my year group by thrashing the ring leaders!

I wasn't sure that I'd heard him right so asked what he meant. It seems that Harry had booked "Vampire Circus" for the senior school that particular year and "The Square Peg" for the juniors. First to watch the movie were Year 11. Dougie the technician set the first reel rolling and then disappeared. For some reason Harry was left in charge of the whole year group, other staff sneaking off for a brew or quiet chat. The movie began with a prolonged lesbian interlude culminating in a vampire fest. Harry hadn't quite nodded off and became acutely aware of naked ladies cavorting about and fondling each other in a provocative and lascivious manner. The Year elevens had become very quiet (thinking no doubt this was a bit different to the usual Norman Wisdom guff they got). Harry. God, bless him, jumped up and tried to see if Dougie were in the hall, he wasn't – there was just Harry. Then he turned his attention to the projector and after moments of indecision he managed to turn the focus down enough to mask Count Dracula smacking his blood stained lips having already done away with a whole circus full of scantily clad, nubile women! The Year elevens had seen it all. Dougie eventually returned and adjusted the focus, this time he stayed with the film in case there might be anymore nudity (it was decided that the damage was done and the best way to minimise it would be to act as if nothing had happened). The Year elevens watched the movie in much anticipation of further frolics that failed to materialise and left the hall to tell the Year tens they were in for a treat. Mine were the Year tens! Of course in the meantime a powwow had been hastily summoned by management and it was decided that the Year tens would have normal lessons that afternoon instead of watching the pornographic movie they were all looking forward to, so obviously they went on strike! Ross and others dealt with the ring leaders of the strike, who tried to barricade themselves into the Maths rooms, by dragging them off and slippering them. Needless to say I was very popular the next day when I settled my year group down to Norman Wisdom in "The Square Peg" – Mr. Grimsdale, help!

Ruth Hyham who later became Ashworth made up the final cog in the year system. She specialised in the Year 7's and she was an exceptional person. Ruth and I generally got on like a house on fire and appeared to care about the youngsters we had in our care in a similar fashion. She was of course much more efficient than me at things like the necessary paperwork but we sang from the same song sheet and generally saw things in a similar way. Ruth was a terrific sounding board and I count her as one of my closest colleagues and a good friend.

Life at Suthie was never predictable and in order to survive for any length of time you had to be on your toes but if you liked the students and they took a shine to you there was no better school on God's earth.

I loved my years as a Head of Year. Obviously some memories are better than others and some of the things I managed to do were more successful than some of the other things I did or failed to do.

In those first years at the school we were desperately trying to get the money together to purchase a mini bus – now most schools have two or three all on the budget – back then if a school wanted such a luxury it had to be worked for. The first big money raising event was a Rush Cart Procession. I think it was the brainchild of Dave Cook (Geography) who was also a Morris dancer. Rush carts were a traditional activity in ancient times where parishioners pushed a cart decorated in rushes through the village or town and then spread them on the floor of the parish church.

Obviously a rush cart needed rushes and what better use of ROSLA kids than getting them down to one of the local farms to cut rushes with sickles made in the metalwork shop with the help of George Naylor (affectionately known as Noddy). Teachers took it in turns to give up the odd double free period to baby-sit these rush gathers and to make sure they weren't decapitating themselves.

I remember on one of my stints with them they came across a rabbit in the final stages of myxomatosis. It was a sad and terrible sight as the rabbit stumbled blindly along in obvious pain unable to find its warren (myx is one of those terrible man made diseases created to keep rabbit populations in check and it surfaces every so often). The lads were obviously concerned and wanted to do what was right. The consensus was that the poor thing should be put out of its misery, especially as there was no cure. I agreed and asked which of them would do the deed. Two of the tough guys who'd appeared on stage with David were with us (David I think must have been approaching the end of his tattoo apprenticeship with the fair) and one of them volunteered to do it in. What to use? The sickle was the only appropriate tool to be had so that was decided upon. Fifteen minutes later he was still building up to it. Eventually I pulled him quietly to one side and asked if he'd rather I did it and he agreed he would – he certainly didn't want to be seen to be backing out by the others. Sad to say I do have some experience in killing rabbits having shot a great many during holidays in Ireland (I never hunted with traps only with a shot gun) so I took the sickle from him and using the heavy blunt side brought it down sharply on the rabbits head which immediately finished it's terrible ordeal.

Funnily enough I was quite proud of the boys that day – they'd all been up for killing it to put it out of its misery but when it came down to it not even the toughest of them, who wouldn't have thought twice about clobbering another year eleven, could bring themselves to doing it! It kind of gave me a bit of faith in just how decent they really were. Not that I am suggesting I am not decent – it's just that I had a little experience and believed, like the boys, it was the right thing to do for the poor thing!

Raising the money for a mini bus seemed a never ending task. I remember suggesting we held a Donkey Derby, something they did at St. Dominic's and Cardinal Langley, raising in excess of a thousand pounds when they did so. Ross Gavin was horrified, he said many of our parents were old style Presbyterians and Methodists for whom gambling was the ultimate sin. Catholics could gamble their souls away but not the parents or progeny of Suthie!

So I organised a 10K run officially opened by Mike Sweeney of Piccadilly Radio fame. It was planned for Mike to actually run but on the day he was ill and although he turned up and set off the Claxton he was unfit to run. We presented him with a T shirt and an army of helpers printed his son's name on the back. The event was so successful it led me to organise an half marathon which I did for the next five years, sometimes raising quite a bit of money for the mini bus fund and later to keep the mini bus on the road. The first couple of half marathons were hugely successful but then peripherals like having to pay for signage, St. John's Ambulance, adverts in running magazines and various other sundry costs became quite staggering and I eventually allowed it to run out of steam after the fifth one - that may have made an actual loss.

I met some wonderful people that I still call friends today whilst organising the half marathons: Norman Quint and Neil Rowcliffe (they owned Summit Washing Machines) are just two who not only volunteered unstintingly during the events but also stumped up some magnificent prizes during its five year existence. Norman was always a guy who put his money where his mouth was and he was for a lone time a leading light at Darnhill's Boxing Club. Norman was the kind of parent who helped make schools quality places by showing that they cared and would support the school. I am proud and pleased to say that all of his girls did well out of the school – two of them since becoming PhD's. God bless you Norman, he's still as lovely as ever he was and still reminiscing about his Navy days!

Eventually the school did raise the funds to purchase a mini bus and Norman Rowlands (Head of Maths) became its keeper and protector. If you wanted to book it out you went through Norman, when you brought it back in, Norman inspected it. He arranged its maintenance and looked after it as if it were his own – I belabour this point because since then I know that now many teachers treat their schools mini buses with contempt and rarely does anyone take responsibility for it! I've seen mini buses that have obviously been involved in accidents where someone has driven it into a wall or scraped the side and although others have used it after the accident the damage hasn't been reported until someone uses it and goes through the pre-use inspection. By this time the damage has started to corrode and it's impossible to go through the insurance company because no one knows what happened to it and whoever did it doesn't own up! God help you if you turned up with a scratch on Suthie's mini bus whilst Norman was on the job! As a result of his vigilance that mini bus remained in pristine condition well beyond its best by date!

I must admit I became very involved in my job and perhaps became somewhat complacent although I prefer to think of it as contented. Julia became pregnant with my only son sometime in 1976 and Neall was born in January 1977. I was still a kid in my mind and must have obviously made mistakes and misread things. I thought his birth would cement our relationship and bring us closer together. I was already looking forward to his sister or brother. It wasn't to be. Julia entered a period of post natal depression that eventually culminated in her informing me that she no longer loved me and that she wanted to separate.

I am not going to try to analyse the rights and wrongs of the thing, nor will I attempt to apportion blame – there's always two sides to any story. Suffice to say that despite trying everything I could to get her to change her mind we did separate and eventually divorce. I did visit several solicitors, once I accepted that we were going to split up, wanting a positive answer to just the one question, "Could I get custody of Neall?" I was told at each one I visited that if I couldn't prove a mental problem with Julia than I had no chance! So my marriage came to an end. Neall was just over two years old and for his sake I attempted to choke my pride and try to be amicable about it. Thus began what I refer to as my life as a weekend dad. At first I visited mid week for about a year and collected him on a Friday evening, delivering him back on Sunday afternoon. Then I started a Pastoral Care course led by the great Douglas Hamblyn (Swansea University) that clashed with my Wednesday mid-week visit and I think much to Julia's relief I cut out the mid-week visit. Neall remained a pivotal part of my week end and holiday life from that time onwards until late into his teenage years when he started to visit me on his terms.

I'm proud to say we had some terrific times, great holidays in France, some school holidays he came on, and with family in Ireland, by then my sister had moved over to Ireland to make a new life for herself and her girls with Sean. I believe that I still have a good relationship with Neall and I think our love and respect for each other was developed over those tough years when I was a weekend dad!

I do remember breaking the news to Ross Gavin. The breakup coincided with strike action called by members of the union that catered for school caretakers and Rochdale Authority in its usual understanding way decided that although they accepted that no teachers, being union members, would cross a picket line they still had to turn up to school to be registered. It was a petty requirement that people like Ian Geary thought was insulting (Ian got a doctor's note stating that he was too ill to attend on that day). I turned up with the rest of the staff and met in St. Paul's car park. I asked Ross to come and sit in my car, which he did, and then despite rehearsing what I wanted to say I broke my heart and told him what was happening. He was more than understanding. I can never express how much Ross helped when I'd had my collapsed lung. Not only did he get me to the hospital but he picked up Julia and brought her there and back, he even loaned her his car so that she could visit me. She'd passed her test but we didn't have a car on the road at that time – I was still into motor bikes! He certainly did more than your average deputy might be expected to do!

So I began a new life which meant that I threw myself into work more than ever before. I acquired some disco equipment from Keith Fane and started running year dances, senior school and junior school dances and despite some objections from one or two of the older staff I managed to get Christmas Year parties off the ground. I never managed to get the idea of a Prom off the ground – it was before it's time – although I did try – having seen and enjoyed 'American Graffiti'. There was some resistance to these ideas brought on by fears of what the ROSLA kids would be like at such events. I also started running Friday lunch time discos to raise money in order to keep the record collection current. Students trained as DJs and some of them were fantastic, no names mentioned (if I mention one I'd have to mention them all because there's still some currency in citing who was the best at such and such as evidenced in recent Facebook quarrels – which was my best year group? etc.)

The student body definitely benefitted greatly from these social extensions to school life and so did the staff because we were able to run staff and PTFA parties and dances, whilst providing our own music free of charge. The end of each half marathon was followed by a dance presentation all run in house. It was terrific.

Following my separation and eventual divorce I decided to get back on track with the degree I had put on hold when my dad had his first heart attack. I did two nights a week for a year ('78/'79) and managed to obtain a secondment for the year 1980/81. I treated the year really professionally. I said to myself at the start that I should be working nine to five so that's exactly what I did. I worked nine to five. If I wasn't in a lecture, tutorial or seminar I was in the college library. It meant that I never missed a deadline and was on course to achieve a First, which I missed by only three marks! Story of my life!

I did manage a two, one, which is considered a good honours so in the end I was happy enough. That Christmas was also a bit special because it is the only one I ever spent out of this country. I went to Benidorm and had a terrific time. I wouldn't want to be there in the summer but I did have a lovely time that Christmas and New Year. Midnight Mass in the Basilica was something very special and will forever remain a very fond memory. Brian Kenny was supposed to be going but backed out at the last minute. I ended up with John Walsh the son of the Catholic Clubs one time steward and he was a bundle of laughs – he became home sick before the plane left Manchester and managed to get a flight home just before new year!!!! I stuck it out and had a blast thanks to a couple of very nice Irish girls, a girl from Kent and a publican and his good lady wife from the East End. They all set out to befriend me and ensure I had an extra good time – which I did. We did a lot of mourning for John Lennon I recall!

Marilyn Whitehead (RIP) was given acting responsibility for my year group whilst I was on my year out and, having finished my exams, I offered my services to accompany her on the year trip she had organised to Rhyl. I was very conscious that she was in charge and so tried very hard to keep a low profile by spending an hour or two in a local hostelry (I was a volunteer after all).

That summer was also quite special because I maaged to book myself onto one of Douglas Hamblyn's university courses at Swansea. If I had my time over I'd have chosen to go to Swansea - a university where the gates open out onto a beautiful white sandy beach – yes please. I must have made it up with Brian for leaving me with John Walsh in Spain, because Brian travelled down to Swansea with me for the ride – he was going on to London to stay at his brother Terry's (RIP). It was a 1981 and I was on the course during the Royal Wedding which was marked by a royalist versus Republican football match. The Republicans won! It was a valuable and enlightening week made all the more interesting because the university is close by the Gower Peninsula where Dylan Thomas hung out at the Antelope on the Mumbles mile. He had long been a personal favourite of mine – I suspect part of it was because of his resemblance in terms of his life to Brendan Behan whom I was named after.

I enjoyed a wonderful Year out and returned to school refreshed, ready to work hard and because of the standard of my degree much better off financially.

On my return to school I started running short outdoor walking breaks. Brian Kenny, who was teaching at St. Dominic's by this time, had invited me, whilst I was out for the year, to join a party from Dominic's to a place in West Yorkshire called Cragg Vale. I went and fell in love with the place. Brian explained that the school charged the children (about thirty of them) around £15 each for two nights at St. John's in the Wilderness Sunday School, which had recently been opened by Jimmy Saville for use and hire by schools. Hugh Morgan ran the centre on behalf of the church and it brought in some very useful funds for the church. Brian explained that they did their own cooking and provided transport as part of the package.

I talked it over with Mervyn Lee and he agreed I could give it a go if I got staff support. Our first ever trip had four or five staff, including females, and we charged the students £12 which covered everything. We ran our first trip on the first weekend of the October half term break in 1981. Friday night was settling in, Saturday was a walk to Heptonstall via Stoodley Pike. Ray Riches walked with us pointing out landmarks and he had arranged for lunch to be served in The White Lion in Helptonstall – the kids loved it. Saturday night we had a sit down meal with three or four courses and no one was permitted to leave before the end of the meal which was followed by a penny concert. Every student was encouraged to do something either solo or as part of a group to entertain us. The concerts were always brilliant. I can still remember a group of seniors performing the 'Dance of the Dying Slugs' which involved them staggering around the stage (the stage was upstairs in what we termed the boys dorm) in their sleeping bags and dying dramatically. I cried with laughter – on paper it doesn't do justice to how funny it was. Sunday we cleaned up and headed back home around two or three o'clock. I always made a big thing about leaving the centre cleaner than we found it!

That first venture was so much fun and whet so many appetites that I planned a longer one for the Easter break. Five days, four nights, at £25 per head. Once again I had no problem getting staff to support me. Paul Wood (Woody or occasionally Jasper Carrot because of his resemblance to the comedian) was always my most faithful supporter and remains one of my closest friends to this day. During the Easter break, because it was spread over a longer period, everything was much more relaxed. I would get the students to the Vale during the late morning, early afternoon, usually in two mini bus trips. Staff usually brought their own transport so that they could make a fast getaway at the end of the week. Monday would be spent settling in followed by a midnight hike which would take us along moorland and passed reservoirs in the blackest of nights as far as the White House Pub near Blackstone Edge and then we would walk back along the roads. Tuesday it was Bradford where we visited the Imax Cinema and the National Photographic Museum, occasionally finishing off at the Ice Rink with a chippy for dinner (thirty two lots of chips please, ten fish, seven steak and kidney pies, eight meat and potato pies, and seven jumbo sausages please – the chippy loved us!) Wednesday we walked to Heptonstall via Stoodley but on the way back we stopped off at Walkleys Clogg Factory which back then was a fantastic tourist attraction in the area and had much more than just clogs in it! Thursday we visited Keighley and Haworth. Cliffe Castle in Keighley is a terrific place to spend a couple of hours being in a lovely park and with loads to see inside. The house, which has the appearance of a castle, was donated to Keighley town by a nineteenth century mill owner. Downstairs it has rooms with magnificent furniture from the nineteenth century. Also downstairs there's an industrial revolution museum displaying a variety of nineteenth century machinery which then leads into a geological display and wild life of the area section. Upstairs there's a display of nineteenth century children's toys. Well worth a visit and free to enter. The afternoon was spent in Haworth visiting the steam railway exhibition and the Parsonage Museum. A truly fabulous day for all – in those days a little prior negotiation got great deals on entry to the parsonage. Thursday evening was the sit down meal where we always tried to pull out all the stops even though the fair was usually Irish Stew for the main course – vegetarians were catered for by being told to avoid eating the meat! This would then be followed by the penny concert which was always a highlight for me. Friday was the big clean up and repatriation.

Although prices necessarily went up over the years the content remained much the same. I know that the youngsters who accompanied me on these jaunts still talk about those times with great affection. They have obviously forgotten all those occasions when I dragged them out onto the moors in driving rain, sleet and mud, with precious little in the way of drying facilities back at the centre. One particular midnight hike was appallingly bad. Ray Riches led us on a short, very frightening walk to Stoodley Pike where we somehow managed to get a paraffin stove lit and made a brew before returning soaked to the skin and barely conscious. I don't think we lost anyone or if we did they haven't been missed yet!

I've deliberately not mentioned any students by name up until now but I feel I must mention one in particular, Simon Mellor. Simon came on every trip he could to the Vale from Year 10 (fourth year) to Upper Sixth, both the short breaks and the longer Easter breaks. Simon is a teacher himself now and he has also begun introducing some of his students to the joys of walking the hills and moors.

It's funny because when Simon was at school I often spoke to him about what he wanted to do when he eventually left school. "Banking" was all he wanted to do and all he ever aspired to, I felt it was a terrible waste of a young person who had displayed the right temperament and patience to make a fine teacher. However he did leave school and he did go into banking. To cut a long story short he got in touch with me after a couple of years in banking and told me he'd made a mistake, he didn't like banking and wanted to try to get into teaching which meant university and would I consider giving him a reference for John Moore's in Liverpool. I gave him the finest reference I could and he duly went to John Moore's where he qualified as a teacher and has made an excellent career out of it - as I knew he would. I know that like many teachers today he feels put upon by how much he is expected to do by governments and Heads who could care less about the individual and that youngsters are not getting easier to teach but he needs to remind himself regularly that it's the children who count and he has a vocation that they need to share with him. I am very proud of Simon as I am very proud of the vast majority of young people it was my privilege to work with at Suthie.

I must admit that I witnessed an enormous number of changes in the profession whilst at Suthie most coming under Maggie Thatcher's governance. Kenneth Baker introduced the Baker Days or "B" Days as they were christened – everybody knew they were there but nobody knew what they were for! It was the government's way of snatching back five days of time when we could be called in to school for training. I'm not sure if you have ever been involved in any kind of modern training but an enormous amount of it is about individuals or groups devising specific training for a particular niche and charging the earth for the session.

Training for teachers is no different to any other kind of training out there; 10% is excellent, 10% is of some value, 10% doesn't insult your intelligence and the rest are in it for the money! I saw lots of so called specialist training for students in my final days in the profession and the vast majority of it was appalling – it's no wonder youngsters lose heart. Training for teachers is equally 'iffy'.

Qualities like loyalty, generosity, individual creativity, passion, kindness and the courage to step out of the box are no longer valued in almost any type of employment today, including teaching. Instead the qualities of toeing the party line, teaching for the result and using any means to get it, keeping your distance from children and parents, following the prescribed curriculum even when it proscribes works that you have always found inspirational and engaging, and playing the promotion game which rewards those who don't make waves and who support any measures that enhance their own importance. It's not the vocation I entered thirty-eight years before retiring from it! I strongly believe that the type of country we have today with the emphasis on dog eat dog and do unto others before they do unto you is very much the legacy of the Thatcher years.

By the way I would hasten to add that in all of my years teaching I never confided to my students anything about my political beliefs or leanings. In that I am of the old school who believes that if you are in a position of influence over young people you should not use that influence to brain wash them into following your politics. It should be enough to teach them wrong from right and how to judge between the two coupled with love and respect for your fellow man. I had no problem with stating that in a sensible world we would always treat other people in the manner we would like to be treated.

The only occasions when I broke my silence in political matters was whenever I came across an extreme fascist. Children aren't fascists they simply believe what their parents tell them and I certainly came a across a good number who were being brainwashed into accepting the drivel of National Front, EDL, and others of their ilk.

I recall one conversation with one young man whose name wasn't a million miles away from the name of one of my oldest pals (I'm sure he won't mind me using it to illustrate this point) Latowsky. A general election was approaching and young Latowsky was spouting NF propaganda with great vigour and noisy support from his classmates; demanding my opinion. Didn't I agree that we should send them all home? Who are we sending home I asked? The P***ies and the b***ks. You mean like the Asian guy who runs the corner shop? Yes he declared as if he'd proved his point. He was born in this country I pointed out which makes him at least as British as you. I went on to suggest that if NF ever got into a position of power after they had repatriated all those who were obviously non European they might start looking at those with Eastern European names or Irish names – in fact with a name like Latowsky I suggested he might be one of the first thrown out. I twisted the knife a bit then by then telling him that with a name like Ramsbottom I'd probably be offered a cabinet posting with them even though I was the son of two immigrants. He was outraged, I'm English, he cried, they wouldn't throw me out. At this point I quietly suggested that what he was really saying was that if their skin isn't lily white they don't belong and that quite rightly we call that racism which is exactly what NF is or was.

I could never keep quiet about subjects like this. I am very proud of what the men and women who fought against Fascism did for our country and it literally breaks my heart to see fascists roaming around freely spouting off their unchanging diatribe of hate. Why is it these neo Nazis are permitted to despoil the very graves of the heroes who defeated their ideology in WW2?

Anyway, by and large I don't believe any student could ever have said that I voted this way or that. Obviously the more intelligent and more politically astute would have been able to make an educated guess. It's funny which principles meant a great deal to me – any ex pupil reading this might well be shocked to hear how strongly I felt about certain issues.

My years at Suthie were exciting and very fulfilling. After my divorce I made a promise to myself that I would never get involved with any woman who didn't display undying love and devotion for me. I didn't want to be hurt again; although I never discounted marriage.

In the early 1980's I became more and more involved with the school's Parent, Teachers and Friends Association. Len Taylor pointed out one of the parents who was always very active in her support for the school. She was called Sandra and he fancied the pants off her. I thought she was quite tasty, but married, so I thought no more about her until a couple of years later following her own nasty divorce I found myself working closely with her on the organisation of one of the half marathons. She was busy visiting local businesses and enlisting their financial support by getting them to buy space in our programme. She was very successful and it became abundantly apparent to me that she was also very interested in me.

At the time I was dating three or four girls (women) intermittently. Under pressure from Derek Gooding (Head of Music, RIP) I found myself getting involved in the local amateur dramatic scene. He knew that I had appeared in several pieces and that I could sing a bit. I'd been in stage plays and shortly after my separation I had become involved in Middleton's Amateur Operatic and Drama Society in "Guys and Dolls" which is still one of my favourite musicals. I had discovered that involvement in such groups opened up access to some beautiful women and the really great thing was that there were always more women than men involved in shows.

Derek convinced me to play Big Chief Sitting Bull (whom I played on two separate occasions) at the Gracie Fields Theatre (I've always had a fascination with Amerinds and couldn't resist the opportunity to play such an important character even if it was just for laughs) and later he persuaded me that I could handle Bill Sykes in "Oliver".

I wasn't so sure but I gave it a go. Bill Sykes is the role that Oliver Reed played with such gusto in the 1950's musical but Reed didn't sing in it, I did! It was great fun. I remember during the Saturday matinee tricks were being played by cast members on each other. I had a really strong bull terrier playing the part of Bullseye and as I prowled onto the stage to sing "Strong men," I was to pass Bullseye to Cyril Greenwood a local business man I knew well and whose daughters I taught. He was to take the lead and control the dog until I finished and they moved into "Oompapa". Unbeknown to Cyril I placed lots of the doggy treats Bullseye loved in Cyril's jacket pockets. As I came on stage Bullseye nearly pulled me over in his haste to get to Cyril and Cyril was almost knocked off the flimsy bench he was sitting on. How I got through the song that afternoon was a true miracle. Cyril took it all in good part and played some evil trick on me in the final performance that night!

I think I realised that Sandra was smitten when she came to near enough every performance of the show – she was a single woman by that time. Our relationship blossomed from around about there on in. Early in 1987 I decided that Sandy (my name for her, seemingly she'd never been called that before) met my criteria for a woman to get involved with. With that in mind I proposed to her one Saturday afternoon whilst I was having a bath – it seemed like the right thing to do at the time! She accepted. I explained that having been through the rigmarole of the full wedding thing before I wanted something low key – so we got married in Gretna Green on our way to Ireland for a holiday with my son Neall and her youngest daughter, Lisa. We told no one, except our immediate family – I had to tell my mother and her sister because we were going to spend time at their home in Galway and it wouldn't do to turn up with a woman and two children expecting them to put us up! We had to be legitimate!

Gretna Green was a sketch. We had no witnesses obviously, so the registrar popped out to the Tourist Information Office and asked a German couple if they would act as witnesses. They agreed and when the registrar left them telling them to turn up in ten minutes they spent the time looking for the hidden cameras! They explained later: "Oh ya, ve come to Gretna Green and someone comes and says be a vitness at a vedding. Very funny. Ve think ve are on ze Candid camera, ya?" (His English by the way was actually better than mine, he was an English teacher in Germany). The registrar had to run out and grab them as they left the tourist Information Office and drag them in to her office! They were absolutely thrilled, as were we, I think they saw the potential after dinner chat that would accompany their experience for years to come – "Yes we visited Gretna Green and do you know we were invited to be witnesses at a wedding!"

Outside they tracked us down and presented us with a lovely box of chocolates and thus began my second marriage which is rapidly approaching our New Furniture anniversary (don't tell Sandy) – so I think I might have made the right choice there! Next year it will be Pearl – oh dear!

Ireland was an interesting introduction to the family for Sandy. My mother was at that time living with her younger sister Mairead whom we all called Babe (being the youngest) and she, a widow, lived on a lovely farm in Galway close to the town of Glenamaddy. They had been forewarned that we were married and arriving with Neall and Lisa. The youngsters were around nine years old, there's only a month between them in age and they were to sleep in a tent in the garden of Babe's house. This was the first thing that caused consternation between the two older women so much so that my mother approached me and asked if I wouldn't rather put the tent up in the bathroom for the children. They couldn't get their heads around the idea that Neall in particular was well used to camping out and that as a regular camper I considered their home safer than almost anywhere I'd ever camped before.

My mother then showed us up to the room she had prepared for us. Babe's house was a big rambling affair although it only had three bedrooms. Mum had spent the morning airing the room out because it hadn't been used in years and smelled kind of musty. As part of the airing process she had lit a fire in the grate and placed the bedding around the fire to ensure it was completely dry. She then left the room to see to other things and when she returned the bedding was quietly smouldering and burning. The room was full of dense smoke and a total disaster was only narrowly avoided. Consequently when we were shown up to the room the odour of a recent house fire was choking and there was a black ring around the wallpaper where the smoke had blackened it! Welcome to Ireland Sandy.

The very next morning we were awoken at the crack of dawn by my mother banging a tin pot underneath our window – she didn't hold with any hank panky even if you were married!

It may sound less fun than it actually was but I think I can truthfully say we had a terrific holiday. After a week with Babe and my mother we pitched our own tent and the kids tent in the field directly opposite my Uncle Mark's home in Mayo.

Neall and Lisa were washed out one night the rain was so hard. We were all awakened very early one morning by a rampaging donkey – the Black Donkey he was known as locally. We were camping inside a field and the donkey having escaped the confines of its own field came pounding along the road adjoining the field but when your head is in close proximity to the ground, as it is in a tent, the sound was enormous and sounded much too close for comfort. Plus we had no idea what it was that was thundering towards our tent!!!! Later in the week the weather cleared enough for us to invite all of the family for a barbeque. The first in the history of Ballykilleen I like to think. Everyone came including my cousin Eileen who brought a bottle of poteen (illicit Irish whisky – or moonshine). We had an absolutely fantastic time of it although Padraic's (my cousin) wife Marian has never forgiven me. She had just given birth to her youngest, Dana and had to stay home with her. Story of my life.

We finished our stay in Ireland with a few days at my sister's home in Monaghan where Sandy and I tried to complete a pub crawl of all of the pubs in Castleblaney by way of celebrating and found it was impossible to complete! All in all we had a wonderful holiday.

Just before we left England to get married we had bought a house in Todmorden and it was to here we returned. First priority was to announce our wedding, which I think took everyone by surprise, and to throw a house party. Needless to say it was a cracker and we settled into our new life in our new home and we remain there to this day!

I'd fallen for the house as we walked through the front door. It was built in 1826 and had once been two weavers' cottages which had been knocked into one house in the 1930's. It was full of charm and eccentricity, it was also a terrific base for exploring the Calder Valley which we started doing with a will. In the good weather we walked the hills in the evenings as well as at weekends. It was terrific.

I didn't know it at the time but my time at Sutherland was coming to an end. Rochdale Authority was planning a major reorganisation of schools and in 1990 I was shipped out to start again at the Queen Elizabeth School in Middleton (I'd gone full circle).

I'm not sure how thorough or how scientific the selections made by the authority's advisers were but I found myself moved from the school I loved and with an effective demotion on top. Although they were at pains to inform me that I wouldn't lose any money as my salary was protected – what it meant in effect was that I was going to have to prove my worth all over again to a new Head and management system and one which didn't believe in Pastoral systems other than Form groups!

I'm afraid I don't recall a great deal about those final months at Suthie. My confidence had been dented and I felt badly devalued whilst attempting to put on a brave and nonchalant face. It was hard. I didn't get too involved in the final goodbyes – I know that others were too tied up in their own experiences to notice how badly affected I was.

I do know that I left an English group that broke the mould in terms of examination success and the group that was partially responsible for the school's turnaround in terms of academia. The group I left were at the end of Year 10 when I took my leave but I had taken them from Year 8. Their Year group (the Chernobyl kids) were appalling when they joined the school in Year 7. A radical re-think ensued and it was decided that we would strictly stream their Year group (individual subject settings had been in use until then). The top group in the year was 32 in number and I was selected to take them for all of their English lessons. They were lively but I managed to win them around and towards the end of Year 9 I took the whole class to Cragg Vale on a Creative Writing Course for a week which was a tremendous success – every student completed an original piece of writing; some were actually quite good. The real value though was in the closeness we all felt from that moment on. They became a joy to teach and the GCSE work we did in Year 10 was excellent. I didn't want to lose them but I did and when they took their examinations, under a new Head, in a newly named Heywood Community School, all but one or two passed both Language and Literature. Ray Riches, who had been taking the second group, also got a few good GCSE results and suddenly the decision taken four years earlier to strictly stream that particular year group was vindicated and for the first time the school was achieving

40% of students with 5 GCSE's at grade 'C' or better! My babies – for which I received no kudos!

To add insult to injury I attended preliminary meetings at my new school and met my new Headteacher, David Lack, who informed me he wanted me to teach Drama! But that's another story altogether.

20. The Blow-in.

Mum lived for twenty-six years after dad died. Twenty-six lonely and occasionally eventful years!

These, her final years, were spent attempting to find her niche. She lived for a while back in England, where I worried constantly about her safety and then fought with her when I made the mistake of moving in with her on the breakup of my marriage. Eventually, with encouragement from me, she moved back to her home place having purchased a mobile home and here she settled in next to the home of her brother Mark. It didn't work out and she next moved in with her sister Margaret (Babe) who was also sadly, widowed early. This didn't work out either and she found herself living in the town of Glenamaddy in County Galway, close by her sister's place. I remember asking her if she was now happy living in her own little home, in such a nice little town and she answered, "I'm nothing but an auld 'blow-in' to them". A 'blow-in', seemingly, is someone who settles in a town that they weren't born in! I thought at the time there's an awful lot of us in that boat mum.

Here she grew old, sometimes gracefully and occasionally disgracefully. I visited her two and sometimes three times a year, especially as she became less able to cope and more and more forgetful.

In the late nineties she proved herself unable to fend for herself any longer and the family took the decision that she would be best looked after in a nursing home and so she ended her days in the

Meadowlands Nursing Home in her home town of Cloonfad. The window from her room looked across to the lovely graveyard a mile away where dad had been interred.

Meadowlands is a lovely home and she had the best of everything except peace of mind. To her Meadowlands was a prison where she'd been incarcerated. The nurses and owners were her jailers and we were individually the Judases who had put her there!

Mum had always been a very strong willed woman, used to getting her own way. To find herself dependent upon "black strangers" as she described the staff from time to time was hard for her to bear. She had the canny knack, certainly in later years, of being able to sew dissent where there was harmony and unhappiness where there was joy. This is why none of the places she tried to settle in those final years worked. She was intolerant of other women and was always vying for the top spot, not a recipe for congenial living! Yet she could still make me laugh, as well as cry, at times.

Thus began a twilight period of anxiety for me. I suffered from terminal guilt whenever I left her even though I knew deep down that were I to try to look after her it would almost certainly have cost me my marriage. Many are the times I stopped the car and cried because she looked so frail and desperately unhappy at our parting. I can see her now looking at me as if in accusation, "How can you leave me here?"

Time passed and Sandy (my wife) and I visited mum regularly. We visited her together for the last time in the Autumn of 2001. By this time she had begun a deterioration that she would not recover from.

Sandy is a terrific observer of human kind and she has tolerance to spare for all. As we were leaving she told me to prepare myself because mum wouldn't be around too long now. Mum had been asking me, on a daily basis during our visit, how dad was and what he was up to today, did I see Mark and. . . All the great but dead men in her life had come back to be a part of the end. Sandy had witnessed such conversations before and knew that the end was approaching.

We came back to England and got on with our busy and cluttered lives and mum gradually fell into decline.

I got the call early in January and was there at the end, just as she'd been there at my beginning.

I sat with her, keeping vigil, for two nights and on the third night I was persuaded to get some sleep by Marion, my cousin Padraic's wife, before I fell over!

I believe my head had only just touched the pillow when I was summoned to Meadowlands. She'd taken a turn. I arrived about eight-thirty.

Mum drifted in and out of sleep her breathing ragged. Around her bed stood all who could be there with her. Tony my brother was on his way over. Her sister Babe, Kitty (Mark's widow), Pat (my sister) and Sean (her husband), Marion and Padraic, and my cousin Eileen stood around the bed.

Hushed conversations and occasional group prayers kept my mother company during these her final hours on earth.

Around eleven-thirty, mum had been sleeping for a long while, she awoke. The nurse had already told us that she believed she could no longer see. Now she opened her eyes and looked towards the bottom of the bed. She appeared to focus above the heads of Eileen and Kitty and a partial smile stole over her sunken face and she clearly mouthed the words, "O. K." Both Marion and I noticed it and quietly wondered who she could be speaking to. Next she looked directly at every person surrounding the bed. Her gaze lingered and she looked as if memorising that person. She moved her head, something she hadn't been able to do for some time in order to better see each of us; despite us having been informed that she was blind.

At just before mid-night the nurse came in and told us she needed turning and would we pop out for a moment.

No sooner were we out of the room than the nurse was at the door saying, "Quick, she's going". We tumbled back inside and I threw myself down kneeling at her head. Patsy was to my right and Marion was directly behind me. Mum's breathing had further deteriorated and her eyes, sunken and shadowed as they were, bulged as they stared and appeared to plead with each of us. I have no doubt that she was aware she was about to depart.

Kit began the rosary and we intoned the responses. Never before did I recite the rosary with such conviction. I held mum's hand tightly. The rosary ended and a moment of silence descended.

I repeated some prayers I had said with mum earlier in the day and during the nights I had spent with her. When I finished mum was still breathing raggedly, her eyes still implored. Patsy said, "Don't be afraid mum," and that triggered a repeated mantra in me. "God loves you mum. We love you", I repeated aloud.

"God loves you mum. We love you," I prayed and slowly she slipped away. She took a last breath and then stopped. Her eyes were opened. A moment passed. I heard tearful goodbyes and whispered prayers and then Patsy said, "Close her eyes" and I did. No sooner had I closed them than mum took another shuddering breath and snapped her eyes open again. As she released her breath she lay still and calm and failed to breathe again. My mum had gone after eighty-seven years walking this earth. At the end it was actually quite peaceful and inspiring – there was nothing frightening or ugly about the moment. My mother was gone and already reunited with whoever she had earlier whispered "O. K." to. Perhaps dad and Mark were there to ease her passage. I'd like to think that was the case.

The intensity of the moment is with me now. I felt fit to burst the emotion was so tight in my chest. "Well done son," whispered Sean as we were eventually ushered out by the nurse.

My mum with all her human faults and frailties was gone. Never again would she "give out" to us, never again would we be exasperated by her behaviour, never again would she make me laugh although she still retains the power to make me cry.

Love her or hate her, and there were some who did, she lived a long and eventful life. She embarked on an adventure that took her away from all that she knew and understood. She made a life for herself in an alien country. She raised a family of three, who wanted for nothing during sparse times. And she never forgot where she came from and who she was.

I recall enquiring of dad once why he stayed with her because she could be so contrary and he said, "She was great fun when she was younger and you know that she'd lay down her life for any of us". I know she would. I also know she'd have killed for us and that occasionally she might have swung for us!

My mother the contrary blow-in. Despite all of her contradictions I still miss her.

21. Homage to Jack.

Since I remarried and moved to Todmorden I have had the good fortune to meet a great many characters; all with stories to tell. None made a greater impression on me than Jack Diggle (R.I.P.). There are wonderful people to be met wherever you may be and Jack was wonderful.

Jack was an old man when I made his acquaintance. He enjoyed a couple of pints on Sunday afternoons with his lovely wife Barbara keeping him company and he enjoyed telling a good tale. Barbara is a character in her own right and has achieved a degree of fame with her recordings of "auld dialect".

One of Jack's tales in particular tickled my fancy. It concerned a mate of his called Tom Howden.

Tom was a regular at the Masons Arms on the Bacup Road and a good friend of the landlord's, Jack Smith.

Jack told the tale beautifully. I hope my attempt to retell it whilst attempting to capture Jack's phrasing does it justice.

He took a sip from his beer and then he "were" off, as they say around here:

"It t'were after t'war. Late 1940's anyroad. Jack had never had a day off from pub and he'd been invited to a licensed victuallers do in Blackpool for t'weekend. So he asked Tom if he'd look after t'pub like.

'You don't have to do much', he tauld him, ' just collect glasses at t'end o' nite, put empties in crates in t'yard, and throw a bit a sawdust down 'fore sweepin' up and run t'coth over tables 'n bar 'n such.'

Tom were game and he agreed to help Jack out.

Anyroad t'weekend arrived and Jack were ready for off. He handed keys over t' Tom and said, 'Help yourself to a pint when you want one lad and when you do just put a mark on't bar. O. K.?' He had a stick a chalk on bar fer Manchester darts like.

'O. K.' said Tom and Jack took off. It were Friday teatime like.

Anyroad, Jack had a right good weekend and returned happy to the Masons late on't Sunday afternoon. Tom were there and t'pub looked a proper treat. Pubs used to close in them days for a break in't afternoon, until seven of a Sunday. I think it were before opening Landlord came back.

'By 'eck,' said Jack, 'you've done us proud.' He looked around and everything were nice and neat like. Floor were clean and swept. Glasses were washed and stacked. Bottles and crates were in't yard. Everything were spic 'n span. Eventually he looked at t' bar and saw three chalk marks in one corner:

/ / /

'By 'eck you have been a good lad, only three pints over t'weekend?' asked Jack.

Tom were never shy in coming forward. In fact he'd drunk one hundred and eleven pints between ten o'clock Saturday morning and five o'clock Sunday afternoon! Aye he had a thirst did Tom and he had a right good time looking after t'pub."

"I don't think Jack ever went away again."

Jack sat back and took a sip of his pint the twinkle in his eye a treasure to be hoarded. I miss Jack and his lovely tales. Happily Barbara, his lovely wife, is still with us and still as chirpy as ever. I met her coming out of the local doctors' surgery last time I saw her and asked if she was alright. "Aye love, it's just that they think I might be pregnant again!"

At eighty something – I personally wouldn't contradict her.

Sadly since I first wrote this Barbara has passed away. I was privileged to attend her funeral where the backdrop to the proceedings was her recorded voice telling hilarious tales of her childhood in Todmorden. Oh how we laughed.

Barbara had been in great demand to record the talking newspaper for the blind and also by linguists who wished to hear and retain the broad dialect of yesteryear.

Funny how you can laugh so much on such a sad occasion, but I suspect that's exactly what Barbara would have wanted. She was a lovely person.

22.Third Post, 1990 – 2004.

I started at the Queen Elizabeth School in September 1990 determined not to enjoy my time there. I felt rejected and that all the hard work I had put in at Suthie counted for nothing!

Preliminary meetings at the school did little to assuage my concerns. I remember at one of these we had a presentation of what a Student Record of Achievement profile might look like and something that resembled a concertina was unfolded to the titters of an embarrassed staff. It looked like the kind of thing a group of students might dream up with little knowledge of the practicalities of collecting and collating information. A bad start I thought.

The Queen Elizabeth (QE) was on two sites initially. The grammar school site that I knew, on Alkrington and the Hollin Lane site where Hollin's Junior High had stood. An extensive refurbishment was being completed which included some new buildings at the Hollin site and the new QE would be sited there. David Lack had been the Head of Hollins and some of the staff who remained had little experience of the senior end of secondary education post thirteen – hence the concertinaed ROA.

I left that meeting with a feeling of dread. I'd met some interesting colleagues and some I would become quite friendly with so there was some hope on the horizon. For most of us this was new territory and everyone felt a little nervous about the way things would pan out. I left this particular meeting with a heavy heart.

The next day at Suthie I received a note stating that David Lack wanted to meet with me at Heywood's Teacher's Centre - so after school that evening I arrived at the centre around 1700. David asked me how I felt about things and I told him the truth. I was unhappy. I'd spent years proving myself, had loads of pastoral ability and skills, hadn't taught drama in years and didn't particularly enjoy the experience when I did, I felt I had been demoted, and the prospect of teaching on two sites wasn't at all appealing.

David commiserated with me but reminded me that none of this was his doing. He had lost people he wanted to hold onto and he was expected to run two sites as efficiently and effectively as he could and to crown it all the people responsible hadn't given him anyone with drama skills or experience, or anyone who could run a Careers Programme – apart from me. The mention of careers had me in a state of panic – I hated the idea of trying to interest youngsters in careers – I'd always found it a paper chase. The only way I would consider careers was if I had control of the Work experience programme which was in its infancy at QE (they had never had a year group out on work experience.).He asked me to trust him and asked me to please act as head of drama on the understanding that he would try to get in a specialist as and when he could. He also agreed that I would be kept on the one site (the senior site on Alkrington) and that Work experience would be part of my brief. I think I had mentioned to him that I hadn't had a great deal to do with Year 7 children for several years.

What was I going to do? I agreed. As it turned out it was probably the saving of me, but more of that later.

Fourteen years earlier I had been told that Suthie was the toughest school in Rochdale bar none and that they would eat me alive there. The Suthie kids were 'pussies' (in the nicest possible sense of the word) compared to what we all encountered at the senior part of QE. The first day was like entering some kind of Bedlam. To say that it had ever been a grammar school was extremely hard to believe. Years 9, 10 and 11 rampaged around the overcrowded buildings in a manner reminiscent of the world's wildest rodeo! The word pandemonium comes to mind whenever I think of that first day and the weeks that followed.

I believe several things were at play: youngsters asserting their ownership of the site; new staff unsure of themselves; the absence of protocols for dealing with simple things like movement around the school; bad behaviour and very bad manners. In effect those early days were very much 'every man and woman for themselves'. You and your colleagues were either going to sink or swim and if you didn't learn to swim fairly quickly you were destined to drown very rapidly. I lay a pound to a penny that the sale of alcohol to members of the school staff increased exponentially in those early days! I know I downed more than a few as a personal coping strategy!

As it turns out I was a swimmer and made my own classrooms into oases of calm, dealing with bad manners more than anything else initially. Movement between my classroom and other parts of the school involved moving through a tide of rowdy, noisy, aggressive and rude teenagers – it was horrid. My feeling in the classroom was that you couldn't really talk enthusiastically about metaphor in an atmosphere of grunting bad manners – therefore my students learned early that I would not tolerate displays of ignorance. I think my size helped me a lot and the fact that I was well used to contacting parents and speaking to them in a manner that they could accept, understand and believe – a number of my pupils went home to meet the kind of parental wrath that could well have landed the parents on the wrong side of social services and me along with them as a co-conspirator!

I signed up to an Educational Psychologists course at Salford University and met up with an old colleague, Mike Henstock who had taught at Saint Wilfrid's all those years ago. He was terrific and I ended up with more letters after my name. I became and Associate of the College of Preceptors. So I was now officially: Cert. Ed. Dist.; CTC; B. Ed. Hons 2:i; and ACP. I may have them inscribed on my tomb stone but only if it doesn't cost too much! The only use they have ever been has been when completing someone's passport application. Anyway back to the mad house.

Slowly but surely my students began to realise that if they displayed appropriate respect for me then that would be reciprocated. If they didn't it would be dealt with. Students I didn't teach also began to either give me a wide berth or began to approach me with respect and displays of good manners.

I had one or two early successes in the classroom. One young man in Year 11 was very weak. My aim was to try to ensure he got English and English Literature – early on I realised that to get much better than a double 'U' (unclassified) would be nigh on impossible. He was part of a mixed ability group where the most outstanding student was potentially a double 'A'. I had to get this group through their Shakespeare text as well as the bulk of their poetry and the novel – their previous teacher who had seized the opportunity to take early retirement on reorganisation had tactically avoided doing anything with the group that might have involved teaching or any form of hard work.

I'm going to call the young man in question Geoffrey Chaucer (Geoff for short) because his real name was the same as that of a very famous poet.

I always introduced 'Macbeth' to my seniors in the same way, "How would you like to read something with loads of sex in it?" – most of the girls and a few of the lads would put their hands up. "Something with loads of violence in it?" – the majority of the lads would put up their hands. "Something with the supernatural in it?" – a majority of the class would put their hands up. "Right we're doing Shakespeare's 'Macbeth' next!" – groans all round.

I began work on 'Macbeth' believing that if I could get the class through Shakespeare the rest of my work with them would be comparatively easy. After the initial battles, which I anticipated and expected (almost every class balks at the prospect of Shakespeare), they settled down and seemed to come to terms with the Bard. Geoff in particular appeared to have one of those moments of epiphany where his eyes and levels of understanding suddenly took off. Whatever I was doing ignited in him a desire to discover more of Shakespeare's work.

At the end of one particular lesson he came to me and his conversation went something like this:

Geoff: Sir, sir, sir, you know I work part time in the video shop? Well they had this video of 'Henry V' (he actually said 'V'.

Me: Yes Geoff I know it. I think there's a new version of it.

Geoff: Yes well I got this one with Lawr. Lawr. Lawrence Oliver in it and it was brilliant. What I wanted to ask you was whether it was better than the one with Kevin Brannigan in it, 'cos I've got that one out now?

Me: Well Geoff, the Lawrence Olivier version was made during the second world war so it emphasises the patriotic themes to encourage the war effort. I'm not sure about Kenneth Brannagh's version because I haven't seen it yet but I'm sure it will be very good and will emphasise themes with a relevance to today!

With that Geoff left me only to return several days later.

Geoff: Sir, sir, sir, I watched that 'Henry V' film with Kevin Brannigan in it and it was brilliant I think it was even better than the other one I watched. Have you seen 'Hamlet' with Mel Gibbons in it, 'cos I've got that out to watch now?

Me: No I haven't watched that yet Geoff but I heard it's very good. It's very different to 'Macbeth' and 'Henry V' you know. I believe Mel Gibson does a good job in it.

Geoff: Yeah I know but I thought the others were pretty good so I thought I'd give this one a twirl.

And give it a twirl he did reporting back that it was the best yet. I think he ended up with an 'F' and a 'G' and I know that when he left at the end of Year 11 he took an apprenticeship as a mechanic – he was a big hefty lad. I bumped into him about two years after he left and enquired how the apprenticeship was going.

Geoff: Oh I quit that after a year or so sir 'cos I hated it. I only did it 'cos me mam and dad wanted me to do it.

Me: So what are you doing now Geoff?

Geoff: Hairdressing sir, its brilliant, I always wanted to do it and now I am.

Its funny but whenever anyone asks me what my greatest successes were as a teacher Geoff is one of the first people who spring to my mind. I am proud that I must have done something partly right in inspiring him to take up the pursuit of film versions of Shakespeare – a young man who could barely read two lines without help! He had obviously listened when I suggested that if Shakespeare were around today he would be very much like Stephen Spielberg wanting to reach as big an audience as possible and giving the public what they wanted. Shakespeare was after all written to be performed and not just read and Geoff appeared to have bought into that. Yes I am very proud of that. He was a lovely lad as well – one of those who didn't need reminding that manners maketh the man or woman!

I found myself teaching a deal of English, Drama in dining rooms and some careers. Graham Smith was Head of Music and had been involved in selecting the Performing Arts (PA) course that was on offer – it was a horrible course that failed to engage the students or me. I set out to discover whether there might be a more appropriate syllabus for the type of students we were working with – it took me two or three years to opt out of that course and into a pure Drama course. It took so long because David Lack really wanted the Performing Arts course to take off – I basically said if that's what he wanted he should try teaching it himself! I believe it paid immediate dividends once we switched – that year the Year 11 students took both PA and Drama, the Drama results were better.

In the English team I met a lovely guy called John Simpson. John was an Oxbridge graduate who was dedicated to his classes but who did have some difficulties with discipline and on reorganisation discipline became a bigger not smaller problem. John and Graham were 'old timers' from the grammar school and they decided that as I had been thrust upon them as the titular Head of Drama I should continue the tradition of a school production!!!

The prospect filled me with dread. Although I had done plenty of performance work and had helped direct the odd sketch I had never taken responsibility for a full school production. I felt a bit like a sacrificial lamb and I also felt that John and Graham were setting me up for a fall – the loud mouthed new guy who really knows nothing! Our relationships did develop over the years by the way and I am proud to say that I was able to help John (as his Union rep. when he went through a particularly harrowing time some years later).

They convinced me that I had to keep the tradition alive. I wasn't easily convinced because I had witnessed very little talent in the so called PA group we had. I shopped around until I found something that looked easy (nothing by the way is easy about a school production) and settled on, Willy Russell's 'Our Day Out' – at first glance it looked like everything happened on board a bus – how hard could that be to direct? We began with auditions and assembled a motley crew of youngsters willing to give up some of their time to appear in a 'show' – all of them wanting to be top spot whether they had talent or not.

I soon discovered that Russell didn't give any advice on the position of people on the bus – it was a nightmare trying to work out where such and such a body should be. I'd make a decision as to where someone should be only to discover that they couldn't possibly be sat here if they were to do such and such a little later. Somehow I bluffed my way through, usually bullying uncooperative youngsters to do it the way I wanted it doing.

I was lucky in that the little girl chosen to play Carol developed wonderfully as we rehearsed and I knew would deliver a top performance. Mr Briggs was extremely willing but quite wooden and had to have almost everything demonstrated. Digga and Reilly played themselves and the girl playing Susan had a wonderful voice but was highly disruptive in that she wound up the others so much so that we spent a lot of time trying to appease the rest of the cast whilst trying to prevent her from sulking. Needless to say the staff proved the best attendees at rehearsals!

Somehow the show went on and was surpassingly successful. At the dress rehearsal I sacked the girl playing Susan and juggled the rest of the cast to cover the change and it worked. The cast were happier, I was happier and the show was good. The whole experience only added around twenty to thirty years to my life. What a learning curve

> *"The whole experience only added around twenty to thirty years to my life."*

Somehow I had made it through my first attempt to direct a show and despite times when I really didn't believe it would come together it did and it was generally thought to be very good. For me it was a baptism of fire but it did bring me much closer to John and Graham in terms of wavelength. They were already making suggestions for our next collaboration whilst I was still considering a hot bath and opening my veins! Careers was much more problematic. I had always been dubious about having careers lessons timetabled across a whole academic year. I'd had to listen to youngsters at Suthie complaining bitterly about how bored they were despite Val Spencer trying to make the lessons as interesting as possible. Now I was faced with the prospect of running a careers programme across Year 11. I needed help and it came in the form of one of the hardest working and most enthusiastic people it's ever been my pleasure to work with, Fiona Hilton. She acted as my mentor, adviser and support throughout the early years at QE. With her help I managed to get through my first year in charge and in the second year at QE I became confident enough, with her help and efficiency to pull me through, to devise something wonderful.

Fiona and I had talked a lot about equality and trying to get girls in particular to hold higher aspirations, as well as encouraging the lads to think outside the predictable box!

Our thinking and discussions eventually led us to put together something that I am still very proud of and that was a tremendous success.

We planned, organised and ran a full day for all senior students to take part: an Equality/Stereotyping Awareness Day. Fiona using her vast array of contacts invited twenty-two individuals from a wide range of careers to come and spend the day with our youngsters. The overriding feature had to be that the individuals concerned bucked the stereotypical image for their occupation. For example we had a male hairdresser, female police inspector, male ballroom dancer, female truck driver etc. etc.

The whole day went brilliantly, more thanks to Fiona than yours truly, but the morning was especially good. Each of our guests was invited to say a few words about themselves, their background, where they were from, their educational level and so on, but they were not to give any indication of their occupation. Following their personal input we sat them down on the stage facing the students who had been encouraged to take notes. Each individual was given a number and the students were given a sheet with twenty-two occupations listed. I acted as the MC and reintroduced each of our guests and invited the students to place their number against the occupation they believed they represented. The outcome was absolutely fantastic. The student body was in equal measures stunned and amazed at the disclosure of who was who. There were gasps as each person declared who they were. The eighteen year old ballroom dancer whom all the girls fancied created one of the biggest stirs because he also shook other perceptions that the boys in particular had about dancers in general!

The guests stayed for lunch and in the afternoon we split into small seminar groups and moved the students around in small groups chaperoned by staff to meet with our guests. I was present when one of our boys suggested that all male dancers must be 'You know, er, you know er', 'You mean homosexual?' suggested the young man in question who went on to add that he got into dancing at the age of about thirteen when he was just becoming aware of girls and that since then he had been all over the world dancing with some of the most beautiful girls you could hope to meet, wearing some very revealing outfits, and no he wasn't homosexual. It was a real eye-opener for the lads in particular and I was already anticipating large numbers declaring they wished to be ballroom dancers at their respective career interviews.

At the end of it all I basked in the success, which as I said was mostly due to Fiona's efficiency and contacts. David Lack was over the moon, it was terrific press and I don't think it did my stock in the school any harm. That venture led Fiona and me into doing a major project that we shared with all of the Rochdale secondary schools involving the production of an Equal Opportunities Photographic Teachers Pack. More success thanks to the most gifted careers professional I ever worked with. She went on to bigger and better things at Manchester University when the government started meddling with the careers service to make it cheaper and less effective!

David Lack must have thought me really difficult way back then because I never failed to remind him that I was a reluctant careers person and that if he wanted me to be more effective I would need to get involved in something the government was quite keen on then – work experience for teachers. My insistence on involvement resulted in me spending several two week periods experiencing life in another occupation. Fiona had introduced me to one of Whitbread's most senior women who arranged for me to spend a week at the Forest of Arden Hotel in the midlands (brilliant – a single room was £125 per night in 1991) and a week at a Trust House Hotel off the M62 (hard work). I later managed to wangle a two week slot with the Manchester Opera House which was producing 'Phantom of the Opera' (unbelievable), I arranged for the Phantom – Mark McKerricher (a Californian with a wonderful voice) to come into school to officially open the new drama studio and meet my drama students.

During my first year at QE I had the pleasure of organising and running two work experience placements for Year 11 and Year 10. Hard work but extremely rewarding especially as I got out to visit a large number of the youngsters who generally did really well – if they'd geared themselves up to making realistic choices. I recall one student who was placed at Carcraft (when Carcraft was on Water Street in Rochdale, opposite Robinsons Motor Cycles). I got a message late one morning that one of our students had fallen at the work place and could someone come out to see that he was okay. I went and arrived there just after lunch. It seems that he had climbed inside a car and fallen asleep and not noticed when they lifted the car six feet off the ground to work on the chassis. Waking abruptly and panicking that he might be in trouble he opened the car door and stepped out into thin air. He landed with a bump and caused the service manager to have major conniptions – I'm sure they saw some kind of law suit in the offing! By the time I got there they had already begun their staggered lunch. My lad was sent off to enjoy a long lunch where they hoped he'd stay out of bother. As he walked out of the garage he spotted another lad from QE who happened to be placed at Robinsons and he called out for him to wait for him as he started to run across the road straight into a passing car! He bumped off the car leaving the driver in a state of trauma, brushed himself off and continued on his way to the local chippy. All of this was waiting for me when I got to the garage. I eventually met up with the young man in question and discovered he was totally oblivious to all the commotion and was simply relieved that he wasn't getting into trouble for falling asleep in the car. There wasn't a mark on him. I gave strong reassurances to the service manager, begging him to let the lad finish his experience with them and suggested that where there was no sense there was no feeling. I pointed out that the lad appeared to have forgotten about falling from the car and was just concerned that he wasn't in any trouble. I felt sure they'd hear no more about it. They didn't.

David Lack, I think, was beginning to see me as some kind of miracle worker. Our press releases for the show, the Careers Day, and the work experience painted the new school in a very positive light which kind of balanced out the persistent complaints from those who lived literally within throwing distance of the school! The hatred on the faces of those who lived close to the school is hard to describe and they watched every morning and afternoon as the school filled and emptied, lodging complaint after complaint against the manner in which our students conducted themselves. I know that a lot of the staff would have welcomed a return to the good old days of thrashing your wards into submission. The bus drivers didn't help matters on the many occasions that they either refused to pick up or drop off at the school or refused a student entry on to their bus! They were interesting days!

By the time I started my second year at QE I had decided to take the bull by the horns so to speak and having read that the rights to "Grease" were to be made available to public performance I decided that I would have a shot at that. I was outraged when I realised we had to pay heftily for the pleasure of spending three months of our lives working with difficult and occasionally uncooperative young people to put the show on.

I worked very hard on the show. First I spent time selecting who would play Danny and managed to convince one of my English students to give it a go. Bill Mc was one of the most significant young men in the school. He was a terrific footballer who went on to play professionally and had a group of admiring tough guys who followed him in everything. I knew if I could get him on board he would bring another half dozen very significant lads with him, which he did. The fact that he could barely sing a note didn't matter a jot! I teamed him up with a beautiful singer called Sally who took on the role of Sandy.

Once again the rehearsal period was a fraught time. Bill had to juggle his school and town team football appearances with rehearsals which really meant I worked around him. A couple of our lady teachers Sue MacLoed and others worked on the dances (one area I never came to terms with) and we put together a pretty good cast. I have a vague recollection that in total the cast numbered 125 when they were all on stage – I thought that will guarantee good box office!

Again we were working with some youngsters who seemed to thrive on winding the others up and didn't appear happy if they hadn't reduced someone to tears by the end of a rehearsal! Rizzo was very volatile and another of the Pink Ladies drove me to distraction. Kenickie although probably the best of our male singers and dancers was very touchy and I remember he didn't arrive for our matinee performance on the Saturday until half way through the intermission and then acted as if he was doing us a big favour. As his big number (Greased Lightning, I'd sung the song and read in his lines) had already been on I told him to sit out the rest of the performance and that he better find another school if he attempted to leave the school before the evening performance.

It was a fantastic success. Our parents were blown away and once again the praise and salutations were music to my ears. It made my next decision much easier.

At some point during year two David Lack asked me to accompany him to the old Hollin site where considerable work was being done. The old part of the school was being refurbished and a new purpose built Performing Arts extension which included a Drama Studio and a Dance Studio was almost complete. David took me into the building site that was to be the drama studio and explained where everything was going. He went on to explain that he had a budget of several thousand pounds to set the place up and he needed someone to sort out the studio. He went on to talk about his dream for the school which saw Performing Arts at its centre. Now as I had become somewhat disillusioned with the set up in English at QE this opportunity looked to be gold plated. I had the chance to set up a kingdom within a kingdom. I made it clear that he must never expect me to take on dance as a responsibility but that if he agreed to that I would willingly take on Drama. By this time I'd found the ideal course for our youngsters so everything was beginning to look rosy.

I spent a lot of time that summer in the school setting up the studio and even if I do say so myself I think I did an excellent job. I mastered skills like lighting, sound, video recording and an array of other skills that would be useful. I began work on schemes of work for every year group, taking advice where I could and interpreting it for application at QE. The new block would have me working very closely with Graham Smith, Celia Davies (who like me had been redeployed from Suthie) and Brian Shaw who had worked at the old Hollin and before that Langley High School. I got to know and appreciate Celia much better at QE than I ever did at Suthie and Brian was a soul mate – it helped that he was deeply interested in Native American History, which is one of my passions.

I could spend a great deal of time working systematically through productions but I don't intend doing that. Although I will mention a few.

My first major production on the new site was "The Wizard of Oz" which remains one of the productions I enjoyed most and was technically, for me, one of the hardest to complete. There was no stage at the new QE so I had to devise a set in the round. Brian designed three sets of flats that were absolutely brilliant and this helped me a great deal to see how everything would and could work. On top of the staging and directing I had to learn how to operate the ultramodern lighting console, direct the lights and programme them for the production – ouch! Another major learning curve. Graham was in his element because the numbers are so well known and loved. We had already more or less selected the cast by running a 'Wizard' break at Cragg Vale where we had two teams of twenty students rehearse and present a 30 minute version of the show each. The residential was terrific and we ended up with a largely terrific team of youngsters.

Obviously back at school we held auditions, just in case someone with superior talent hadn't been on the residential. Students were given a short piece of dialogue to learn and asked to rehearse a song from the show. One young man turned up and not only had he not bothered to learn the few short lines but he had a voice to kill for and I mean that you would want to kill him if he tried to sing in your presence – he was appalling. At the end of his presentation (he hadn't rehearsed a song and appeared to be chronically tone deaf) I thanked him and said if he didn't get the part he had auditioned for (he'd tried out for the Tin Man) would he accept another role. This was a stock statement at the end of each audition and a means of measuring commitment to the show rather than the role. His response left me speechless for quite a while after he'd left the studio. He said, *"If I don't get the Tin Man I'd probably do the Scarecrow or the Lion, but not the Wizard"*. His arrogance stunned me – I remember thinking had he ever heard what he sounded like when he opened his mouth to sing. I must admit I've said the same thing during early auditions for 'X Factor'.

The show was an enormous success and I personally believe it was probably the best musical I did whilst at QE. It certainly gave me the greatest satisfaction although once again we had one or two students who seemed to wallow in the wind up and weren't happy unless they were upsetting the rest of the cast. I informed the girl who played the Lion (she was very talented and perfect for the role) that she should never consider being in one of my shows again unless she radically changed her ways.

The sequence of the shows I worked on is lost to me somewhat but I do recall that the young lady who played the Lion also auditioned for "Bugsy Malone" when I did that and hers was by far the best audition for Tallulah. Graham and I argued about the role for a long while and in the end I suggested a compromise. One of the other girls had delivered a fairly good audition but her nerves had let her down – I knew she was a cracking dancer from our Christmas Concerts (which were a terrific opportunity to vet the talent coming through the school). I suggested that we offer them both the role and that they would perform on alternate nights, joining the chorus line on the nights they weren't Tallulah. I explained to our ex Lion that the other girl would be given the role for the run of the production if she stepped out of line at any point during rehearsals. It worked and both delivered superb Tallulah's.

The cast of 'Bugsy' was one of the best I ever worked with because the principal roles were largely made up of the class to die for.

I think every teacher gets at least one class in their life time, if they are lucky, which is absolutely outstanding. I had mine the year I did 'Bugsy'. I had been delivering excellent results for the school from once we moved on to the pure Drama course and I think those results encouraged some real high fliers to opt for drama that year. Out of a mixed ability class of twenty-one, nineteen passed with 'C' or better; eight had 'A' grades and four of them were 'A*'. I can truly say that I never enjoyed going to work as much as I did that year – it was one of the great pleasures of my life – every lesson felt like fun and our relationship was outstanding. Some of those students are still in contact with me and I am proud now to acknowledge them as friends.

During the time they were in Year 10 I put on "See How they Run" a farce set during WW2. I liked to alternate between a straight play and a musical – the straight pays were much less demanding in terms of time. Traditionally youngsters handle farce badly but these youngsters lapped it up and delivered a wonderful interpretation of the play, especially my two leads: Carl D and Mary R. Mary was in Year 11 and she was an outstanding student in her own right, certainly in her class.

I'm not sure but I may have begun my Primary School Shakespeare around this time. In one of my mad moments I thought it would be lovely to introduce our feeder primary schools to Shakespeare, an abridged version of course. With the Year 10 group I had - I believed anything was possible.

Over several years we did, 'A Midsummer Night's Dream' (twice), 'The Tempest', 'Macbeth', and 'The Twelfth Night'. Each play lasted between thirty and forty minutes and they were presented in the round. We only ever used the Bard's words but out of necessity they were much abbreviated. I think they were appreciated by the primaries and in promoting the school to youngsters and parents. I won't say it was always a very pleasant experience with all of the classes I took out on the road – some worked hard against the idea of tackling Shakespeare but they always delivered.

I did 'Grease' a second time but didn't enjoy the experience as much the second time around. 'Little Shop of Horrors' and 'The Dracula Spectacula' were big hits with our parents although I didn't enjoy the music or story lines too much. I will mention a young man who appeared in 'Dracula', Adam H.

Adam had come to us from Boarshaw Primary School. I had been pals with his Uncle Dennis year's earlier on Langley. Adam was a lovely lad but not particularly academic although his comic timing was incredible. He could have the whole class in stitches, including me, for just about as long as he wanted but he had very little confidence in his ability to do anything other than ad-lib or improvisation. I needed an Igor, Count Dracula's side-kick and began to work on Adam – I knew he'd be perfect for the role.

At first I asked him if he would try out for the pilot, he was terrified because he didn't think he could learn the lines. I pointed out that he knew several popular songs and that learning lines and lyrics would be little different. He said he'd give it a go and then turned up for his audition absolutely word perfect. I then pointed out that I didn't have a driver for the coach and felt he'd be perfect. The same scenario followed. So he was the pilot and the coach driver, then I dropped the bombshell – I'd have to drop the show because I didn't have an Igor. After much persuasion and begging he agreed to try it and again he came to the first rehearsal absolutely word perfect. He was the star of the show which we performed at the old Hopwood Hall theatre. It's the only show that I felt totally relaxed with when watching because Adam had me helpless laughing at ad-libs we hadn't rehearsed but which worked beautifully. He was a real natural when it came to comedy.

He once confided to me that his Head Teacher at Boarshaw once told him he'd amount to nothing and I remember being shocked and outraged. I couldn't believe that anyone working with young people could say something so damaging to a young spirit. I worked very hard on his self-confidence and he definitely grew in stature in his last two years. I pulled a few strings with pals who worked at Hopwood to get him a place in their Performing Arts set up – we knew that despite him getting a 'B' in Drama his grades would never get him onto the BTEC course. They took him on because they recognised his potential and accepted my recommendation. They ensured he got the kind of intensive support that enabled him to qualify for the course in his second year at the college. I saw him in 'The Crucible' and he was excellent.

During his third and final year his tutors asked if they could bring in a group to perform an assessment piece in front of an audience. It was absolutely superb. Adam played a Dutch guy with an accent better than many of the Dutch people it's been my pleasure to meet. After the performance he hung around to speak with me. He is one of very few students who ever reduced me to tears.

I shall never forget the conversation. First he thanked me for all I had done for him and for having faith in him. He then said something that choked me. He said, "I just wanted to tell you sir that I am the first person in the history of my family to go to University!" I am filling up just writing about it now! Earlier I mentioned Geoffrey Chaucer and said that he is one of the students who spring to mind when I am asked about my successes as a teacher – if Geoff is the first then Adam is the second. I was proud of him then and I remain very proud of him today.

In parallel with the work we were doing in class and for the Christmas Concerts and shows or plays I also pushed David Lack to permit involvement in the Rochdale Festival where we had years of tremendous success. By this time I was supported by a person who became a good friend of mine Neil Davenport.

Neil first turned up as part of the Fickle Theatre group. Mark Johnson was another member of the group and Mark remains a great friend of mine and I see him fairly regularly. I booked them to do something at the new site once we were in and I got talking to Neil and Mark about the possibility of doing some paid support work. David Lack had given me permission to approach someone to support some of the work I was doing in Drama and more especially to introduce a bit of dance to the curriculum. It turned out Neil was quite skilled in terms of choreography. I managed to get him a couple of days a week and he contributed greatly to the continued success of the department. As a graduate in the performing arts he was invaluable to me. I treated our relationship very much as one in which I acted as his mentor. I immediately saw his potential for teaching and encouraged him to go for his PGCE pointing out that he would command more in terms of salary if he had that. I am very pleased to say he followed my advice and became a qualified teacher, my only regret is that once qualified he took off to Australia – my fault I'm afraid.

Neil had been with me a year or so when I heard that we had an Australian girl on supply in the school. I think she was doing PE or something. I saw Neil at break and told him we had an Aussie on site and that her name was 'Kylie', which I thought amusing because of Kylie Minogue and Neighbours. I informed him that her main subject was dance and that she'd expressed a wish to look at the drama and dance studios. I told him I was delegating the responsibility for looking after her to him.

Neil was a very attractive young man and it seems the two hit it off so famously that they eventually married. I was instrumental in bringing them together and Neil asked for my advice on proposing to her. I knew they were scheduled to go up in a hot air balloon and so suggested that once above the Lake District the time would be as right as ever and if she said no he could always throw her out! For some reason he couldn't bring himself to propose once they were up there and so it fell to a trip to Venice when he hid the ring in such a way that it popped up at the appropriate time and she said 'Yes' – I'm not sure she could have said anything else by that time. England's loss is Australia's gain.

By far Neil's most impressive work were two things he did whilst supporting me. He did a mini-production of Macbeth that had moments of real class – his ability to see an image and incorporate it into a production was excellent and he did a thirty minute dance version of 'Scrooge' which was truly breathtaking and stole the show at one of our Christmas Concerts. Those concerts were always something special and I was very proud of what was achieved by people like Neil and all those other staff who supported the productions so unstintingly.

During our first year on the new site I tried to get David Lack to explore how the new GNVQ (General National Vocational Qualification) might be a Godsend to a school like ours but his feeling was that with the new school and other government initiatives the staff had enough on their plates. He did give me permission to seek qualifications to run the new award which I did becoming an Assessor and later Verifier. I managed to convince people like Celia Davies and one or two others to gain the Assessor qualification as well so that when I went back to David he agreed and so we launched Health and Social Care and Travel and Tourism at Level 1 (worth 4 GCSE's at grade "D"). I delivered the Health and Social Care initially. In retrospect I think that although we had some success with the award it was always heavy on time and short on substance and understanding. It was one of those short lived educational wonder qualifications designed to sort out once and for all the differential between the academic and vocational, it didn't work.

David Lack retired following a bout of poor health – he'd already had a quadruple bypass. Before he left we had our first Ofsted Inspection and for some reason I was one of a few members of staff who were recognised by the Inspectors as an exceptional teacher – it did my morale a great deal of good. I still have the citation which I treasure, and my de-brief was again one of those very few occasions when I was reduced to tears. For the first time in my teaching career someone sat me down with the Head and described why they thought I was an exceptional teacher. It was very humbling but also very welcome; I was approaching 50 at the time! Story of my life!

I believe I stated that 'Wizard' was my most satisfying production but there is another that I am unbelievably proud of because it's one of the stories that I loved as a child and if you can't indulge yourself sometimes then life isn't worth living. I'm referring to 'Toad of Toad Hall', based on the wonderful 'Wind in the Willows'.

If 'Wizard' was my favourite show then 'Toad' was my favourite stage play. For me it was a labour of love and I was lucky enough to put together a very fine cast. Right from the start I had a very clear vision of how it would work, even down to creating the illusion of a river using silver paper and lighting devices such as gobos! I was beginning to matriculate as a drama teacher, even coming to terms with the terms!

The story of 'Toad' is so beautiful and it was a real joy to work on it. Again the majority of the main roles were taken by members of that year's GCSE drama students, another terrific class. I really was blessed in some of the students who opted for Drama because elsewhere the school was struggling in relation to general behaviour and discipline. My classes appeared keen to attend and keen to get involved; lapping up the challenges I threw at them which is not to say I didn't face the odd challenge myself.

The young man I gave the role of Badger (a crucial role in the production) whom I had great confidence in decided that the night before we went into production was time enough to learn his lines!!!!

That I didn't drown him in our silver foil river is a tribute to my patience although he was threatened with a much worse end than that! Anthony E knows who I am talking about! We brought the primaries into school to see the production and it was excellent. I was very proud of the way it turned out.

I left an enormous number of fabulous photographs at QE when I eventually left in 2005, I hope they were distributed to students or are kept as an archive somewhere.

David Lack had come to the end at QE and we now faced a period of uncertainty. I had come to respect and appreciate David because his heart was in the right place. He always wanted the very best for his students and whenever I went to him a with a hair brained scheme requiring expenditure he always appeared to find a way to fund it. However when he left us the authority suddenly became conscious of the massive overspend and decided to claw back the money David had spent trying to compete on a level playing field with other schools in the authority. Times of sever austerity were upon us.

Ed Collins, a deputy from Oulder Hill, served as our acting Head, until Tony Peckham was appointed. Although I didn't know Ed he had heard a great deal about me from the likes of Mervyn Lee who had joined Oulder Hill on reorganisation. He appeared to respect me and I respected him but the school was in trouble and sinking deeper all the time.

Tony Peckham came to us from Whitehaven (I think) and he was a real nice guy but for some reason our student body chose his start as a period of dire unrest. On his very first day the fire alarm was set off at least fifteen times before the system was disconnected! Like Mrs. Hindley the feeling of staff was that Tony would have made a brilliant Head of a grammar school – although I feel that he was never given any kind of chance by either the disgruntled staff or the increasingly barbaric students. It must have felt like he'd entered some surreal world designed around Bedlam when he took over the reins. A snap Ofsted decided the school needed to go into Special Measures and Tony was given a very short time to take his leave.

I recall my last conversation with him in his office. He was a fine teacher and he'd been treated abysmally by his new authority. He'd taken on a difficult school at the best of times and an impossible school at the moment. He was given little or no support that I am aware of – but he was given a massively reduced budget (pay back the deficit was all the authority appeared to care about) and told to get on with it. Staff already near breaking point suddenly found that the budget wouldn't run to hiring supply teachers and cover had to be carried out in house, practically all staff training that required staff attendance outside school was suspended and departments were expected to deliver better results with huge cuts to their budgets!

Things had already reached an impasse before the damning Ofsted report and the unions (I was the rep for the National Association of Schoolmasters and Union of Women Teachers) balloted for a work to rule. The National Union of Teachers (NUT) worded their ballot slightly differently to NASUWT which caused a great deal of grief when the results came in. Both unions had agreed to slightly different things which meant that NUT members would cover substantially less than NASUWT. It was a bitter, bitter time at school. Poor old Tony was piggy in the middle. Terry Piggott the chair of education for Rochdale came into school and effectively tried to bully the staff into accepting conditions that were unacceptable and vaguely couching his words in threats to our jobs. The whole staff sat and listened to the dark picture he was painting and no one felt they could stand up against him. Eventually I could take no more and started by pointing out that the majority of our staff was quite young and very frightened of opening their mouths for fear of blotting their copy book with him but that as an old lag with no ambitions to move into senior management I would explain to him how we felt. I then spoke quite strongly about staff feelings and how his veiled threats were designed not to get the school back on track but would actually result in total breakdown because people couldn't take anymore. If looks could kill I would undoubtedly be dead and buried now. Fair play to Tony Peckham he then came in and sided quite clearly on the side of his staff. Piggott was furious and I honestly thought that this marked the end of my career, it was actually the end of Tony's. When I met Piggott a year later with the Union Secretary at a presentation, he was extremely friendly and had even remembered my name enquiring how I was doing. Don't be afraid to stand up for yourself I thought!

Anyway Tony Peckham had me in his office the day before we finished for Christmas 2001. He looked pale and appeared to be in shock. He explained that he had been given only so long (I think 24 hours) to leave the school. It made me wonder whether Ofsted ever arrived at a school with a pre-arranged agenda – getting rid of the Head! I was shocked and upset for the man. It seemed more than a shitty way to treat a good professional who had given his life to education.

He'd actually called me into his office to finalise something he had been asking me to do for some time. One of our most difficult year groups was Year 8, they were seriously off the wall and had some extremely nasty intelligent youngsters in there who were absolutely determined to maintain the state of chaos the school had descended into. He had been working on me and asking me to take them on. I'd already laid out my conditions – I wanted total support on any decisions I made and wanted to consult all of the parents of the named most difficult and objectionable students in the year group. He agreed and so I agreed to take them on after Christmas. As I was about to leave his office he thanked me and told me that he'd be giving me an extra point, which meant more money.

Tony left under a cloud and to the disbelief of the staff. I was pleased to hear a year or two later that he had found his feet again and was working somewhere in Yorkshire and probably doing a brilliant job.

My mother died in Ireland just before I returned to school and following her funeral I came down with a dose that turned into pneumonia. My return to school was delayed by two full weeks, a good start with a new acting Head and a new role!

I believe the new acting head was called Ron Dixon and he was definitely one of the finest heads it was ever my pleasure to work under. I know he was from Stockport and he was considered a super head although he was only with us for two terms.

He welcomed me to the school and asked me to outline what I intended doing and he gave me his full and unconditional support. I summoned forty parents into school. The staff had already identified the ring leaders and most difficult youngsters. I was told by staff that very few of them would turn up but with the Heads support I advised the parents that if they didn't attend the meeting their son/daughter might well be sent home until such time as I could fit them in for a private meeting. All but one parent turned up and I saw them before the start of school the next day.

The no nonsense and zero tolerance approach with these selected 40 youngsters made all the difference and before long the staff had started to win the school back from the brink of the abyss.

I mentioned the school had been placed in Special Measures just before Tony Peckham was so poorly treated and I was disgusted that Celia and I had to jump through the same hoops as everyone else in the school despite our two departments: Drama and Art being the only departments to pass the inspection. There were no exceptions to the draconian measures that apply to a school in these circumstances so as a staff we all faced a massively increased paper workload. Lesson plans submitted in triplicate, schemes of work spelling out the obvious, attendance at a plethora of meetings and courses – all designed to put the average member of staff into an early grave and little of it to do with actually handling disruptive and wilful youngsters.

I struggled on like everyone else and tried to keep a clean sheet. The funny thing is that because we were in special measures money was suddenly no object – why had it been so important before? I trained during this period to become the Lead Behaviour Specialist which I duly became and started cascading strategies and methodologies to staff, including some of the senior staff but I was entering a dark phase at QE. First Jim Bleakley was appointed acting Head and for whatever reasons he decided he didn't like me. I might have had something to do with that. At an early staff meeting he presented himself as a saviour fresh from turning around another failing school in the authority. He actually used the phrase 'little

Beirut' in relation to what Suthie was like when he was reorganised there – I walked out of the meeting. I wasn't going to listen to someone telling me that the school I had enjoyed teaching at for fourteen years was like Beirut. My relationship with Bleakley was doomed from that point on. He didn't last long and he certainly didn't turn the school around despite his high blown claims to have the formula.

He was replaced by Eric Jackson who definitely didn't like me. He was appointed to the Headship on a massive salary and immediately revealed that his management style was and would be dictatorial. He was a systems man and I blotted my copy book with him on his first day in charge.

Letters had gone out to parents advising them that a policy of zero tolerance was to be observed at the school. As our students arrived on that first day in September I found myself in the company of Wendy Robinson (also ex Suthie) and opined to her that we'd soon see what the new man was made of when he came into contact with the usual suspects who were arriving without complete uniform on. Jackson overheard my comment and later that morning sat me down and basically sealed our relationship.

My last year or so at the school was not a happy time for me. I felt I'd proved myself time and time again but no matter what I had done in the past it counted for nothing in the present. Luckily there was something bubbling away in the background that I was unaware of and which proved my salvation.

23. Bye, bye Baby.

My mother's sister Mairead (Margaret in English – pronounced Mi-raed in the Gaelic) was the youngest of seven. She had three brothers – Park (Patrick), Stephen and Mark; and three sisters – Julia, Norah, and Mary Ellen my mother). She was born in 1923 and because she was the youngest in the family, she became known as Baby (naming the youngest Baby was quite common in Ireland).

The three eldest: Park, Julia and Norah all emigrated to the United States before 1929. There were previous generations of the family who had made the journey before them and who made her older brother and sisters' welcome. Stephen headed for England as did my mother. Mark took over the running of the small farm from his father Mark, who died quite young in the early 1930's. Babe (Aunt Mairead) remained on the home place and was the only one of the brothers and sisters to have the opportunity to finish her schooling. She won a scholarship to the convent in Tuam and from there she won another scholarship that took her to a teacher training college in Dublin. Babe became a teacher – a profession that now appears to run in the family.

My earliest memories of Babe were when I was a youngster going home on holidays raising holy murder with my cousins Padraic and Rita. Padraic and Rita were a tad younger than me and generally very well behaved and obedient – until the brat from England arrived! I am sure they received many lectures on what would happen to them if they stepped too far out of line whilst I was at home. This did not stop them from joining in some of my crazier adventures: eavesdropping at Jim Mahon's the local smithy where all the men of the village used to congregate for men's talk (gossip); losing all the nails on one hand through rolling inside barrels on the street outside the house; throwing objects through neighbours windows; experimenting with cigarettes; and all manner of wicked activities like scrumping from the Maguires orchard.

I recall one incident involving Baby, who in those days always appeared cross to me.

My brother grew up on the land, having been evacuated there during the war and staying on when the war ended (I thought that this was unique until quite recently when I discovered it was actually quite commonplace). Padraic, Rita and the others treated him as their brother – in fact I do recall having a row with Padraic over whose brother he was. On this occasion it didn't matter whose brother he was – he was in trouble!

My sister Patsy had an invisible friend whom she called Joey. Joey went everywhere with her. She included him in everything – he was obviously better company than her young, curly blonde troublesome baby sibling! She even demanded that an extra place be set for him at the table and ministered to him during meals. I was only a child at the time but reports suggest that Tony found this highly amusing and used to tease her about Joey regularly. His teasing would regularly result in Pat's tears and Tony would find himself in the dog house.

On one particular day it seems Tony took his revenge because he announced to Patsy that he had kidnapped and buried Joey and he wouldn't tell her where, even if she tortured him!

I can imagine the uproar that followed. Patsy was mortified. Tony realised immediately that he would be in very serious trouble and made himself scarce. Screams and agonised tears alerted the adults to Patsy's heartbreak. Through huge sobs she informed them of the heinous kidnapping and internment of the innocent and beloved Joey.

Tony was sought high and low. The screams of my sister motivated the adults to a frantic search of out buildings, fields and haystacks to see if they could find the guilty party. Babe was the one who found him and brought him back to the rough justice of the gathered adults who were attempting to pacify a screaming Patsy. Tony's arrival turned her sobs into howls of indignant fury – "Kill him", she screamed or it may have been, "I'll kill him". Tony was quite nervous by this time.

Dad, who as always tried the peaceful and calm approach first asked, "Where did you bury him son?" Tony looked at him askance. Did he really hear dad right? He was being asked where he had buried an invisible friend of my sister's! I think it was at that moment that Tony realised his goose was cooked!

He led them all up onto what we called the garden but what was actually a neatly tended field in which the hay stack stood and various farm implements that were under cover.

"Here", announced Tony, "I buried him here." He indicated a neat and obviously virginal piece of ground.

"Good lad," said dad, and to Pat he said, "we'll soon have little Joey back with you." Patsy sniffed hugely and continued her inconsolable sobbing. Mark brought the shovels and they dug. And they dug. And they dug. Soon a great excavation had opened up. The digging was sporadically stopped whilst Patsy was questioned as to whether they had reached Joey or not. Joey had become elusive.

"Are you sure it's here you buried Joey?" dad pleaded with Tony. It was he said, so they dug some more. "Do you see him yet Patsy?" Patsy didn't see him. At some point as the hole took on the appearance of a grave Tony eventually admitted under ferocious questioning from Babe, mum and Kitty that he might have buried Joey somewhere else. "Show us," was the cry as they marched poor Tony off to identify possible burial sites. Six or seven large holes later, Joey was still interred. In fact Joey remains interred to this day. He was never found. Patsy remained inconsolable for days but eventually succumbed to the delights of being in the company of Babe and Eileen. Tony remained in the dog house for the foreseeable future.

Babe had the knack of getting to the truth with all of us kids; young or old!

For me she was part of the fabric of the home place, just as much as Uncle Mark, John Marten Mongan or my cousins were.

Then at the age of thirty-six she married an older guy called Joe McLoughlin who had 110 acres in County Galway. Her new home was in the district of Lehurick which was part of the township of Kilkerrin close by the larger town of Glenamaddy. Her marriage, to me, an occasional visitor to Ireland, was a surprise - I found it hard to imagine Baby married and living elsewhere, I had thought she was a spinster.

She settled quickly to the rhythms of married life. Moved schools from Cloonfad to somewhere closer to her new home and eventually moved onto the National school in Kilkerrin itself where she taught for many happy years.

In later years her husband Joe suffered with emphysema and he eventually died of a heart attack, driving his new tractor in one of the fields close to the house. Babe had been his wife for 26 years and for the next 26 years she lived as his widow remaining in the house up until the last years of her life.

My wife Sandra and I had the pleasure of visiting with Babe often and she came over to us on several occasions. She was a lovely lady although sorely tested by my mother!

When Joe died my mother was living at the home place in a mobile home. At first her return home had seemed like a good idea and everything had gone O.K. for a year or two but then problems began.

My mother was one of those women who, wherever she was, she had to be the dominant female. Kit, Uncle Mark's wife, was a powerful and dominant character in her own right and wouldn't roll over and let my mum displace her in her own home. Uncle Mark and

I had many discussions about why mum was the way she was – but never reached any real conclusions.

When baby's husband Joe died mum saw another opportunity – I have no doubt she had dreams of inheriting Joe's land and home or of dominating Babe and lording it over Lehurick. Within the year she had moved in with Babe and once again for the first few years' life seemed grand until the pair of them found it impossible to live together and Babe insisted on a parting of the ways.

The time my mother was at Babe's coincided with me marrying Sandra (Sandy). In 1987 we married in Gretna Green and with my son Neall and Sandy's youngest daughter Lisa we travelled from Stranraer to Larne and made our way to Lehurick. We had a lovely honeymoon with the two matriarchs. Neall and Lisa were camping in Babe's garden (perfectly safely by the way). I remember Babe and mum pulling me aside and very seriously questioning whether the two young ones should be camping. "Why don't you put the tents up in the bathroom?" suggested Baby, "and let them sleep in there!"

That same year, mum had sought to air the bedding in the room where we stayed and had nearly burnt the house down when the bedding caught fire. Our room, in Baby's quirky three bed-roomed house, was marked with a soot line around the walls and we slept with the smell of the recent fire burning into our nostrils! Some honeymoon. I'm not sure what Sandy made of the family she had just married into!

Mum, as I mentioned, eventually moved out of Babe's and settled in Glenamaddy. Babe continued to rattle about in the draughty pile that was Lehurick.

Sandy and I visited Ireland often in those years and Babe always made us most welcome despite the fall out with mum. In fact they did bury the hatchet (thankfully not in each other's skulls) and we had many days out with the pair of them.

Out of the blue Babe asked me if I would accompany her to America in 1993 to visit with her only surviving American sister, Norah. "Does a bear shite in the woods?" I heard myself muttering before agreeing wholeheartedly to the proposal. God bless Sandy because she encouraged me to go.

We flew to the States from Shannon and met my cousin Norah (Noreen) and her husband Joe, whom we were to stay with, at Kennedy airport. They lived in New York State in a small town called Tuckahoe. Now Noreen lived in a two family home which at that time she shared with her sister (my cousin) Mary Anne and her husband Frankie. Babe was given a room off the hallway in Mary Anne's house and I had the run of the basement which had its own bathroom, TV and all mod cons! I was deliriously happy.

We had the most wonderful time together sampling and visiting the delights of New York, Connecticut, Manhattan and a hundred other places including the then magnificent twin towers. I had long harboured dreams of visiting the States.

The house was beautiful. Just what I had imagined an American home to be – having grown up on a diet of "Mr Ed", "I love Genie", "Bewitched", "The Walton's", and countless other shows it lived up to my expectations a thousand fold.

Everything was terrific. I loved every moment. Frankie took me out for a spin and bought me the hottest "dog" I have ever had and Joe gave me a stretch limo tour Manhattan by night and by day! Wow!

The only recurring hiccough was that Frankie regularly forgot to engage the house alarm when he went out. Almost every time Frankie was left in charge of the house he forgot to engage the alarm as he left! I heard him being reminded of his responsibility several times.

On one particular early afternoon Noreen and Mary Anne went off to the beauty parlour for a makeover. Joe, who was a service manager at two Lincoln dealerships, was working. Babe and I were left in Frankie's care.

Frankie decided to take his new car for a wash and polish – he lavished love on that car! He didn't mention to Babe and me that he was going out. She was napping in her room on the ground floor whilst I was flicking through the channels on the cable TV in the basement.

I slowly became aware of a noise. A repetitive noise was coming from upstairs somewhere. I mounted the steps to the ground floor and as I climbed the noise got louder and louder. I opened the door to the hallway and realised it was the house alarm blazing through the house.

"Babe," I shouted, "Frankie?" There was no response. I walked across to Babe's room and knocked on the door, no reply. I tried the door, it was locked! "Babe? Frankie?" I called edging towards hysteria. The alarm was deafening. Then the phone started ringing. I went to it. I stared at it. Was it my place to pick it up? What will I say to whoever's at the end of the phone? I decided not to pick it up. The phone was in Mary Anne's kitchen off the hallway. I made my way back to the hall.

"Babe? Frankie?" No answer. Both of them must have gone out, forgetting I was alone in the house. Babe's door was still locked. I saw some movement outside on the street. A police car had just pulled up outside the house. I went to the front door and opened it. The long front lawn was divided by a concrete path to the steps leading up to the front door. I stepped out onto the stoop. A police officer stepped out of the passenger side of the vehicle nearest to me, whilst a second officer was climbing out of the driver's side. It was then I did what you should never do when facing American cops – I slapped my right hand onto my chest in a melodramatic gesture to indicate my relief at their arrival. I was thinking, "Boy, am I glad to see you." Quick as a flash the cop nearest to me moved to place the vehicle between him and me whilst drawing his service revolver!

"Keep your hands where we can see 'em," he snapped, whilst levelling his pistol at me. Both officers had their guns pointed in my general direction! Oh me!

I immediately threw my hands into the air and felt extremely vulnerable and not a little frightened. The two officers came from around the vehicle and moved towards me, one holstered his piece as he walked, and the other carried it by his side.

"You live here?" asked a particularly young and very well built officer.

"No, err no I'm on holiday," I managed to stutter.

"Where's the owner of the property?" the same officer enquired whilst his older and more brutal looking colleague appraised me with all seeing and knowing eyes.

This is where things started to go just a tad pear shaped for me. I realised how little I knew about the situation I was in and how stupid I was going to sound. My ignorance was appalling and when coupled with the growing fear I felt I found myself jabbering.

"Who is and where is the owner of the property?" he barked at me before I could get my thoughts in order.

"I'm err, not sure," I muttered, "it's a two family home. Err Joe Rossi is one and . . . . ." If my life had depended upon it, which in some ways it felt like it did, I could not have told them Frankie's name at that point; which is rather ironic because his name is Polici! "And err . . . ., my err cousin Mary Anne is married to Frankie but I can't remember their second name," I lamely announced.

The two cops exchanged a glance that said, "Likely story. As if you wouldn't know the names of the people you're staying with!"

The younger one looked me over; I was wearing shirt, pants and flip-flops, "What's your name fella?"

"Err," (I never say err), "Ramsbottom sir, Brendan Ramsbottom"

"O.K. Mr. Ramsbottom," he said in a manner that suggested he knew that this was an alias, "would you please show us into the house?"

This felt a little easier. "Of course," I said and turned to return to the house.

"Slowly," the older cop insisted. He was still holding his pistol by his side. I moved slowly to the steps and up them, the younger of the two closely shadowing me.

We entered the house.

I stood facing the two officers in the large hallway. "Is there anyone else in the house sir?" asked the younger of the two. He managed to make the "sir" sound kind of insulting.

Things were going from bad to worse.

"My aunt Bab . . . ., I mean my Aunt Mairead , I mean Margaret. At least I thought she was here. In that room." I pointed to the little room off the hall. "And Frankie . . . . (I still couldn't recall his name) I thought Frankie was home."

The older cop tried Babe's door, turned and shook his head to his partner.

"You got any ID buddy?" asked the senior cop.

"Err (here I go again). I have my passport if that's any good?"

"Well let's see it," he demanded.

"It's err, it's in the basement," I almost said cellar!

"Lead on fella," he prompted.

I took the older officer, who had at last holstered his weapon down the steep basement steps. My suitcase was on the floor behind the settee that I had been watching the TV from. Ironically it was the movie "The Kray Brothers" that was now on as we got to the couch, one of the Krays was cutting some guys mouth open with a sword. I searched for the remote and killed the telly.

The cop stood and watched, saying nothing. I felt the need to speak, I think it was nerves. The silence frightened me.

"I err, (again) keep it in my case," I muttered, tugging the case up from behind and throwing it onto the couch. "I err, (!) keep it locked, for security," I jabbered.

I don't know if you have ever been in a situation where you're frightened, it feels like the clock is ticking, you're being very carefully scrutinised and assessed, and you have to perform some simple task – well let me tell you it is possible that you could begin to fall apart. That's exactly what happened to me.

It took me what felt like an age to find the key, which was where I always kept it – in my jacket pocket on a key ring, with other keys. Once I had found the keys I entered into some kind of keystone routine where I couldn't for the life of me work out which key it was to open the case (it was the smallest key on the ring). I tried three different keys, almost managing to jam one of them into the lock, before finding the right one. I could sense the officer holding his frustration in check, thinking to himself this "jerk" is stalling for time!

At last I got the correct key in the lock – but the pantomime continued because I couldn't turn the bloody thing! At last, after what seemed like an hour, the locks popped open. My agony didn't quite end there because I then couldn't find the passport. "Had I left it in my jacket after all?" I thought. Just as I was about to check my jacket the cop leaned forward and said, rather sarcastically I felt, "What's this?" as he picked up my passport which had been standing to one of the sides of the case.

"It's my, err, (not again please) my err, passport."

He studied it evidently convinced it was some kind of neat forgery.

He escorted me back up stairs, passport in hand. As we reached the hallway his colleague was returning from the kitchen where he had evidently been on the phone to someone. The older officer handed over my passport and said to his colleague, "He says it's his passport!". It was blazingly obvious he expected his partner to identify the tell tale signs of an illegal document. God, I'd be an illegal immigrant – what would they do to me?

It was at that precise moment that Babe chose to open the door to her room.

I couldn't speak. My mouth hung open, my eyes popped, and my mouth began making fish like motions as I mouthed but couldn't speak the word, "What?"

In unison the two officers doffed their caps, smiled at her, and the older officer spoke directly to her, "Hello marm. Sorry to disturb you, but do you know this individual?" indicating me with his thumb.

Individual, individual – I wasn't even a named person to these two guys who had pointed guns at me, made me sweat, shake and stammer!

"That's Brendan," she answered, "what's he done?"

I was flabbergasted. What's he done? I managed to close my mouth, collect my dysfunctional thoughts and to speak for the first time since she appeared, "Babe? Where were you? Didn't you hear me shouting for you?"

Quick as a flash she came back with, "I didn't know who it was?"

I was back to mouthing, "What?"

The two officers who had been so surly and disbelieving with me took to Babe as if they had known her forever. They chatted like old friends. They covered where she was from, how long she was staying, who were her relatives, how long her brother and sisters had been in the U.S., whether this was her first time in the Sates and so on. They were particularly enamoured over the fact that she had visited America previously. They wanted to know what changes she had noticed, whether the family was O.K. and doing well. One of them even asked her if she lived anywhere near Athy (pronounced Atie) in Ireland which was where his people came from.

After they had exhausted what seemed to me to be innumerable pleasantries the younger of the two explained that when the alarm went off the company it was wired to had phoned the house to see if it was a real problem. He looked at me accusingly and asked, "Why didn't you pick up the phone?"

"I err, (oh dear I thought this is me for the rest of my natural) I err, didn't like to," I answered very lamely.

"Well when no one answered they called us to check the place out. So that's how come we're here. Anyway whilst you were down in the basement with Donnie I checked out the rest of the house and rang the security company. They ring alternative numbers see, to check if maybe there's a valid reason for the alarm going off. They got through to (he took out his notebook and read) Eileen Pellegrini (Noreen's daughter who was at work) and she told them that they had guests from Ireland staying and that they probably tripped the alarm. That would be you two? So which of you tripped the alarm? Was it you?" he asked of me in a most belligerent manner.

"I err, (bugger) was down in the basement watching TV so I don't think it could have been me."

"Marm?"

Babe looked at the two officers. She appeared to have shrunk in size so that she appeared older and much more vulnerable, I swear her voice quavered a little as she admitted, "Well, I did get up to go to the bathroom."

"That explains it," old cop said, "you must have trodden on a pressure plate which triggered the alarm."

"I'm terribly sorry officer," Babe answered.

"No, we live to serve marm. We live to serve. There was no harm done. Glad to be of service. Are you alright now marm? You must have been very frightened?" he asked.

"I'm sure I'll live now officer and thanks for your trouble."

"No trouble at all marm." The younger officer agreed with his colleague and they both took their leave of us with a great many exhortations to have a nice day and a great vacation. Both gave me a good hard look before leaving as if to say we'll see you again; or perhaps more likely we better not see you again! They hadn't asked Babe to verify her name or demand that she produce a passport! I couldn't believe what had happened – the two cops must have been fully aware that we were legitimate guests in the house even before Baby showed herself, because of the phone call, but not once did they ease up in their manner with me! I must look the illegal immigrant type – either that or they didn't like the Limey!

As they went I turned to Baby. "Why didn't you answer me? Didn't you hear me calling for you? Didn't you notice me knocking on your door and trying the handle?"

She thought for a moment and said, "When that auld alarm started off I got a bit of a fright and all I could think of was to lock myself in the room, don't you know?"

I shook my head. "You were frightened, you were frightened. Baby I was almost shot!"

"Ah now don't be exaggerating. All's well that ends well as they say," and with that she promptly turned around and went back into her room, a moment later the sound of the key turning in the lock could be heard putting a final full stop to the matter.

Noreen and Mary Anne got home before Frankie. They had been contacted by Eileen at the beauty parlour. They fussed around Baby for the rest of the day. Poor old Frankie got it in the ear again –

this time for putting the alarm on as he went out. Joe, I believe, couldn't stop laughing about it for the next couple of days. I had to retell the story from my perspective several times and Babe's only contribution to the tale was to add the final remark, "Well I didn't know what he (me) had been up to! Did I?" ? ? ? ? ? ?

Despite our adventure with New York's finest I had the most wonderful holiday with Babe. If it was a bonding exercise we certainly bonded. I felt much closer to her after New York.

Back home life went on at its slow retired and refined pace.

Mum sadly passed away in 2002. Babe was there with her on the night she died, as were myself and Patsy along with many of Uncle Mark's family. She passed away surrounded by love and prayers. Her's was the first death, and only, death I have witnessed. Babe was one of those who helped me to come to terms with it and she never brought up their fall out again; only ever speaking about mum with sadness at her passing. Despite everything Babe missed my tempestuous mother, as do we all.

Sadly Babe herself passed away this year (2011) the same year as my sister Patsy (who was one of her closest friends along with my cousin Eileen – the three musketeers whenever they were together). She was eighty-eight. She lived longer than any of her siblings – something she was quietly proud of. Mum had been eighty-seven! Is it possible Babe hung on long enough to beat mum who had been the eldest survivor up to then?

Since retiring I generally go swimming each morning and on the morning she died I returned from the baths to find Sandy in tears at our half door. That night we sailed for Ireland.

Babe had died incredibly peacefully in her sleep. She had been ill during the summer but had seemed to be recovering. The week before she passed away she appears to have made contact with everyone she loved. On the Sunday before she died she phoned me. This was a rare call because normally I phoned her. I spoke to her on the Tuesday and she sounded in great form. She instructed me to contact Noreen in America and to chide her for not writing! On the night she died (Wednesday night/Thursday morning) she was up until midnight watching a programme on the election of the next president of Ireland and discussing the merits and demerits of those standing for the office; she always had very strong opinions. At three she visited the toilet and by 0730 she had drifted off. There was no sign of trauma; her body was quite relaxed indicating that she did just drift away.

During her final two years she had moved in with Uncle Mark's youngest daughter Mary and her husband in Dunmore, County Galway. It was in their house that she died. And it was to their house that her body was returned for the waking at around four o'clock the next day, Friday.

Her waking in the house was for family only. The principle behind the Irish wake is that the living keep company with the deceased until the removal from the house. So until around four in the afternoon of the next day (Saturday) she was kept company by her family. Her body was then taken to Kilkerrin Community Centre where around three hundred of her neighbours and ex-pupils paid their respects. At eight thirty that night we accompanied her to the church in Kilkerrin and as we approached the church the senior class of the National School lined both sides of the road with lighted candles – she would have been so proud of that little mark of respect. All of us there were moved by the gesture – these youngsters who had not been taught by her had given up whatever they normally did on a Saturday night, at eight–thirty in the evening, to stand in the cold to say goodbye to someone they didn't really know!

Next morning, Sunday, requiem mass celebrated her life and the priest – Father Tom, whom she had known for a great many years delivered the most wonderful eulogy before a huge crowd accompanied her, for the last time, to the local cemetery where she was at last interred with Joe after twenty-six long years apart.

There are many wonderful memories I have of Babe and like my mother and Uncle Mark before her, I shall miss her terribly. I know that my brother will miss her greatly because she always had a great soft spot for Tony. He was always the, "poor gossoon". She rang him twice a week for years and I know her calls meant the world to him.

With Babe's passing we sever the last remaining link to my mother's generation of the Cunniffe family. Now we; Tony and I, are the auld ones. Will we be remembered and missed as fondly as the likes of Babe? I wonder?

24. Final Post, 2004 – 2011.

As 2005 dawned I was generally unhappy and basically trying to see out my final years with as little heartbreak as possible. I was serving as a moderator for the examination board and that was taking me out of school quite a lot visiting other schools. I'd had to step in a year or two earlier to take over the Leisure and Tourism when the previous teacher left. I guess I was feeling tired. The internal politics in the school were not to my liking and the staff felt exhausted and fearful for the future.

Around Spring half term I had a visit from one of the authorities advisors who asked me had I heard of the Headways Project? I hadn't. Apparently it had been set up the previous September to see if an alternative curriculum could work with those students the three Heywood secondary's felt they couldn't handle or who were likely to be permanently excluded. Their time tables consisted of a mixture of sessions at Hopwood Hall College (vocational training), Middleton Technology (Midd Tech) School (I. T.),various other sites like the Magic Centre at Heywood indoor market (English, Maths etc.) and some work experience. There were thirty-two students on the project and it wasn't working.

A lot of money had been expended in setting it up and the authority felt it was being forced into a decision as to whether to wrap it up before more money was lost or whether it could be salvaged. I was asked if I might be interested in trying to salvage the situation.

Initially I was terrified. I didn't believe that I had the necessary experience and working only with the most problematic youngsters wasn't something I relished. An old friend from Suthie, Clive Rotheram, would be my immediate line manager if I got the job.

I didn't commit to anything but asked if I could see the youngsters in action and whether I could visit a well established project in Sheffield. I was given the nod to do both.

I applied for the job and although there were several other applicants I got it. I started after Easter 2005. By then the group had been thrown out of the Magic Centre and Middleton Tech were ready to pull the plug on them. I guaranteed Midd Tech that I would solve their most pressing problems – they couldn't handle all 32 students on site for a full day (Wednesday). I said they would never have to handle more than 16 at any one time and then only for half a day at a time. They reluctantly agreed to try this out. I managed to get rooms on the Middleton Campus of Hopwood Hall and taught Maths and English from there. I had observed the vocational provision at the college and was very impressed with the Hairdressing, Brickwork and Motor Vehicle but less impressed with Engineering and Woodwork. Woodwork in particular caused me serious concern. I had meetings with the various managers and with the woodwork manager, I informed him that I wouldn't accept what was happening – near enough joinery was no preparation for industry and that's what they had settled into. They were simply trying to keep the students amused, quiet and less disruptive by failing to challenge them when they submitted shoddy work. Tutors were afraid of correcting them and so all of the work, no matter how poor, was being judged 'near enough'. I asked would it be acceptable on site and the answer was obviously 'No'. I insisted that they be made to work to the industry standard. This continued to be an issue throughout my time in charge of the programme.

It really was a baptism of fire. The nature of the youngsters was such that their first inclination was to look for any weakness and to attempt to tie you or the system up in knots. In their nine years in mainstream education they had become exceptional manipulators – understanding and sharing how to: avoid hard work or work of any kind, wind up teachers, get themselves suspended, disrupt in any or all situations and generally present themselves as a pain the school's posterior. A school having emptied itself of such time consuming characters could only improve their value added for all of their children.

I set out first and foremost to win over the parents and began a series of meetings with all of the parents that ran on for maybe five or six weeks. This became a feature of the later Headways Programme when it was rolled out as a permanent provision. All parents had to agree to come on board and to support us no matter what their youngster might say – I insisted that we could only help them and their offspring if they found they couldn't divide and conquer – something they were exceptional at doing!

Jayne Nutt had been with the project from its start and was an invaluable help. She had worked with the previous manager and I'm not sure what she thought of me initially. I think that when I took over she felt that for the final month or so before Easter she had carried the whole thing so a new guy coming in and altering so much so quickly must have been difficult for her. Jayne had been a very effective Educational Welfare Officer in various schools before moving onto the project.

I tried to make sure that she felt included in all I was doing, for example taking her with me when I went across to Sheffield to see how a settled project was working and including her in the interview process even though they were outside of office hours.

Somehow we managed to nurse the youngsters through the rest of Year 10 and into Year 11. At some point the powers that be decided things were looking rosier and decided it would no longer be a project but would become a programme in its own right – we must have been doing something right.

We began recruitment for the new intake around Easter of my second year on the programme and had a big take up from schools despite the fact that it would cost more to send their youngsters to us than to keep them on their own site. I met with Head teachers regularly and parents on a daily basis. I believe the reason why it started working better than it had at first was because I made great efforts to keep the parents on our side. It seemed fairly obvious to me that if a youngster was so obnoxious at school they must be fairly obnoxious at home and their parents were desperate for someone to show them how to get to grips with young men and women who were now trying to and often succeeding in ruling the roost at home!

I talked partnerships. I talked about pre-emptive action. I talked about support but most of all I talked about turning their son or daughter into a success who would leave school after 11 years with something to show for their time. Most of our parents jumped at the chance to ensure their children achieved something, a few needed reminding from time to time. Our best allies were the youngsters themselves who would try to intimidate their parents and bully them in the same way they tried to intimidate and bully teachers at school. At the end of the day their parents realised that if we worked together we could, as the adults in the triangle, turn their offspring around.

I also insisted that all of the Headways staff have mobile phones so that no issue was postponed and handled at a later date. Contact could and was made within minutes. I can remember calling a parent in the middle of an English lesson and simply saying that such and such had just informed me the didn't intend doing the work set. I then pointed out that I would be keeping them on site until the work was completed and did I have their agreement – the answer was always "Yes" – end of strike!

For the next several years we went from strength to strength. At one point we had 66 year 10 and year 11 students on our books, enough to get me another member of staff, Carol Newton. It was hard work but for some reason I loved it. I loved second guessing them and informing them that the tactics they had honed over nine years at school just wouldn't work here. Exclusions would be rare; begging me to change my mind wouldn't work even though it was a tactic used by them that had ground parents and other teachers down by their relentless 'Pleeeeeaaaase'; not finishing a piece of work was not an option; failure was a choice that was not tolerated; whining and whinging would be dealt with as if they were babies; parents would support a decision made by me if it was to support progress and so on.

As Carol, Jayne and I all had phones we were in regular touch with each other regarding the progress or lack of progress of individuals. Everything was immediate. Suddenly the youngsters were faced with a situation where it didn't take a week or two to deal with the problem they presented – it could be dealt with within moments.

I recall the odd lesson where I would quietly phone a parent in the middle of a lesson – didn't matter whose lesson – and invite them to listen in to their son or daughter. It was an eye opener for some of them and certainly gave them no grounds to defend obnoxious behaviour nor did it provide wriggle room for their offspring to deny their behaviour or to accuse me or Jayne or Carol of lying to their parents.

I had a maths teacher who was being given a torrid time by the small groups I arranged for him to take and I remember setting up my FLIP (a mini camera that records up to 30 minutes on a small battery) surreptitiously so that it would record their worst excesses and then inviting the odd student into my office to view their performance before I invited their parents in to see it – it worked a treat – few were keen to let their parents see quite what they were really like. I had already received parental permission to photograph them. I used every trick in the book including blackmail, to ensure compliance. The tutors who took them for their various vocational courses of course wouldn't agree that they were managed effectively (certainly in woodwork) but they were managed sufficiently for them to succeed by and large.

It's tempting to write about some of the antics these youngsters got up to but I do firmly believe that despite the way they were, the majority will have turned out to be valuable and hopefully hard working citizens. They were certainly given the necessary start to make it in the world of work. Writing about their stupidity, ignorance, bad manners, and disruptive tendencies would simply embarrass them now because they will all be young adults with worries (perhaps their own children) of their own by now. Hopefully the Headways Programme helped them to make a good start at some point when they rid themselves of their rebelliousness. I remember saying to their Head teachers at various presentations that I enabled their students to achieve despite their best efforts – which always seemed to go down well.

I will mention one of my students who came to me from his school unable to read, write or add up. He was a quiet and fairly well mannered boy. He was not stupid but he obviously had learning difficulties. He came to the programme without a statement (students with learning difficulties were generally statemented which enabled me to channel more support their way). I was angry and horrified that s youngster could reach the age of fourteen in our modern system without being picked up by his primary school or secondary school. The way his high school dealt with his problems was to pass them on to the programme. I won't name the school or the young man in question but if ever a person was let down by our educational system it was that young man – luckily he was enabled to achieve some limited success with us despite the lack of funding that followed him! It's easy to see what had happened – the children who created immense problems and the parents who made the loudest noises about support were the ones who got the statements and support – little boys who didn't disrupt, who were quiet and whose parents were only semi-literate – these were ignored! A damning indictment on modern day ed.

One of the things I did build in was a presentation evening at the end of each academic year and in our last presentation evening our student of the year achieved the equivalent of 17 GCSE's, some at grade 'C'. This was a young man who had been told by his Head that he would never amount to anything. He had GCSE English 'C', Maths 'C', Literacy 1 & 2, Numeracy 1 & 2, IT 1 & 2, GNVQ Brickwork Level 1, Btec Building Level 1 and Plumbing Level 1. Thanks to some support work I bought in we had also rekindled his interest in soccer and he was playing regularly again. He had some kind of personality clash with the Rochdale Town Team manager in his early years and that was when he began to disrupt! I sincerely hope that he has made use of the fine start he made to working life and I feel sure that he has. Although here's an example of how short sighted the system can be. The young man's Plumbing tutor felt that he was one of the best trainees he had ever had – he described him as 'a natural'. The boy wanted to carry on with his Plumbing. Even so he could not get a place on the Level 2 course (which Rochdale didn't run) because he wouldn't have the necessary five GCSE's at Grade 'C' or better (because Plumbing was in such demand the grades would need to be much better). Our system lets down our youngsters in all sorts of ways. I could write a book on it but I won't – it would just make me too angry.

At this last presentation evening Colin Lambert was present to hand out certificates. Colin had been the CEO (Chief Education Officer) when I was appointed and had been in on my interview. Our presentation evenings always had a full turn out – perhaps because their youngsters had rarely achieved anything a school could reward them for until now. I broke the news to our parents and students that I was retiring that year and an audible gasp filled the whole room; our leavers and Year 10s didn't cheer or applaud as I thought they might. I explained that they would be well taken care of and that the college was taking over provision.

Colin asked everyone to stay where they were at the end and delivered a lovely valedictory in my honour. His kind words were the second time in a career spanning 38 years that I felt moved, almost, to tears. He said a great many nice things mostly in relation to the achievements of our students and what they owed to Jayne, Carol and me but then he went on to state that my appointment had been the best decision he had made whilst CEO bar none. I was moved greatly. He then went on to say that he had made arrangements for me and Sandy to be taken on a private tour of the Palace of Westminster with an MP of my choice – the Right Honourable Jim Dobbin (RIP) was my only choice because he had been a great friend of the programme. Colin asked me what I thought about that and I answered that it was one of my unfulfilled ambitions, especially as I had studied Government at 'A' Level – I was thrilled. He then said, "You don't think that's all do you?" I obviously didn't know what to say so kept quiet. He went on, "It's also in my gift to nominate someone to attend one of the Royal Garden Parties, and I am going to nominate you and your lovely wife. What have you got to say to that?" I thought for a moment and knowing that one of Sandy's wildest unfulfilled ambitions was about to be met said, "As a Republican I thank you and accept on behalf on my Royalist wife." I was blown away and for a short time – you may not believe this – I was speechless.

At the end of the evening lots of parents and their youngsters came to say farewell and thank me for all I had done. I knew that most of the students wouldn't appreciate any of this until maybe ten years on from that point when on looking back they would realise how wonderful the opportunities they had been presented with actually were.

For a month or two before that night I knew I would be finishing. The Programme by this point was bringing in around £250,000 per year in terms of what the schools had to pay for their youngsters to attend and that kind of money meant that the college was very interested in taking it over. We were subjected to an Ofsted and passed with flying colours, much to the chagrin of the college – I think they were hoping we could be faulted and they'd get the programme by default. I was also aware that the authority was already in the throes of the recession and looking for ways to trim its budget – my salary would be a nice reduction. So I was offered various options to enable the college to take on the programme without me – their thinking was that they had a plethora of managers and that they would absorb the job of dealing with our students.

A period of negotiation ensued and I realised that if it went on too long whatever was on offer this year might be radically changed next year as the recession bit deeper. I was offered an absolutely plumb job teaching English at Siddal Moor without any responsibility and on my present salary to take me through to retirement in 18 months. I informed them that that filled me with dread – the prospect of facing 30 Year 7's was something that had me trembling. They couldn't understand how I was prepared to work with the youngsters I was working with and couldn't face 30 keen fresh faced youngsters. I pointed out that I knew where my students were coming from and didn't find that stressful! They eventually let me go on an actuarially reduced pension, I lost 15% of my annual entitlement but money isn't everything is it? Story of my life!

I made a promise to myself that I wouldn't retire and go straight back into supply work which so many retired teacher's do. I have a number of reasons for this and I think I made the right decision for me. Ron Dixon had a conversation with me just as I passed fifty and he said that male teacher's in secondary schools who are still teaching post sixty rarely lived to retirement age! It kind of focussed my mind and I was quite happy to be getting out at just under fifty-nine, although I would have carried on, quite happily, had I not been given the option. I knew there were lots of things I wanted to do before I was finished with this old world and finishing a little early might just have given me the opportunity to pursue those dreams. One of them was to finish writing a bit of a book that I had started years before!

Hopwood Hall College took over the Programme and gave its management to various existing and proven managers within the college. Sadly it only survived for a further two years. I suspect that the type of skills acquired over thirty-eight years in the business that enabled me to deal with youngsters of this type are not common to all educators.

In 2011 I began a new phase in my life and one which didn't involve spending hours preparing, marking, assessing, reporting, managing and being generally answerable to a wide range of other managers whose understanding of the type of work you were doing wasn't always sympathetic.

I enjoyed my time on Headways. I think that many of the staff and agencies I worked with or came into contact with couldn't understand where I received my patience from in dealing with these youngsters and their parents. I enjoyed the freedom I had to make decisions without interminable delays. I enjoyed the support I received from the thirteen schools I dealt with – the fact that they accepted my assessment of a situation so that on the rare occasions when I felt exclusion was inevitable they rarely questioned my judgement. I enjoyed the fact that I was no longer involved in the everyday politics of particular schools. In fact I probably enjoyed the time I spent on the programme much more than I can really say which is difficult for some to understand, especially those who came into close contact with the youngsters concerned.

I finished knowing that the youngsters I worked with in the final seven years of my teaching career would never admit they received any help or support, that they would never say 'Thank you,' and that they believed any achievement was theirs alone. I finished knowing that maybe ten or twenty years on most of them would be able to look back and appreciate that their school spent a lot of money on them and that they were given chances others didn't get and that then they might be thankful! Time will tell and I wish them all well. I know that some of them without the intervention of Headways would have already spent time at Her Majesty's pleasure and that being a part of the programme may have taken them through that period of their lives when they were most at risk of offending.

In my last year I was able through some contacts to arrange a visit to Styal Open Prison where some of my seniors had the chance to meet and listen to two prisoners.

One of them was a young man who had progressed from a Youth Offenders Institution (YOI) and who had caused the death of his best mate whilst driving under the influence of alcohol. He was very open and adamant that the YOI was very tough and frightening and that under no circumstances did he ever want to spend time in prison again.

The second was much more fascinating. He had been a senior member of a gang of Liverpool Gangsters who were smuggling and dealing in drugs. He had received a life sentence and had worked his way through the prison system from Category 'A' to open prison and it had taken him 16 years to do so. As one of the top dogs he had thought he was completely insulated but when the edifice toppled he was caught up in it and sentenced accordingly. At the height of his career he had owned three homes (one in Spain), two shops, three or four top cars and had lived a millionaire life style. The way the law works today had meant that he not only received a life sentence but all of his collateral was confiscated. His wife, who was totally innocent, was reduced to a council flat. He was in prison when his mother died; and when his daughter got married and had his first grandchild. He would in the next eighteen months be allowed to leave prison on license and try to get back on the straight and narrow (no way would he ever offend again). He explained that being under license meant that he could be lifted at any time for any infringement and returned to complete his life sentence; that he couldn't hold a passport and if he wanted a holiday in Wales where some of his family lived his first port of call would be the local police station to register his presence on their patch.

I felt it was one of the most rewarding experiences I ever had and certainly that my youngsters could have. Some of them regularly expressed admiration for the so called 'Gangstas' who supplied drugs in their areas. At the very least it gave my lads something to think about – they'd been inside and seen for themselves, they'd heard accounts straight from the horse's mouth so to speak. It was the kind of session I believe would be valuable to roll out to a great many senior students in our so called tough schools. We played 'I Spy' in the mini bus on the way back to Rochdale and one of my lads had us all guessing for ever such a long time – because I never am prepared to give up without getting it. We were looking for something beginning with 'R'. This time I had to say "I give up; what is it?" "Wrapper" he beamed pointing at the offending article on the floor of the bus! Ah me!

As I walked away from Rochdale Education after almost 39 years working for the same authority it was with some smug satisfaction. I felt that I had on occasion made a difference. Some of my youngsters would almost certainly become shakers and makers in their own right because of the guidance, teaching and support they had been offered by me and others of course. Some of my youngsters might not fall by the way side and offend - losing their place in society because of experiences I had provided. Some of my youngsters would have a love of walking the hills, reading for pleasure, writing poetry (if only haikus in some cases), travelling abroad, acting, dancing, singing, going to the theatre, exploring possibilities and so many other activities I encouraged them to pursue. Some of my youngsters would almost certainly believe in themselves and what they might achieve if only they gave themselves the chance. Some will be better people for having come into contact with me (I hope) and I do hope that some of them look back in fond memory of the time I taught them in whatever capacity I taught them! I wish all of them happiness and satisfaction in life. As Charles Dickens said so eloquently, "God bless us. Every one."

25. A Life.

I guess we are the sum total of the life we live. Elsewhere I think I may have said that it's the people who make a place interesting and I firmly believe that. Places are interesting, even fascinating but it's the people you meet along the way or that you share the experience with that make the places endearing and memorable. I'm lucky to have experienced a great deal with a great many wonderful people.

Looking back on my life thus far I recognise times or periods that were the highlights.

I believe that moving onto the Langley Estate in 1965 was a game changer for me. I fell into the company of guys who remain close to this day, although I don't see them too often now. From around the age of fourteen to well into my twenties and beyond Andy Scanlon, Brian Kenny and Phil Noonan were almost my constant companions. They were all and still are intelligent, humorous and knowledgeable. I'm glad they took me under their wing so to speak. The closeness of our friendships increased exponentially when I joined Cardinal Langley in 1968 and there I met others who influenced and made my life more exciting and interesting, at least to me!

I was a little surprised that they accepted me at Cardinal Langley especially after having spent a holiday with the school and Andy Scanlon in Biarritz, France. On our first full day in this, one of the most chic resorts in France, I purchased a bottle of rough red wine. "Une bouteille de vin rouge" being one of the phrases I had prepared earlier. The older guys with us and Andy were all too smart to drink more than a mouthful of the revolting stuff, but I was brought up to 'waste not, want not', and drank the remaining two or three glasses! Disaster! We got back to the 'pension' around dinner time. I was trying hard to hide the fact that I had quaffed a substance I had never had before, when they placed the bouillabaisse in front of me. My stomach counted, 'One, two, three,' and completed a triple somersault. One of the members of Upper Sixth, Ivan Rankin, I think, reached over grabbed me and dragged me up the few stairs to the first floor toilet where I made a collect call on the big white tellingbone! I was fined the equivalent of five pounds – a huge amount (the wine had cost about six pence for the bottle) and I thought that it marked my last best chance of ever getting into Cardinal Langley. I was sure that the teachers on the trip would report my drunken adventure and thus nip my prospects in the bud. But no, I was allowed in and no one ever said anything unkind to me about the episode. Come to think of it not even Andy has taken too much time to tease me about it!

For some reason I loved Cardinal Langley and am proud to tell those who know nothing of the school that Steve Coogan (the comedian and film star) and of course the diminutive Paul Scholes (of Manchester United and England fame) went to my old school. I met guys there who would go on to become world shakers in their own right traversing the world and reaching the top in their own field. Of course over time you lose contact with a great many of your old school friends and what remains then are the hard core of people you can call friends.

I mentioned Trevor Cook (whom I later met again in Todmorden) who shared a terrific few months of his life with me when at Cardinal Langley. Kev Haughton became a good friend and one I enjoyed clubbing with and visiting Manchester Central Library with.

There were others: Bra (Brian) Statham who played for the school's senior rugby team when I was playing second row. In those days I guess I was a bit cocky and outspoken (hopefully I've matured a little although there are those who tell me I'm still a bit on the gobby side). Anyway Bra took exception to something I said or the way I was acting one day in our social area and we arranged to meet behind the bike sheds that afternoon to settle our differences. I was quite relaxed about the whole thing and thought (incorrectly as it turned out) that I'd settle Bra in next to no time. I managed to get in the first swing as Bra launched himself at me. I connected with a haymaker to his left ear turning it into a vegetable for the next day but his momentum caught me and took me off my feet and planted me firmly on my back with Bra and his knees firmly astride my shoulders. I couldn't shake him off. He seemed upset and was shouting something about not wanting to fight but... As his head got closer to mine I tried to use my head on him (it was the only thing not pinned down – kneeing him in the back or trying to kick him wasn't working). Bra obviously took exception to this and started to pummel me in the face. Paddy the old Irish school's grounds man came along at that point and broke up the one sided battle whilst I still had some face left.

Overnight I developed the most beautiful shiner I've ever had. I was in two minds as to whether to venture into school the next day. I'd be laughed at, but if I didn't go in that would be like saying that I hadn't won or that I had been beaten. I went in and so did Bra – his crumpled ear was a delightful black and blue. We both laughed on seeing each other and that broke the ice. I wouldn't say we became bosom buddies after that but we tolerated each other and perhaps I wasn't as annoyingly 'gobby' again. The teachers ribbed us both that evening when we turned up to rugby practice – I think we were playing De La Salle Salford that Saturday and they suggested that we'd rearranged our features a little early and that if we'd done it to frighten the opposition we needn't have bothered we were much more frightening to look at without the battle scars. Ha, ha, ha! Teachers and their sense of humour! De La Salle thrashed us that weekend. Story of my life!

Brother Austin was the Head of Cardinal Langley whilst I was there and his sobriquet was 'Creeping Jesus' because just like the Lord himself he seemed to be able to appear anywhere just out of the blue. I was a smoker and smoker's always attract other smokers and so it was that on this particular day four of us had ventured into the area behind the Brothers home. The Brothers (De La Salle Brothers) lived on site. We had just sparked up when he was in our midst. "Go home gentlemen and await my invitation to return." We were all in Upper Sixth which means we were all either seventeen or eighteen years old. For the life of me I can't recall the names of all four of my smoking buddies but I do remember Damian and Peter. Damian went on to become a Buddhist lecturer at LSE (? I may be wrong on the university) and Peter, like me, took up his vocation in teaching. The other lad (whose name is gone) ran away and never returned to school although he did return home I was assured, at a later date.

I went home and prepared to face my early execution. My mother was not the most tolerant of mothers and I had been vexing her greatly around this time – being excluded from school would surely mean death! 'Teacher's right or wrong' was always one of my mother's favourite expressions. In primary school when I'd been strapped for something I didn't do and indignantly told her on getting home, I'd gotten a good slap from her for being in the wrong place at the wrong time! This was more serious so death was definitely on the cards. Patsy my sister was a teacher at the Assumption Juniors on Langley at the time, so I threw myself on her mercy. She extracted several babysitting promises before ringing Brother Austin and explaining that my life was in the balance. She vouched for my future good conduct and basically begged him, on my behalf, to let the matter drop. He agreed after treating me to two Saturday morning detentions and I was back in school the next day. Eighteen years old!!!!! I'd much rather have had the cane or the strap immediately! Damian and Peter returned to Sixth form within days.

Damian was a fascinating character. He was taking English, French, Spanish and Russian (I might be wrong about the Russian). He was obviously a gifted linguist. He appeared to sleep through most of our English classes and rarely handed in essays on time. I'm guessing he was the same in his other classes. Languages at that level were largely about the ability to function in the particular language in terms of literary appreciation. I think that the only work Damian ever did was to read the texts and then turn up to the exams and answer the set questions on the texts in whichever language he was being tested in. He passed everything, perhaps not with outstanding grades but he passed with ease everything he ever sat. I was in awe of him; it all came so easily to him.

I remember during our final exams when I was staying up all night trying to get on top of whatever was confusing me he spent his time killing time. One day he was in Manchester it was raining quite heavily and feeling bored he called in to the Army recruiting Office on John Dalton Street where he was questioned by whoever was on duty there, to begin the process. By the way Damian did not look like a brilliant guy nor did he carry himself in a way that would suggest intelligence lurking somewhere behind those sleepy eyes. The officer explained about the type of life available to an infantry man: how he would visit exotic places, meet exotic people and if he was really lucky he would get the chance to kill a few of them! Following his prepared spiel the officer got to the bit where he had to mention that if a lad came to them with a few qualifications he could apply for officer training and bypass some of the basic training given to recruits. He skimmed over this section fairly briskly. Looking at Damian it was obvious to the chap interviewing him that he had little or no education and would be perfect cannon fodder.

"What qualifications?" asked a laconic Damian. The officer explained that if a young lad came to them with four or so GCE's he might be able to apply for this so long as he had English and Maths. "I've got them," Damian offered. The officer looked at him closely and collecting his wits suggested that they needed to be pass grades. "I've got them," persisted Damian.

"Right," said the interviewer getting a little cross – he knew that Damian must be taking the proverbial, "you better tell me about these so called GCE's and the grades you say you've got."

"OK," said Damian.

"Go on then," he challenged, "I'll write them down as you tell me and don't forget I want the grades!"

"I got a one in English and in English Lit. and I got a one in Maths." In those days GCEs were graded 1 -9 where 1 – 6 were considered pass grades and 7 – 9 fail grades.

The officer stopped writing and stared hard at Damian. "You're telling me you got a grade one in Maths and English?"

"And English Lit.," Damian offered.

"You know we can check on all this don't you?"

"You can if you want. Do you want to know what else I got?"

"You're telling me you have more than this?" He was beginning to sound a bit ruffled.

"Yeah," he paused for effect, "I got ones in French, Spanish, Russian, Physics, Geography and History as well as twos in Art, Biology and Chemistry."

"We can check all this you know lad," the officer muttered almost to himself.

"Yeah, I know," smiled Damian.

"Wait here," said the chap who'd been interviewing him and he returned a few moments later with a real officer who informed Damian that he was taking over the interview from here on in.

Damian glanced out of the window, "Nah," he said, "you don't believe me so I'm going to the Russians they might believe me," and with that he left the office never to return. The British military had missed the chance to recruit one of the most naturally intelligent and laziest individuals it ever had the opportunity to recruit!

Damian had us all in stitches as he related that story to us – I may have embellished it a little but it's in keeping generally with the tale he told us! I clearly remember him telling us that he appeared too well qualified for the first guy who needed to get his superior to carry on the interview!

We had a careers convention that featured the military I remember. We all attended. At that time we were all more or less committed to doing as little as possible for the rest of our lives for as much as we could get! At this convention I spoke to the Army careers guys (this would have been 1969 or maybe 1970). The Troubles were in the news nightly. Several of us displayed inordinate interest. Eventually I asked about the Intelligence Corps. Yes we'd be eligible we were told, coming in with A levels we were exactly the kind of lads they might be able to use. What if you've got Polish or Ukrainian parents we asked – you'd have to be vetted like anyone else but that might well serve as a reference in intelligence. What if both your parents are Irish Nationalists I enquired as seriously as I could. I suspect that if they'd had their armalites with them I wouldn't have survived too long after that question – end of nice guys, come and join us!

I applied for a course at Tudor House in London to become a journalist but didn't go to the interview and when I finished sixth form I didn't really know what I wanted to do. Mum told me in no uncertain terms that the building trade was not going to be an option so I, by default I guess, applied to De La Salle Hopwood and was offered a place to study English and History. One of the few good decisions I believe I ever made.

Between Lower and Upper Sixth I got a job on a building site at Bury Precinct. I was building a very big police station. Richard MacNicholas, who was lodging with us, had got me the job. It wasn't great pay but it was a job and that's what mattered. The work was very easy in comparison to many of the other site jobs I'd had.

Richard was a brother of Paddy and Vincent, mentioned earlier. Paddy had been one of Patsy's boyfriends before she married Sean and Vince had been a great friend of my brother Tony. Richard had been in the U. S. And had returned to make his fortune in England! I suspect he left America before he was drafted; Vietnam was becoming a very serious war by then.

Everybody liked Rick. He had a strange West of Ireland/American brogue peppered with Americanisms and he used his index finger to punctuate a lot of what he said, especially after having a few. He got on with the guys like a house on fire – I think we reminded him more of life in America which I believe he had enjoyed until they wanted him to die for the right to live there!

He had a pair of nail clippers (I'd never seen anything so clever in my life before) and he gave me a little black plastic loose leaf ring binder folder that would fit in your back pocket – very nifty. He also carried around with him several topless pictures of someone I assumed was his girl friend when in the States. I thought America must be a terrific country if the girls gave you snaps of themselves like that to remember them by!

Shortly before I finished for the summer Rick had had to face a serious threat on his way to work. He used to walk to Hollin Lane of a morning to catch the Bury bus. This involved half to three quarter miles walk through the estate and a couple of short cuts through ginnels (passages between houses). At one of these ginnels he was met each morning by a vicious looking Alsatian (German Shepherd) dog which bared its teeth and barred his way until he parted with the lunch my mother had made for him. This went on for a couple of weeks despite trying to vary his times, and trying to avoid that particular ginnel. It was as if the dog knew where he'd be and at what time and nothing but his lunch would get the animal to let him be on his way.

One morning he left tooled up as they say. He had stashed about is person a metal bar around eighteen inches in length and when the salivating, rabid monster blocked his way he gingerly held out his lunch pack and as the animal began its preparatory sniffing he rapped it smartly over the snout as hard as he could. The dog did the splits with its front legs before setting up the most humongous wail – Rick took his leave super fast carrying his salvaged lunch with him. The dog did not lie in wait for him again so that when I joined him later that summer he could only point to where he had encountered the Hound of Bonscale Crescent.

It was during that wonderful summer I stayed up all night to watch Neil Armstrong and Buzz Aldren walk on the moon whilst Michael Collins covered their backs in the craft that would return them safely to earth. I remember Richard coming in that night and being annoyed with me for using electricity at that time of night and that I should be ashamed of myself. I remained awake for almost the whole night but missed the opening of the hatch and only woke with a start as Neil Armstrong appeared to leap from the bottom rung of what appeared to be a ladder (very sci fi) and moments before he said, "That's one small step for a man, a giant leap for mankind". My heart was thumping and I felt that I was living an enormously important moment in the history of the earth – it was an unbelievable moment. It must be hard for those born after this event to truly appreciate the enormity of that long ago moment. All I can say is I am saddened that you can't experience the intensity of the experience but even more saddened when I hear youngsters speak about space exploration or achievements as if they are minor events or achievements – something that doesn't have a relevance for them. I'm glad I was around to witness such a thing and I still get a thrill when I think about what those pioneers did. I still managed to get to work later that same morning. Tired as I was I wouldn't have missed it for the world!

The 1967 satellite broadcast around the world which featured the Beatles singing a live version of "All You Need is Love" was a similarly exciting and momentous event that would be difficult for youngsters today to appreciate fully.

The day that I was born, Thursday January 24th 1952 Kay Starr was top of the UK charts with, 'Comes A-long A-love' which I think just about sums me up but the more important date was Friday, January 14th 1977. That was the day my son Neall was born.

In the weeks since Christmas Johnny Mathis had been top of the charts with, 'When a Child is Born' and I was quietly praying it would still be number one when the promised child was delivered. As providence would have it Mathis was displaced that week by David Soul and 'Don't give up on Us' – there may be something in charting what was number one on the day a person was born!

I went to work as normal that Friday morning and got a message at lunch time telling me that Julia had been taken in to Crumpsall Hospital (now North Manchester) with the start of labour. At that time I was riding a little Honda 50 (she's rapid and she's nifty) – the only vehicle that I ever got booked on (once for speeding – honest; and once for carrying Julia on the pillion without a helmet, the day after I picked up the bike - on an empty street in Blackley). I'm not sure how I got home but I must have ridden home and then on to the hospital. Neall was born mid evening and I was present for the birth – it was magical. I thought my heart would burst through my chest I was that excited and keyed up. I recall the nurses telling me to look when his head started to show and I nearly broke Julia's neck trying to raise her head so that she could look between her legs! Nothing prepares you for moments like these, just as nothing prepares you for parenthood.

My subsequent separation and eventual divorce tore me apart for ever such a long time. I did what I usually did at tough times in my life I threw myself into my work. As a coping strategy it does work because it gives you so little time to mope. I will always regret having to become what I describe as a weekend dad but Neall has turned out to be a son to be proud of – what more can I say of someone who presented me with twin grandchildren, Olivia Patricia and Sophia Elena, on Saint Patrick's day 2013? Life goes full circle. Procreation is perhaps the most ultimate purpose of life. I am still bursting with pride when I look on these two bundles of joy – I must admit I do feel a bit sorry for them having an old grump like me as their Pappy (their name for me)! Born on Saint Patrick's Day – oh my!

Julia informed me shortly before Neall's second birthday that she no longer loved me and wanted us to split up (it was on Boxing Day to be precise). I think I spent the rest of that year numb in mind and body. Eventually I admitted defeat and we split.

That summer I joined four other guys in a trip to the South of France: Brian Kenny, Mick O'Rourke, Dave Carling, and John Walsh. I borrowed the car I was still paying for and that I had left with Julia – an Austin Allegro (one of the worst cars ever made) and

John Walsh took his car. We attempted to make it in one go and drove straight across France using 'N' roads only. By ten in the evening on that first day it was pretty obvious we weren't going to make it to our destination 'Camping Les Pins' near Frejus. We pulled into a small village where they were busy celebrating some festival. We had already set up a bet whereby whoever managed to be first to dance with a French girl would win a tidy amount. I was quickly out of the car with my "Voulez vous, dances avec moi?" and won the first bet of the holiday. We slept that night in a smelly bus shelter – it was actually very early morning when we turned in and Dave Carling and I couldn't stand being in the cars for another minute – I think the others slept in them. Dave and I would regularly end up sleeping outside of the tent to escape Kenny's snoring – how he didn't wake the rest of the campsite I'll never know.

I think it was the next day or certainly within a couple of days of getting there that we took a spin to the next resort along; Saint Raphael. John carried us in his car so I was able to have a drink. We ended the night in a bar with a pool table which I wasn't keen on playing. Outside the bar I'd started chatting to some Dutch girls who were joining a beach party. I joined them and perhaps drank a little too much wine (not at all like me) and stayed a little longer than I should because when I eventually got back to the bar it was closed up and John's car was nowhere to be seen!

I didn't have a clue as to where I was or which direction to follow. I was also a bit inebriated although I believe that I was beginning to sober up out of pure fear. I bumped into a French guy who also appeared to be slightly the worse for wear and in my best Franglais managed to explain to him that I needed to get to Frejus and didn't know which way to head. He indicated that I should follow him because he was heading that way and then he proceeded to head out of Saint Raphael in exactly the opposite direction to Frejus – although I didn't realise that until the next morning!

We strolled for perhaps three quarters of a mile when I was caught short and needed to pass water in the most desperate way. We'd been walking along a paved area with steps leading down to the sea on our left hand side. I crossed the road and found access to a corn field just a stumble down from the road. I staggered down and began to pee. My new mate followed me; obviously he was caught short too! As I was busy sighing with relief I felt a hand slip into my back pocket. I quickly turned, zipping myself up as I did so.

I remember it was a beautiful clear night with a magnificent full moon shining down on us in our little section of the corn field. My erstwhile friend had stepped back and looked at me with a sheepish expression on his face that seemed to say to me if you're so silly as to get drunk and separated from your friends in a foreign country you deserve everything that happens to you. He held out his hands, palm up in the universal gesture that accompanies a shrug.

I hit him as hard as I have ever hit anyone in my entire life and he went down like sack of spuds and lay still underneath the moon, stars and bright stalks of corn! I scrambled as quickly as I could out of the field and began running back towards Saint Raphael. I must have stopped at some point because the next thing I knew was that it was early the next morning and I was sat on about the third step down from the paved area above the beach, a stone's throw away from the first signs of human habitation that was Saint Raphael. I checked that I still had my wallet, which I did.

I thought back on the night before. I furtively looked back along the road as if to see if my companion was on his way to join me. He wasn't. I realised that the night before, on our drive into Saint Raphael, the sea had been on our left so that if I wanted to get back to Frejus I needed be on the other side of this town and to keep the sea on my right side!

It was very early and I walked through the small resort of Saint Raphael without seeing or coming into contact with a soul. I actually saw signs for Frejus and started heading that way. I'd walked for maybe ten minutes beyond the town when a decrepit looking 2CV pulled up and the driver, in rapid fire French that was totally incomprehensible to me, enquired after something. He might have been asking me the way to Paris or telling me he had just found the body of a guy in a corn field on the other side of Saint Raphael, but I worked out, somehow, that he was asking me where I was headed and would I like a lift. Not knowing how far I was from Frejus and how to find the campsite I got in and managed to explain to him I was looking for Camping Les Pins near Frejus. His face lit up and we lurched off into the early morning. During the drive he kept up a never ending chatter of which I understood only tiny snippets. Suddenly at a crossroads he stopped and it took me a moment to realise he was nodding his head for me to look to my left and saying,

"Voila, Les Pins". He'd brought me practically to the door. I thanked him profusely in English, French and gibberish and took my leave of him to go find the pals who had left me on my own the night before.

Kenny's snores led me to the tent where I woke them all unceremoniously with accusations of desertion and treachery. O'Rourke shut me up with, "We didn't want to cramp your style. We thought you'd trapped off. We looked for you on the beach and you weren't there! We were going to come and get you this morning!" Oh well that was alright then – I'm nearly mugged, murdered or raped and it was my entire fault that they left me!

Brian is practically fluent in French and I had him scouring French newspapers for the next two weeks to see if the body of some athletic French guy had turned up in a corn field near Saint Raphael. For all I know he might still be there to this day enjoying the moonlight!

We discovered a pool in Frejus where you paid so much per day and could leave and return to whenever you wished. We used it regularly and made great friends with a huge tribe of Dutch who appeared to be spending the entire summer there (lucky beggars).

Kenny was always coming up with snappy expressions that would have us in stitches and we taught a few of these to our Dutch pals. My contribution was from an old John Wayne movie where an old Injun would regularly shout "Swell party, where the whiskey?" Whenever we came to the pool and they were on site they began to welcome us with our own words, "Swell party, where the whiskey?" Kenny's contribution was a little more flavoursome. I don't know where he got it from but it was used by our Dutch friends in spectacular fashion on the day we left for home. About forty of them lined one end of the pool and in unison they screamed: "Faaaaantastic, Iiiiiiincredible, what the f****ing hell is that?" It was a fitting end to a terrific two weeks in the sun.

I breathed a sigh of relief as we packed up the tent and set off the next day – I hadn't come across any story concerning French men prostrated in the corn fields of Southern France!

We slept in a lay-by at the side of the road in our cars that night somewhere on the coast road south of Calais. I was the first one to wake up. Being a smoker back then my first thought was to get out and have the first fag of the new day. Very quietly I slipped out of the Allegro, so as not to wake O'Rourke and Carling. As I stepped away from the car I saw a young fallow deer simply stood staring at me. I stood still and looked at it. It was one of those priceless moments where all sound seems to be suspended and nothing else exists except this one moment in time. We seemed to lock looks for ever such a long time before it suddenly sprang into life and rapidly disappeared in beautiful bounds off the road onto a dirt lane that was signposted. I walked to the lane and lit up – the magic moment had passed – as I did so I glanced at the signpost:"Cimetiere du regiment de Manchester". A shiver ran down my spine. Here I was with four other Manchester lads and we had slept the night within a few meters of lads who never came home! Coincidence? Another precious moment to me.

We got to Calais in the early afternoon and pooled whatever francs we had left and bought several big bottles of blonde and bruncttc beer which we then drank whilst sitting on the grass in a lovely square surrounded by tall houses and trees. Brian was in terrific form and had us chuckling at his ramblings. We sat in a rough circle with Brian at the head. He sat with his legs lightly crossed at the ankles and his two arms splayed out behind him. He was in full throttle when a big St. Bernard trotted over sniffed at his back, cocked a leg and began to pee on his back. We were in absolute bulk and collapsed in fits of laughter. Brian didn't register the damp for a moment or two, so pleased with himself and the effect his story was obviously having. As the dampness grew damper he glanced over his shoulder and found himself staring at this huge St. Bernard which finished its business and with a deadpan expression scraped it's forepaws in the grass before trotting off to Brian's belated roar of, "Dirty b*****d".

It was a holiday to remember and went a long way to helping me survive a dark and hard phase of my personal life.

I delivered the car back to Julia needing four new tyres! That was the last time I drove that particular car!

I had passed my driving test the year before we split up and much to the amazement of my instructor I passed it first time. I used the same guy who had taught Julia and on the day I had my first lesson with him I applied for the test. I actually had three lessons with him prior to the test and he was so angry that I'd jumped the gun because he felt I was nowhere near ready. I had one more lesson just prior to the test and then took it in his car.

The test took place in the shadow of Strangeways Prison in Cheetham Hill. As I set off along Cheetham Hill Road I was stopped at the traffic lights just passed the junction with North Street when another vehicle sped by turning onto North Street. There was a loud crashing noise and then the distinctive sound of wheel trims rolling down the road. "Oh dear," I said, "Never mind," said the test officer, "just carry on with the manoeuvre and take the next right." My left leg started shaking uncontrollably. "Oh dear," I said, "my left leg is shaking." "Never mind," he said, "just carry on with the manoeuvre".

I stalled on the three point turn when another car came rapidly up the hilly street we were on and started honking furiously at me. "Oh dear," I said, "Never mind, just continue with the manoeuvre," he said. After that I thought well that's it, 'I've failed' and I then relaxed into the rest of the test.

Back at the centre he opened his door, with what I thought was unseemly speed to get away from me. "Wait here," he said and was about to go into the building (I have the vaguest recollection it was actually a shed or portacabin). "Excuse me," I said, "have I failed?" "No. You've passed. Just wait here until I get the certificate for you."

As he walked briskly into the office I muttered, "Bloody hell." Moments later my instructor joined me and after his initial enquiry he echoed my words, "Bloody hell", he said.

I'd like to thank the driver of the car that crashed on North Street for his thoughtful actions that day. I've often thought of him and how much I'd like to have bought him another beer!!!!! Julia's first words to me when I informed her that I had passed were, "Bloody Hell." The first thing I did was get in the Allegro and drive to Preston on the motorway on my own!

By this time I was riding an MZ250 which was a monster of a bike – the Trabant of the motor bike world! I once, only once took it to 100 miles an hour on Bury Old Road near Bowlee and it scared the living daylights out of me! Perhaps if I had been on a decent bike I wouldn't have felt so vulnerable.

Handing back the Allegro gave me the urge to have my own car. I'd recently met a guy who would over the years become a great friend, Terry Fitzpatrick. We were introduced by Brian, I think, who was going out with Terry's sister at the time. Terry was a mechanic and he used to purchase cars for Looker's at car auctions around the country. He told me about Preston Car Auctions and he agreed to take me to see if they had anything I might be interested in. They had a Morris Marina which we decided to bid for. Terry did the bidding of course and we managed to secure it for £460. I loved that car it took Neall and I to Ireland the following year and I covered lots of ground in it. It enabled me to get up and down to High Wycombe to see my brother Tony much more often and my constant companion was Neall.

After I'd had the Marina for a year or two Terry took me to BCA (British Car Auctions) near Brighouse where we got my dream car, a red Mark 4 Cortina. I loved that car as well. I remember taking Brian Kenny and Peter Russell to the Simon and Garfunkel Reunion Concert at Wembley Stadium and getting us there in just less than three hours – we stayed that night at Tony's and had an absolutely terrific party there. Simon and Garfunkel weren't bad either. I think Peter was more interested in the price of a pint inside the stadium - £5 in a plastic cup – daylight robbery! Mind you I remember Peter and myself in Alice Kerwin's pub in central Oldham swearing that we'd never drink another pint of Guinness when it reached £1.00 a pint! We didn't keep that promise either!

I had some terrific cars over the years and of course some tugs. I'm the only person I know who owned a Lada Riva. It was only one of two cars I ever owned from brand new!

Brian Kenny travelled to the Vendee region of France with me and Neall, when Neall was around six – it was the year Neall learned to swim unaided. One of the things with the Riva was that when you closed the boot it was automatically locked. I can still see my car keys sitting in the centre of the boot as I slammed the door down. A French mechanic came out and spent around 45 minutes stripping the back seat to gain access to the boot area from inside the car (which luckily wasn't locked). I was expecting an English price from him and was already planning an early return home because I knew it would leave me broke. He charged the equivalent of £5.00 – I gave him the equivalent of £10.00 and he was ever so grateful. It seems mechanics across the world aren't all rip off merchants!

The campsite we were on was crawling in Parisian cops; really big guys with severe crew cuts and bulging biceps. They became very fond of their English friends and we were often invited out for meals. I ate my first bucket of mussels there – Neall eat them as well – I think he realised even at that tender age that if he didn't eat them he might well go hungry. Another day we were invited to a big gathering of the force – I think they stayed together for safety reasons. They were having a main course of couscous. We had the cold meat platter for starters and then they served the couscous.

We began eating the main dish which they served with a tube of highly concentrated Tabasco sauce. Brian hadn't had Tabasco before and plastered quite an amount on a mouthful of food. I tried to prevent him but he insisted he liked hot stuff and downed it. Within a matter of moments he was practically steaming, in fact if I had seen steam coming out of his ears I wouldn't have been surprised. He drank a carafe and a half of water before he continued. The company was very convivial and attentive to our needs and Brian was chatting away with them as if he was French born when he enquired what the stuff that looked like rice was called. "La semoule" they answered. I think Brian suffered some kind of mental block at that because he just couldn't seem to work out what that was, so I eventually helped him – "Semolina; it's semolina Brian". At which he immediately downed tools and could eat no more. Brian had attended a seminary in Leamington Spa for a few years before deciding that the priesthood wasn't ready for him and it seems that semolina was a daily dish served for pudding. He'd had an absolute bellyful of it and couldn't bear the thought of putting anymore into his mouth! I thoroughly enjoyed the dish.

We attended a French/Algerian celebration or festival whilst on this rural camp site. I've tried to find out what it was called but have had no luck – as far as I can recall it sounded like 'michvie' but I haven't been able to track any such festival. On the site which was essentially a farm they prepared for the festival two days before by digging two huge and deep pits – I had visions of "The Whicker Man" and "An American Werewolf" running through my mind. Once the pits were dug they layered the bottom in combustibles, mostly timber from the forest and set it alight, they fed it for quite some time and eventually they covered smouldering charcoal in straw and soil (I think) then they threw a half a side of beef in one and a full pig in the other and buried them. There they smouldered for a day and a half until the evening of the celebration which was held in one of the huge farm sheds. The children were seated separate to the adults and everyone was invited to eat as much as they wished and to drink what they wanted. It was sumptuous – the meat was amongst the tastiest I ever had. Brian waited until we were on the fruit course to tell me that we were all expected to provide some entertainment for the assembled party goers. I very near choked and then considered choking Brian. As it happens we provided the highlights of the night. Brian translated an English joke into French that resulted in loud and long laughter and I sang, "Toetapper" whilst he translated, which I have since put on You Tube if you'd like to hear it! We went down a storm.

We made friends for life and swore to visit everyone at some time in the future. The Parisian constabulary's view of English people in general went up several notches. We were the heroes of the hour and they were happy to share their celebration with us – even though I can't for the life of me remember what it was actually called.

One other thing that happened on that eventful holiday. Our next door neighbours were a lovely French couple from Brittany. They had a modest camper van and a lovely little daughter. They spoke no English but managed to enquire whether Neall would like to accompany them on a trip to the seaside at St Giles – he'd been playing with their little girl for much of the preceding week. I asked him whether he'd like a trip to the seaside and the next day packed him off into the camper van – I can still see his little face peering out of the rear of the van as if to say, "These could actually be white slavers dad. Why are you letting these people kidnap me? They can't speak my language and I can't speak theirs except to ask for milk or bread!" Thankfully these were not white slavers and they returned him to me early that evening having had a wonderful, if conversationally quiet, day out. They even bought him a present. His relief at getting back to the tent was palpable although he did admit that he had enjoyed the day. Ever since then he tells me it traumatised him. I prefer to think it toughened him up a bit and prepared him for adventures to come. That's my story and I'm sticking to it. How times change – you just can't imagine having that kind of trust in anyone these days. Is that a sad reflection on the times we live in?

Between September 1980 and September 1981 I was privileged to be given a year's sabbatical to complete my degree in Education. I'd spent two years attending evening classes, two nights a week, and it was a terrific relief to know that I wouldn't have to juggle teaching full time with completing the course. I treated the year out as if it were a nine to five job. My reasoning was that if I hadn't been so lucky as to get the sabbatical I'd be working those hours! It paid off in my managing to achieve a 2:i Honours. I was informed by my favourite tutor 'Derry' that I missed a First by three points. Story of my life.

The degree presentation day, which should have been one of the highlights of my life, was a bit of a letdown. My mother was in Ireland, I didn't have a wife to share it with and Neall was too young to accompany me. I collected it at the Whitworth Hall on Oxford Street and for the life of me I can't recall who presented it to me. I am still very proud of my achievement and would like to point out that of the seven hundred plus who took the degree with me only three obtained Firsts – they were uncommon way back then!

The summer of 1981 saw me attending a week long course in Pastoral Care at Swansea University, led by Douglas Hamblyn. Hamblyn was a genius and guided my thinking for many years in terms of pastoral care theory. I had a terrific week there and at the end of course party I found myself in the company of the Vice Principal of the College of South East Asia. He'd taken a shine to me earlier in the week when I ran a book on when Hamblyn would say the words, 'boys and gals'. One of his foibles was that he would punctuate his lectures with the expression and so for a pound a go people guessed at what minute into this particular lecture he would use the phrase. I think it occurred around twenty minutes in and the noise from the auditorium put him off his stride for a few moments. He knew something had happened by the collective noise we made and he could see everyone furtively checking the time and their docket. I felt really guilty and somewhat ashamed because it really did shake him for a few moments, but he was a true professional and was very soon back in his stride. It was an excellent week of study and I learned a lot from the great man.

Anyway, at the end of course party, I was chatting to my new found friend who offered me a job at the college based in Singapore. The money was terrific and I got the impression that taxation wasn't as big a problem out there as it was in England at the time. I was extremely flattered and if Neall wasn't so much part of my life I think I would have jumped at the chance. I asked him could I let him know in the morning and overnight considered whether I was willing to miss Neall's formative years. I wasn't, and so a potential adventure slipped away from me. I do believe things happen for a purpose and that it was probably for the best. I did keep in touch for a short while and discovered that British teachers out there were amongst the poor cousins. Ex pat clubs exited but were dominated by the oil industry or others in the super rich league. Teachers existed on the scraps from the tennis, yachting, and cricket clubs all of which were very expensive to join and visit. I think if I had gone out there on my own it would have been a lonely existence and I got the distinct impression that the natives didn't permit assimilation. No, I think that for all sorts of reasons I did better by staying to be near to Neall during these important years.

It took me a while to find my feet after my marriage broke up but I did eventually begin to relax into my new life. I managed to buy a small two bed roomed house in Heywood. I loved the house didn't enjoy living in Heywood. I began to visit the theatre more often and to attend concerts as well as keeping up to date with the local folk scene. If it happened during the week it was okay but weekends were difficult. I used to collect Neall on Friday evenings and deliver him back to his mum on Sunday lunch times.

During this period I became a big fan of Billy Joel, Chris de Burgh, Bruce Springsteen and Van Morrison. I managed to see most of them at one time or another. I'd already seen Elton John, Simon and Garfunkel, as well as Bob Dylan who were still very much in my thoughts. On the folk scene I enjoyed the music of the Dublinners, the Wolftones and Christy Moore. Christy Moore became a firm favourite of mine and remains so to this day. I saw them all, some of them more than three or four times. In fact looking back the only one I never saw in a live concert was Van the Man! Bands like Simply Red, Runrig and Tears for Fears were bonus concerts.

I stared courting Sandra, who had gone through a messy divorce, around 1986. I remember planning a special weekend for us both. I wanted her to meet my brother Tony who lived in High

Wycombe and I knew she had never been to London. So one Saturday morning, very early, we drove down to London where I'd booked tickets to see 'Forty-Second Street' which had a very young Catherine Zeta Jones in the chorus line. We got to China Town around 0930 and paid an exorbitant amount to park the car and then I took her on a quick guided tour of all the places she was keen to see. It was a glorious day, in fact the whole weekend was glorious. We got to the theatre in time for the matinee performance and she immediately fell asleep. I was outraged; the tickets had cost an arm and a leg! I woke her and she watched the rest of the show in awe – her first West End production – we later went to see 'Grease', 'Annie', 'Phantom of the Opera', 'Chicago', 'Evita' and an Irish production of 'H M S Pinafore' which was excellent.

After '42nd Street' we drove to Wycombe where Tony had organised one his famous parties. He liked Sandy straight away. We spent Saturday night and Sunday night in Wycombe and on our way home (it was a Bank Holiday Monday) we visited Stratford upon Avon before stopping at the NEC to see Chris de Burgh who was brilliant. It was a weekend to remember for all sorts of reasons and probably the only weekend I ever organised that took in so much. I think I may have proposed to her not long after that weekend.

I used to really enjoy visiting my brother in Wycombe and would go down at the drop of a hat. Sometimes it would be a stop over after a concert or theatre trip like the Simon and Garfunkel re-union concert at Wembley Stadium with Brain Kenny and Peter

Russell. Other times it would be to attend an England versus Ireland rugby game in the then five nations championship.

Thanks to Mark Ramsbottom, my brother's eldest lad he used to have access to tickets and every two years he would contact me to see if I wanted any. Over the years I went to this fixture often. As both my mum and dad were both Irish I considered myself, for the purposes of support, Irish. My thinking is that through them I am two parts Irish and one part English having been born here. In all the years I supported the greens I only ever saw them win twice at Twickenham. Once in 1982 when they beat England 15 to 16 and in 1994 when they won 12 to 13. The '94 game was fascinating because immediately the game ended an English chap seated behind us tapped me on the shoulder and handed me a printed match report which accurately had the score and the scorers printed up in black and white. As I looked up, having studied the sheet of paper, to question the chap he was already gone. To this day I have no idea how he did that. He didn't carry around a printing press – I am still baffled by it. It had to be close up magic!

As we left our seats we headed for the 'Jacks' (Gents) to empty our full bladders. The toilets at Twickenham, like many big stadiums, are colossal. I stepped down a stairwell where I could see over one hundred men facing the wall and emptying their bladders with others waiting patiently behind them. I took my place in the queue and eventually relieved myself. As I started up the steps leading out I had one of my mischievous moments. The gents were heaving with perhaps two or three hundred men down there; roughly

70% English supporters to 30% Irish. I started singing Molly Malone and before I reached the top step every man Jack of them was singing melodically and in terrific harmony. I've been to a great many soccer matches and cannot conceive of doing anything that would so quickly lead to your immediate death! The difference I guess between rugby football fans and soccer football fans!

In 1996 Sandy and I had a lovely holiday in Ireland; one of the first on our own. We booked a week at an hotel in Salthill, Galway. We were only about a mile from the centre of Galway and the weather was very kind. The Galway Races were on the week we were there and we spent one full day enjoying the craic. I'd never been to a race track never mind a race meeting before so it was unbelievably exciting and interesting for me. Sandy had been to race meets before so she showed me the ropes. The tote betting was so simple that I couldn't make any mistakes in losing the little money I brought to play with. We had a terrific day.

I recall the hotel had a nightclub and they were constantly playing a song that sounded very rude – it was in Gaelic and the chorus sounded like they were singing 'fookinella' – don't ask me what it was all about – someone did explain it to us and it was actually all very innocent, even so evryone in the club sang the chorus with much more gusto than I thought was absolutely necessary. Most of the other guests there appeared to be from the North of Ireland.

I mention this holiday because it presaged the end of my affair with cigarettes. Walking between the hotel and the town centre was puffing me out. Like most people who smoked at that time I bought my 200 duty free when entering the country and I also used Sandy's allowance. I had 400 cigarettes to last two weeks, we were spending the second week visiting family. Now I was normally a twenty a day smoker (too many I know!) so they should have lasted me twenty days! However, like most other smokers I smoked more when on duty free and it was seldom that 200 lasted more than five days. I was smoking twice as many as normal and as a result I was literally gasping for breath. I remember thinking to myself if I don't stop sucking on these things I'll be dead before I'm fifty. It was at that point that I chose to give up (again). I'd given up in my thirties and been off them for several years but somehow managed to re-start! This time I decided I must give up permanently.

I didn't say anything to Sandy or to anyone else for that matter but when we got back to England, a few days before the start of term I made plans and on the first day back at work I called in to the old gym at Hopwood Hall College and paid for a year's membership. Leaving the gym I had about seven or eight cigarettes left in the pack. I looked at them and said to myself, 'I have just spent all the money you would cost me in the next year, therefore I can't afford to smoke any longer,' and with that I crushed the pack and threw them away. Somehow, despite having several failed attempts in the couple of years before this, I managed to quit with very few problems and I have never gone back to them, thank God. I do believe that they played major roles in the early deaths of both my sister Patsy and my brother Tony. I know they could still, even after all these years, still do for me, but at least I've given myself a bit of a chance.

I started going to the gym two or three times per week, arriving at 0700 and working out for around 45 minutes before carrying on to work. It was hard. In October of that year someone told me that they had early morning swimming at Middleton baths so I thought I'd give it a try – swimming's got to be good for the lungs I thought.

Monday's and Wednesday's I swam at the baths and continued to work out at the gym two or three evening per week.

My first visit to the pool was memorable. I managed six lengths roughly half front crawl and half backstroke and came away absolutely exhausted and gasping for breath.

As a teenager I'd visited the pool fairly regularly with Brian Kenny, Andy Scanlon or Tony Grierson. The routine then was swim a couple of lengths and then bob up and down accidently bumping into the best looking girls you could find. I remember Brain and myself falling for a girl called Susan from Middleton Junction and the pare of us practically stalking her for the rest of that summer – or at least cycling across to the Junction in the hopes of spotting where she lived and chatting her up!

Now I set myself targets. I gradually built up from six lengths and by Easter of the following year I managed to swim a half mile (26 lengths in Middleton's old pool). I then set myself what I never thought was something I could achieve – a mile, which I achieved on the first day of that year's summer break. Fifty-two lengths of Middleton's pool – I couldn't turn my neck for the next four or five days. At that time I used to breath every stroke so the constant turning of my head to breath gave me a severe case of neck ache! The mile had taken me one hour fifty minutes to swim and it remains one of the proudest achievements in my life (sad person eh?).

I continued and became more proficient thanks to help and advice of another older swimmer. He must have been watching me for a while – shaking his head and feeling desperately sorry for me. He engaged me in conversation one day.

Him: Do you know what stroke you use?

Me: Yeah, front crawl, why?

Him: It's actually Australian crawl.

I thought to myself – there you go – not just crawl but Australian crawl and me self taught!!!

Him: Australian crawl is where you crawl with your arms and breast stroke with your legs.

Talk about deflated. He took me under his wing and soon had me straightening my legs and breathing to just one side every second stroke. I am eternally grateful to him. He was a retired swim coach and for shame I don't know if I ever knew his name!

I've carried on with my swimming and by setting targets for myself I eventually brought my time for the mile down to forty-five minutes at the Middleton Pool. I can just about do that now in the Todmorden Pool although it takes it out of me even though I am now a much better swimmer than I was back then. The Tod pool is a 25 meter pool whilst Midd's was a 33 and a 1/3 yards meaning that I have twelve extra turns to complete the sixty-four lengths that now make the mile. The turns slow me down. I have improved because four years ago I managed to swim two miles in one hour forty-five minutes – I did it to celebrate reaching sixty years of age! I routinely swim 70 to 100 lengths now when I visit the pool although since I had a new knee fitted in September I've dropped some of the distance and started concentrating on pace.

My thinking has remained fairly constant in relation to the reasons why I swim – the primary reason is to prevent my lungs from deteriorating any more than they have already done so through the years of abuse I gave them smoking. I shall continue to swim and have grown to enjoy my early morning dip. I'm invariably in the pool by 0700 most mornings and I have to be really rough to miss a session. I've also befriended a motley crew of early morning swimmers since transferring to Tod pool. After our swim we meet up in the sauna, steam room or Jacuzzi and set the world to rights. They are a truly eclectic mix of people with vastly different past lives. Many of them, like me have retired a few fit in the swim before work like I used to do. All of them are fascinating and intelligent characters with views that I value enormously. I also occasionally bump into my old Head of Department Ray Riches and one of the many acting Head's I served under, Ed Collin's. It's a small world.

I can't pretend that retirement hasn't been a blessing for me. I was ready for it certainly and I'm glad I didn't do what so many of my colleagues did which is to retire and sign on the following year as supply teachers. I remember a conversation with one ex deputy head who bragged to me: 'I worked five days a week for two days off and now I work two days a week for five days off and I'm clearing more money now. Great isn't it?' I'm still sorry I didn't clobber him there and then. I was insulted by his arrogance and his ignorance. Arrogance because I was still working and putting in a lot more than five days a week and ignorance because he had no empathy for all those youngsters who not having found jobs could have been doing what he was taking up space doing!

No, retirement came at the right time for me and even though I have lost and will continue to lose some money each year for the rest of my natural life, I am still appreciative of a system that permitted me to do that. My heart breaks for those who follow me.

By the time I did retire I'd gone through a long period of caravanning, which Sandy and I loved. In the mid nineties I was looking to reduce the cost of storage and insurance which was costing around £800 per year without even making use of the caravan. I used to store it on a farm in Heywood which was unsafe to say the least and the cost went up annually. Around 2000 I got it into my head that I might be able to find somewhere to leave it in France (George Naylor RIP, had done this when I was still a novice at Sutherland). I remembered a site we'd stopped at on our way to the South of France a couple of years earlier and decided to head back there, my thinking was that if I could store it there it would be half way to the South and I'd save money on towing and ferries.

We decided to camp because it was a half term break so we only had one week and towing a rig would slow us down. It was a wicked week. It rained and when it didn't rain it poured down! We visited the battle site of Verdun (Verdun is what any Frenchman thinks of when you say WW1) and on the way back got caught in the most vicious hail storm – I swear they were the size of golf balls! The pitch became a quagmire so in the hope of retaining some sanity we upgraded to a mobile home for the last four nights we were there.

In the meantime I had been chatting to the lady who ran the site, her other half was in the South of France visiting their villa. She had agreed that we could leave our caravan on the site at a cost of one hundred Euros (about £80) a year. That was a massive saving on costs in England so I had more or less made up my mind to do it when her partner returned and spoke to me. He pointed out he was selling some mobile homes and wondered whether we might be interested. Sandy and I had looked at mobiles in England and knew they were out of our ball park starting at around £25,000 for a good second hand one. Just for the fun of it I enquired how much he was selling for. His answer stunned me because it worked out at around five to five and a half thousand pounds.

On returning to England we were still thinking of leaving the van over there so I enquired about insurance – I was quoted close to six hundred pounds and when I pointed out that this was in rural France where the most serious problem they had faced in the last ten years was the theft of a bottle of wine from a tent I was informed that if I wanted to insure and keep the van in France then I had to pay a premium! I made enquiries with a French insurer who quoted one hundred and sixty Euros (about £130 then) – no debate then? I thought. We had obviously continued to think about the price of the mobiles over there and we made our decision whilst on holiday in Somerset where we spent our last caravan holiday – Andy and Elaine joined us for a few days – lovely.

Returning home I sold the caravan back to the shop we'd bought it from and was able to pay the total cost of the mobile whilst paying for two years site fees at the same time. Site fees were then around one thousand seven hundred Euros (about £1300 then).

It turned out to be one of the best buys we ever made. Since then we've travelled out to France regularly making lots of new friends and touring parts of the country we hadn't already seen. Since I retired I upgraded to a newer model with an apex roof and a longer life expectancy and of course we're able to spend much longer out there now!

Even now as I sit typing I am thinking about what it will be like when we go out there this year – will we head off camping to visit another part of France, should we visit Holland again, what about our friends in the South should we be calling to see them? The pace of life is different, slower; driving is the joy it should be not the toil it is in this country. I'll be able to read more, write more, paint, pursue photography, learn about the local wild life (especially birds), meet up with old pals and generally relax in a way it is impossible to do at home. Friends say would you relocate and I have no problem in saying 'No'. France has a different life style and culture to that which I belong – I admire and respect much of it but I wouldn't want to live there permanently, the UK has too much to offer even when you consider the giant car parks they have the cheek to call motor ways!

La Forgc dc Sainte Marie is our second home (even though it's only a narrow mobile) visiting it and planning visits to it have breathed new life into a retired educator. It is therefore with a happy heart that I take my leave of you – for I have some planning to do before I leave on my next great adventure. Adieu mes amis - jusqu'à ce que nous Mee à nouveau.

Well dear reader, that's it. If you've stayed with it this far you must have gotten something out of it. If you did then please email your friends, say something on: Facebook, Twitter, or even by word of mouth if that's still in use! Because the only way any of them will ever hear about this "E" book is through you.

You can contact me on: *brammy@tiscali.co.uk*
I'd love to hear from you.

If you'd like to hear some of my YouTube offerings you'll find them on:
https://www.youtube.com/watch?v=SRjuT7dOPZU
https://www.youtube.com/watch?v=b1jpMQWkSr0
https://www.youtube.com/watch?v=t98DIS6zYiU

There are a few others if you find these of interest.
The illustrations follow:

Sandy est moi, 2015,
Nous sommes Paris.

1. Cover image: Brendan Michael Ramsbottom (author) around 1957.

2. *Dad (centre with shovel), Blitz clearance around 1945/6*

3. Mum, the Clippie (bus conductor), around 1945.

4. Dad (2nd. from left, seated) with brothers and sister around 1926/7.

5. *Me on Pat's Raleigh bike around 1959.*

6. *My family in Blackpool around 1961.*

7. Patsy with Santa around 1950.

8. Dad, Paddy McNicholas behind, Whit Walks around 1957.

9. My grandmother, Elizabeth Ramsbottom (with cousin Betty) around 1955

10.Pat and me around 1960, Ballykilleen.

11.Me, Patsy & Neddy around 1959 (Noran in background)

12.Dad with Aunty Kit & Uncle Mark around 1960.

13. My mother's mother, Ellen, around 1950.

14.Whit Friday Walks around 1960 – me in front!

15. My first holy communion 1959.

16. Andy Scanlon, Biarritz, around 1967.

17. Me & Trevor Cook, around 1968.

18.Pat & Sean on their wedding day 1964.

19.Pat & Sean around 2000.

20. Me on borrowed scooter 1969.

21. The guys on my wedding day. I'm third from the right standing with Andy resting his chin on my shoulder. Graham of the platform soles peeking out under Mick O'Rourke's chin. I think I can give a first name to most of them. First row squatting (left to right) Brian Kenny, Phil Noonan (told you he was short), Dave Carling, Billy Goulding, Terry Kenny (RIP); middle row standing: Jimmy Foran, Peter Russell, Liam, Richard, Graham, me, Tommy O'Rourke, Sean Keane; rear row: Con, Liam. Paddy (the French teacher), Mick O'Rourke, Andy Scanlon, and Mike Suthaby.

22.

23.Lanngley RUFC around 1970, Danny Pollard (RIP) between me & Mick O'Rourke; Terry Kenny (RIP) between Sean Keane & Phil Noonan; FR. John Walsh (RIP) front row extreme left squatting.

24.Tramps Disco, 18+ group, around 1970.

25. Winner of the Tramps competition, Monica Pollard, me and Maureen Noonan.

26. Mick O'Rourke, swell party.

27. Chase the ace in the Catholic Club, around 1978, Phil Noonan (making a point) me laughing and Mick O'Rourke taking it all in!

28. Me & Terry Fitzpatrick in the Catholic Club around 1980 – I beat him!

29. My mother at 80 (1996).

30. Mum's 80th at Tony's with Pat & me.

31. The first BBQ in Ballykilleen. Passing the poteen. Will Marian ever forgive me?

32. The Sutherland High School staff, 1989. I'm extreme right, top row.

33. Coach trip to France with Ray Riches and his wife. Haven't a clue what she's just seen!

34. Somewhere near the Blue Ball on a Crag Vale trip.

35.Ibiza before the crowds got there!

36. Sutherland High's first half marathon, Norman Quint hands out the trophy.

*37. Mrs Hindley (Head teacher) & Paul Blackwell.
Manager of Heywood's TSB studying certificates.*

38. My brother Tony (RIP) around 1959.

39. Lisa, me & Neall visiting the Cliffs of Moher around 1989

40. Sandy likes her bath, ask anyone, here she's taking time out during a walk in the 1990's.

41.Danny Pollard (RIP) reunion at The Falcon 1990's. I have my hand on Danny's shoulder.

42. The Pahntom and me, 1993.

43. Our Day Out, 1991.

44.Bill & Sally, Danny & Sandy, Grease 1992.

45. The Wizard of Oz, first show at the new QE.

46. Some of the cast of Bugsy Malone, QE.

47.See How they Run, Mary and Carl, QE.

48. A Midsummer Night's Dream, QE.

49.The Dracula Spectacula, QE.

50. *The Tempest, QE.*

51. Toad of Toad Hall, QE.

Students make real headway

STUDENTS who came top of the class after joining a special education programme were honoured at a special presentation at the Royal Toby Hotel in Castleton.

More than 80 parents turned out on the night to celebrate the achievements of their children who have taken part in the Headways Programme – an alternative to standard Key stage 4 curriculum teaching within Rochdale's secondary schools.

The programme is based at Hopwood Hall College, where the students are encouraged to follow a vocational course of their choice while continuing to study for GCSEs in Maths and English as well as having opportunities to pursue IT, Literacy, Numeracy and other recognised qualifications.

Councillor Colin Lambert, who helped launch the Headways Programme in 2003 alongside Clive Rotheram of Siddal Moor Sports College, presented the final awards of the evening to the most outstanding Year 11 students.

The three young people recognised as the most outstanding youngsters this year were Billy Smith who achieved an FCA Level 1 in Joinery, Brad Horton who received an ABC award in Motor Vehicle and Jade Hines who leaves the programme with an NVQ level 1 in Hairdressing and Beauty.

Brendan Ramsbottom Headways manager said: "

"In the programme they get the chance to turn things around and for some it is the first time they have ever succeeded in an educational environment.

"It was another terrific evening – next year the team are hoping for even better results."

TOP of the class ... Councillor Colin Lambert and Headways manager Brendan Ramsbottom congratulate the most outstanding pupils in the programme – Billy Smith, Jade Hines and Brad Horton.

52. Cutting, the Headways Programme.

53. Babe around 1995.

54.Neall marries Joanne, a proud day.

55. Mark Johnson, Joanne, Neall and Jane Handley.

56. Throwing shapes with Sandy.

57. Neall on the Vendee, enjoying French cuisine.

58.Lisa is the rose between two ?

59. Lisa and her boys: Bradley and Declan – hitting the heights in Blackpool.

60. Sophia & Olivia my grandchildren TG.

THE END FOR NOW.

Printed in Great Britain
by Amazon